'Over the last three decades Joseph Palombo has been a major contributor to the integration of neuroscience and psychoanalysis into clinical social work. Working at the cutting edge, the interface of disciplines, this master clinician and gifted theoretician offers a panoramic yet clinically penetrating neuropsychodynamic model of the etiology and treatment of the self-deficits of various psychopathologies. This exceptional feat of scholarship is a valuable contribution to a deeper understanding of both the science and the art of psychotherapy.'

– **Allan Schore,** *Ph.D., UCLA David Geffen School of Medicine*

'Joseph Palombo "mindshares" (his user-friendly concept) his 40-year journey integrating the "self" with the mind and the brain, and their respective and inevitable deficits. He provides an enriched understanding of ourselves, our patients, and our field. He offers unique clinical strategies to empathically respond to our patients. This book is an essential resource for any therapist, psychoanalyst, or student of depth and neuropsychology, who is committed to moving our field forward.'

– **Mark D. Smaller,** *Ph.D., Past President, American Psychoanalytic Association*

'"Mindsharing" is Joe Palombo's term for how people with self-deficits arising from neuropsychological impairments search out others who complement the skills they lack. With this book, he fills in the deficits for psychotherapists who have similarly searched for the missing theory and clinical technique to work effectively with these patients. A fitting capstone to Palombo's work in this area, it is a "mindsharing" of its own, a clearly written, comprehensively explained text to guide clinicians as they navigate the complex border between the innate and the psychological.'

– **Erika Schmidt,** *MSW, President,*
Chicago

The Neuropsychodynamic Treatment of Self-Deficits

The Neuropsychodynamic Treatment of Self-Deficits examines from a psychoanalytic perspective the problems that confront patients with neuropsychological impairments, such as ADHD, dyslexia, and executive function disorder. It explores the latest advances in understanding while also addressing concerns that clinicians may have in providing treatment. These patients can often feel shame and humiliation. They develop defenses as a result of their disorders that can then become overgeneralized and lead to future dysfunctional feelings, thoughts, and behaviors. For therapists, the challenge is to find ways of responding to these patients and to help them deal with their issues at the level of the multiple domains of self-experience, rather than at the single level of their intrapsychic dynamics.

This book proposes a new neuropsychodynamic perspective that is bound together by a metatheory, deriving from dynamic systems theory. Joseph Palombo breaks new ground in his consistent application of nonlinear dynamic systems theory and a levels-of-analysis perspective. The framework brings together elements of a relational perspective as well as concepts from self psychology. A central thesis of this work is that when patients experience such disruptions in their lives, they feel impelled to seek others who can provide them with the psychological functions to complement those that they are missing. When those efforts are successful, their problems recede to the background. However, if the efforts fail, then a cascade of sequelae ensues, which is when some of them apply for therapy. The framework suggested conceives of the therapeutic process as a collaborative effort in which each member of the dyad makes a unique contribution to the process. Change agents that permit patients to benefit from therapeutic interventions include the relationship between patient and therapist, the understanding that emerges from the identification of self-deficits, and the proactive engagement of the patient's sense of agency. The great advantage of Palombo's framework is that it permits the integration of a broad set of domains of experience that include the neuropsychological, the introspective, and the interpersonal. This book will allow the reader to become familiar with the types of patients that have neuropsychological deficits, providing an understanding of the psychodynamics of these conditions and enabling better preparedness to address psychological needs. More important, Palombo also makes the underlying case that an understanding of brain function is critical to any assistance such patients may need.

Covering work with children, adolescents, and adults, *The Neuropsychodynamic Treatment of Self-Deficits* is the first book to offer a guide to understanding and working with patients with a range of neuropsychological disorders from a broadly psychoanalytic perspective. It will appeal to psychoanalysts, psychotherapists, and clinical psychologists, as well as clinical social workers, family therapists, and mental health nurses.

Joseph Palombo is a clinical social worker specializing in the treatment of children, adolescents, and adults with learning disorders. He is the Founding Dean of the Institute for Clinical Social Work, Chicago and Director of its Joseph Palombo Center for Neuroscience and Psychoanalytic Social Work.

The Relational Perspectives Book Series

The Relational Perspectives Book Series (RPBS) publishes books that grow out of or contribute to the relational tradition in contemporary psychoanalysis. The term *relational psychoanalysis* was first used by Greenberg and Mitchell[1] to bridge the traditions of interpersonal relations, as developed within interpersonal psychoanalysis and object relations, as developed within contemporary British theory. However, under the seminal work of the late Stephen A. Mitchell, the term *relational psychoanalysis* grew and began to accrue to itself many other influences and developments. Various tributaries – interpersonal psychoanalysis, object relations theory, self psychology, empirical infancy research, and elements of contemporary Freudian and Kleinian thought – flow into this tradition, which understands relational configurations between self and others, both real and fantasied, as the primary subject of psychoanalytic investigation.

We refer to the relational tradition, rather than to a relational school, to highlight that we are identifying a trend, a tendency within contemporary psychoanalysis, not a more formally organized or coherent school or system of beliefs. Our use of the term *relational* signifies a dimension of theory and practice that has become salient across the wide spectrum of contemporary psychoanalysis. Now under the editorial supervision of Lewis Aron and Adrienne Harris, with the assistance of Associate Editors Steven Kuchuck and Eyal Rozmarin, the Relational Perspectives Book Series originated in 1990 under the editorial eye of the late Stephen A. Mitchell. Mitchell was the most prolific and influential of the originators of the relational tradition. Committed to dialogue among psychoanalysts, he abhorred the authoritarianism that dictated adherence to a rigid set of beliefs or technical restrictions. He championed open discussion, comparative and integrative approaches, and promoted new voices across the generations.

Included in the Relational Perspectives Book Series are authors and works that come from within the relational tradition, extend and develop the tradition, as well as works that critique relational approaches or compare and contrast it with alternative points of view. The series includes our most distinguished senior psychoanalysts, along with younger contributors who bring fresh vision.

Vol. 84
The Neuropsychodynamic Treatment of Self-Deficits:
Searching for Complementarity
Joseph Palombo

Note

1 Greenberg, J. & Mitchell, S. (1983). *Object relations in psychoanalytic theory.* Cambridge, MA: Harvard University Press.

The Neuropsychodynamic Treatment of Self-Deficits

Searching for Complementarity

Joseph Palombo

LONDON AND NEW YORK

First published 2017
by Routledge
2 Park Square, Milton Park, Abingdon, Oxon OX14 4RN

and by Routledge
711 Third Avenue, New York, NY 10017

Routledge is an imprint of the Taylor & Francis Group, an informa business

© 2017 Joseph Palombo

The right of Joseph Palombo to be identified as author of this work has been asserted by him in accordance with sections 77 and 78 of the Copyright, Designs and Patents Act 1988.

All rights reserved. No part of this book may be reprinted or reproduced or utilised in any form or by any electronic, mechanical, or other means, now known or hereafter invented, including photocopying and recording, or in any information storage or retrieval system, without permission in writing from the publishers.

Trademark notice: Product or corporate names may be trademarks or registered trademarks, and are used only for identification and explanation without intent to infringe.

British Library Cataloguing in Publication Data
A catalogue record for this book is available from the British Library

Library of Congress Cataloging in Publication Data
Names: Palombo, Joseph, 1928– author.
Title: The neuropsychodynamic treatment of self-deficits: searching for complementarity / Joseph Palombo.
Description: Milton Park, Abingdon, Oxon; New York, NY : Routledge, 2017. | Series: Relational perspectives book series; volume 84 | Includes bibliographical references and index.
Identifiers: LCCN 2016033810 | ISBN 9781138229143 (hbk : alk. paper) | ISBN 9781138229150 (pbk : alk. paper) | ISBN 9781315390208 (ebk)
Subjects: LCSH: Psychodynamic psychotherapy.
Classification: LCC RC489.P72 P56 2017 | DDC 616.89/14—dc23
LC record available at https://lccn.loc.gov/2016033810

ISBN: 978-1-138-22914-3 (hbk)
ISBN: 978-1-138-22915-0 (pbk)
ISBN: 978-1-315-39020-8 (ebk)

Typeset in Times New Roman
by Apex CoVantage, LLC

To my patients, who taught me to listen and who helped me understand what troubled them.

Contents

Preface		x
Acknowledgments		xix
1	The neuropsychodynamic perspective	1
2	The self as a complex adaptive system	25
3	Self-deficits: the neuropsychological domain (L-I)	54
4	Self-deficits: the introspective domain (L-II)	87
5	Self-deficits: the interpersonal domain (L-III)	117
6	The nonverbal dialogue: mindsharing	143
7	The therapeutic dialogue: an overview	169
8	The therapeutic dialogue: concordant moments	191
9	The therapeutic dialogue: complementary moments	211
10	The therapeutic dialogue: disjunctive moments	242
11	Conclusion	253
	Index	259

Preface

In Plato's *Symposium* (1920), Aristophanes humorously describes the nature of love as our endeavor to find our other half. He then goes on to say:

> Each of us when separated . . . is but an indenture of a man, and he is always looking for his other half. . . . For the intense yearning which each . . . has towards the other does not appear to be the desire of lover's intercourse, but of something else which the soul of either evidently desires and cannot tell, and of which she has only a dark and doubtful presentiment.
>
> (p. 318)

Aristophanes, it seems to me, gave expression to something important about us as human beings. It is as though we go about searching for someone not just to satisfy our erotic longings but to complement us for something that we experience as a deep void within us. We realize that alone we cannot feel fulfilled, but only after finding our complement can we be at peace. The greatest pain that we can endure as human beings is that of isolation from others or other people's unresponsiveness to our emotional needs.

As social beings, we construct human contexts in which to conduct our lives, and by so doing, we feel nourished and sustained. Yet there is another dimension to interpersonal relationships, more silent and less obvious: our need for others to complement our self-deficits by performing functions that we lack, self-deficits that may result from innate factors, trauma, emotional deprivation, or social conditions.

This work addresses the problems confronted by people with self-deficits that result from neuropsychological impairments, whether neurodevelopmental or neurocognitive, that are primarily innate in their origins. Individuals with those self-deficits often feel bewildered by their distress and often have no knowledge of the sources of their suffering. Their experiences are fraught with feelings of shame and humiliation that result in states of dysregulation and failure to accommodate successfully to the context that they inhabit. Not only do their feelings cloud their capacity for self-understanding but their condition also interferes with their capacity to maintain satisfying relationships with others. Furthermore, the effects of those deficits are evident in their unstable sense of self-cohesion and in their inability to meet the demands of their day-to-day lives.

The central thesis of this work is that when people experience such disruptions in their lives, they feel impelled to seek others who can provide them with the psychological functions that they seem to be missing. Their hope is that others will complement their sense of self and help them restore or maintain a stable cohesive sense of self. When those efforts are successful, their problems recede to the background. However, if the efforts fail, then a cascade of sequelae ensues, which is when some of them apply for therapy.

For therapists, the challenge is to find ways of responding to such patients and to help them deal with their issues at the level of the multiple domains of self-experience rather than at the single level of their intrapsychic dynamics. To meet this challenge, I propose that we can best understand the self as a complex adaptive system, which I view through the levels-of-analysis perspective that includes three domains of knowledge: the neuropsychological, the introspective, and the interpersonal. The processes that guide the interactions within and among these domains are associated with nonlinear dynamic systems.

Early in my career as a child therapist in the 1960s, I first became familiar with the existence of learning disabilities, which were then called Minimum Brain Dysfunctions, or Perceptual Deficits (J. Palombo, 1979). At the time, I faced two sets of challenges in my practice. The first was that of understanding the relationship between my patients' brain dysfunctions and the emotional problems they presented. The view, common at the time among psychoanalytic practitioners, was that parents were to blame for the emotional problems of their children. In particular, the belief was that the mothers' unconscious conflicts caused the children's problems. The second challenge was the absence of a clinical theory to guide practitioners in the treatment of these patients.

Since then, changes have occurred regarding the first set of beliefs. Parent-blaming is no longer in fashion. As for the emergence of a clinical theory for such patients, the slow progress in the development of a framework has been due to the resistance of some members of the psychoanalytic community to the integration of our understanding of brain function and dysfunction into a view of human development and psychopathology. A framework that incorporates the contribution of neuropsychological deficits to a developmental psychopathology remains a work in progress.

Much of what I have published during the past 40 years has focused on correcting the early misconceptions about the sources of these children's problems. In addition, my efforts were directed at formulating a theoretical framework for clinical practice that would enhance our ability as therapists to be helpful to the patients, their families, and those that provide them with supportive services.

As clinicians whose primary concern is the treatment of patients with a variety of disorders, we are deeply aware of the need for a clinical theory to guide our work. We are also committed to the view that firmly grounds such a clinical theory on a foundation that includes a theory of development and an explanatory theory for the psychopathology that sometimes ensues. Fosha, Siegel, and Solomon (2009) called such a clinical framework "an *experiential clinical therapeutics* supported by neuroscience and developmental research" (p. viii, italics in original). It is to such a task that this work addresses itself and is dedicated to this goal.

My efforts at reaching this goal were much more difficult than I initially envisioned. It has involved multiple steps. The first step was to make a methodological shift to an evolutionary perspective; second, it entailed a move away from the old Newtonian linear view of causality to the revised view that applies nonlinear dynamic systems of reciprocal causality to development and psychopathology. This shift led to the revision of traditional psychoanalytic views of development, an effort that entailed confronting several issues. Among these issues were those of integrating the recent findings from the neurosciences into a psychoanalytic framework and shifting our view from the position that conflict was central to these patients' psychopathology to the position that self-deficits are the major contributors to their psychopathology. Finally, it required the reformulation of a clinical theory that is suitable for the treatment of these patients.

Accomplishing the goals of this agenda turned out to be far beyond the scope of this work. However, because of the urgency that I feel to publish my reflections, even though they are still incomplete and not fully formed, I decided to share with readers the progress that I have made so far. Of necessity, then, what is included in this work is an outline of some of the major issues with which I have struggled over the years. Furthermore, I found myself being frustrated because I was unable to pursue in detail many of the threads that my explorations exposed; to have done so would have doubled the size of the work, and I would have run the risk of never completing it.

The framework, which I call a "Neuropsychodynamic Perspective," is divided into three sections. The first is devoted to a review of the concept of the *self* as a "complex adaptive system." The second discusses the concept of *self-deficits*, which is central to a view of psychopathology (as defined below). The final section, which is the *raison d'être* of this work, summarizes a framework for the treatment of patients with these self-deficits that emerged from the many years of experience that I have had with these patients. The neuropsychodynamic perspective is bound together by a metatheory, which derives from dynamic systems theory of the interrelationships among the phenomena.

The theme that organizes all three sections is that of patients' "search for complementarity." I propose the concept of *mindsharing*,[1] a ubiquitous form of nonverbal communication, as central to the processes that are involved in that search. My thesis is that individuals with neuropsychological deficits, which are neurodevelopmental or neurocognitive in their origins, such as learning disorders, are beset by deep feelings of shame and chronic fears of the exposure of their inadequacies. They struggle to keep these hidden and avoid circumstances that would disclose them. If these efforts fail, they suffer from narcissistic injuries or at times serious trauma. They then feel caught between instituting defenses to deal with these intense feelings and seeking ways to have others repair their deficient sense of self by providing functions they lack and hence complementing their sense of self. When these patients seek therapy, special approaches are necessary to help them heal the rift in their sense of self. Their search for complementarity becomes central to the transferences they form; consequently, the therapists' responses require modifications from those that traditional theory recommends.

However, I want to emphasize that not everyone with these self-deficits follows the same path to such outcomes. Some individuals are able to compensate for their self-deficits, while others are able to avoid the circumstances that lead to the exposure of their deficiencies. They are fortunate in that they found ways of leading successful lives, untroubled by their limitations.

Some object to the use of terms, such as self-deficits, because they label the person rather than the condition, as when reference is made to someone being autistic rather than having autism. I believe that by identifying the self-deficit as a disorder, we address two sets of issues. First, at the subjective level, we identify for patients the neuropsychological sources of their difficulties, which provide them with an understanding of the reasons for some of their feelings, thoughts, and behaviors. Second, we leave open the possibility of conducting research that may reveal the sources or causes that are responsible for the symptoms. Such investigations may then make possible the development of interventions for the amelioration and/or remediation of the condition, or alternatively, for the compensation of its effects. For example, were it not for the fact that some reading disabilities were labeled as "dyslexia," the research that led to the identification of phonological processing problems as its cause may never have taken place. Programs such as the Orton-Gillingham and the Wilson Reading Program have benefited untold numbers of people who had problems decoding written texts (Shaywitz, 2003).

Organization of the book

In Chapter 1, I offer "The neuropsychodynamic perspective" as the conceptual framework that organizes the data about these patients. I propose an evolutionary perspective based on nonlinear dynamic theory as the underlying methodology for the framework. I outline the neuropsychodynamic perspective as a framework for the treatment of patients with neuropsychological deficits. Central to these patients' psychodynamics are the feelings of shame and the fear of exposure of their limitations. By psychodynamics, I refer to the mental processes that govern the functions of the self as a complex adaptive system. The framework is divided into three major sections. The first deals with the concept of the *self* as a "complex adaptive system" and the implications of this view of the self to theories of development. The second includes the concept of *self-deficits*. In the third, I apply each of these concepts to the *treatment process*.

Chapter 2, "The self as a complex adaptive system," explores the concept of the self as a complex adaptive system. In the first section, I outline the levels-of-analysis perspective that organizes the data of patients' experiences and provides a scaffold around which the conceptual framework is structured. The second section deals with the changes in developmental theories brought about by the critique of nonlinear dynamic theories. It then provides a summary of what a revised view of development would include.

Chapter 3, "Self-deficits: the neuropsychological domain" (designated as L-I), begins with a redefinition of the concept of psychopathology, which I define as an *unsuccessful accommodation* to the context that patients inhabit. These unsuccessful accommodations result from self-deficits that constrain patients' capacity in three domains: their ability to perform tasks that the context requires of them, their emotional well-being, and their social relationships. The focus of the discussion is on the variability or diversity in patients' endowment as initial conditions. These conditions organize the trajectory of the patient's development. I conclude this chapter with a detailed discussion of the case of Ryan to illustrate many of the issues covered in the previous chapters and those that follow.

The discussion in Chapter 4, "Self-deficits: the introspective domain" (designated as L-II), highlights the major processes that govern the activities of the introspective domain, which are the preferences for self-cohesion and self-understanding. An integral part of the patients' psychodynamics is their affect states, in particular the feelings of shame and humiliation generated by the self-deficits and the defenses brought to bear to deal with those intense negative affects. The capacity for self-understanding, on the other hand, may mitigate those vulnerabilities if a coherent self-narrative emerges as an organizer of the patients' experiences. This emergent property requires the exploration of those feelings as contributors to the person's mental processes.

Chapter 5, "Self-deficits: the interpersonal domain" (designated as L-III), begins with a discussion of our interconnectedness with others as reflected in our relational patterns and the types of attachments that we form. I review the encoding of relational patterns in non-declarative memory and the contributions of attachment theory. The discussion of our communication with others through verbal and nonverbal modes represents what I call the dialogue; this permits the exploration of the attractors that organize the experiences of patients with neuropsychological deficits and the derailments in the dialogue with others that may follow.

Each of these three chapters on self-deficits provides a view of people's self-experience and spells out the specific ways in which neuropsychological deficits manifest in the phenomena that patients present. The challenge of applying a nonlinear dynamic systems view to the interaction among these factors is that of providing an account of the multitude of permutations and combinations that are possible. A linear view of these variables runs the danger of presenting a simplistic explanation of what occurs, whereas attempting to account for all the possibilities would obscure the clarity we seek to find through this approach. A balance is found through the selection of a few nodal factors that illustrate the manner in which their interaction manifests in particular patients.

In Chapter 6, "The nonverbal dialogue: mindsharing," I introduce the foundational construct of *mindsharing* that addresses the common means by which we, as human beings, understand others and how they in turn understand us. The concept serves to clarify the nature of the interchanges that occur among participants in the dialogue. Mindsharing not only involves our capacity to feel interconnected with others but also our disposition to be drawn emotionally to complement their sense of self. We respond to other people's self-deficits by attempting to provide the functions that they are missing and by complementing their psychological deficits. This is a reciprocal process in that others in turn complement our limitations. The application of these processes to patients with neuropsychological deficits greatly enhances our understanding of their day-to-day lives. The concept will also find an important application in the discussion of the therapeutic process.

In Chapter 7, "The therapeutic dialogue: an overview," I present a broad description of the therapeutic process as a collaborative effort in which each member of the dyad makes a unique contribution to the process. I review issues related to the uniqueness of each therapeutic dyad and follow with a discussion of what constitutes change agents that permit patients to benefit from therapeutic interventions. Critical to understanding this process are the factors that produce changes in patients' mental processes. One criterion for the assessment of those changes is that of patients' capacity to accommodate successfully to their context. Mindsharing is central to understanding the interchanges that occur between therapists and patients. It represents an integral part of the mutative functions of the therapeutic relationship. Finally, I suggest the concept of *moments* to organize the events of the therapeutic dialogue. In the chapters that follow,

I break down the therapeutic dialogue into three components or moments: the concordant, the complementary, and the disjunctive.

In Chapter 8, "The therapeutic dialogue: concordant moments," I delineate the elements of the therapeutic relationship that concern the establishment of a therapeutic alliance with patients. Since the therapeutic dyad is a system, central to concordant moments are the activities of "fitting together" through which therapists and patients attempt to find a match to accommodate each other. I suggest the use of Spitz's (1959) concept of "diatrophic attitude" and Ornstein's (1986) idea of "the curative fantasy" as the processes through which this match occurs. I then spell out some of the processes in which the dyad engages as part of the initial conditions of the therapeutic dialogue.

In Chapter 9, "The therapeutic dialogue: complementary moments," I discuss the therapeutic process as it addresses patients' core issues, those that relate to their self-deficits. It is during these moments that the transference/countertransference configuration replicates the patient's search for complementarity, while the therapist experiences how others had responded to that patient's search. A central dynamic that recurs in the therapeutic process is that of the enactments by the therapist and the patient of a relational pattern. The therapeutic process involves patients becoming self-reflective and enlarging their understanding of the nature of their self-deficits and the impact those have had on their lives. This process leads to the co-creation of a self-narrative that encompasses both the patients' view of what occurred as well as the therapists' understanding of the contributions made by the self-deficits. Therapists direct their interpretations to the patient's use of defenses such as disavowal or dissociation. At the same time, patients begin to feel empowered as their self-understanding grows and proactively undertake activities that serve to enhance their capacities to accommodate successfully to their context.

Since disruptions of the therapeutic process are inevitable, in Chapter 10, "The therapeutic dialogue: disjunctive moments," I suggest that when these disruptions occur, the treatment is in crisis. In this chapter, I discuss the rupture and repair process that requires urgent attention. Whereas multiple factors can contribute to ruptures, I discuss two factors that are common to patients with neuropsychological deficits: the fear of retraumatization and empathy failures in recognition that result is the loss of self-cohesion. The process of repair can then lead to the reorganization of the patient's dynamics and at times the healing of the injuries suffered because of self-deficits.

In Chapter 11, I review and comment on the major landmarks that were visited in the journey that this work undertook and propose that the validity of any paradigm lies in the possibility of the verification of its hypotheses. Without such a possibility, we would fall prey to the danger of constructing fables that may satisfy our longings for knowledge, but in the end lead to disillusionment in their effectiveness.

Note

1 In this work, I have avoided the use of the term *intersubjectivity*, not because I object to the concept, but because I did not wish to add to the confusion caused by the proliferation of its usage with another definition. As Ammaniti and Gallese (2014) stated: "In the past decades, the interest in intersubjectivity has grown in many scientific fields – from relational psychoanalysis to infant research, from social cognition to neurobiology – each one using its own research methods and theoretical models but nonetheless leading to interesting convergences" (p. xv). Instead, my concept of *mindsharing* covers many of the mental phenomena attributed to it in the literature.

References

Fosha, D., Siegel, D. J., & Solomon, M. F. (2009). Introduction. In D. Fosha, D. J. Siegel, & M. F. Solomon (Eds.), *The healing power of emotion: Affective neuroscience, development, and clinical practice* (pp. vii–xiii). New York: W. W. Norton.

Ornstein, A. (1986). Supportive psychotherapy: A contemporary view. *Clinical Social Work Journal, 14*(1), 14–30.

Palombo, J. (1979). Perceptual deficits and self-esteem in adolescence. *Clinical Social Work Journal, 7*(1), 34–61.

Plato. (1920). Symposium. In B. Jowett (Trans.), *The dialogues of Plato* (Vol. 1, pp. 301–348). New York: Random House.

Shaywitz, S. (2003). *Overcoming dyslexia: A new and complete acience-based program for reading problems at any level*. New York: Vintage Books.

Spitz, R. A. (1959). Countertransference – Comments on its varying role in the analytic situation. *Journal of the American Psychoanalytic Association, 4*, 256–265.

Acknowledgments

The debt of gratitude that I owe for the ideas contained in this work extends to a large circle of friends, colleagues, students, and patients, although I bear full responsibility for their final formulation. Each group has contributed to their development and helped shape the direction they took. Among these are the members of my LA study group: Lou Cozollino, Zeb Little, David Meltzer, Hans Miller, Gloria Mucino, Jonathan Salk, Renee Schwartz, John Watkins, Jeff Weinberg, and Sandy Shapiro; and the members of my Chicago study group: Anne Berenberg, Lynn Borenstein, William D. Gieseke, Jordie Kleiner, Gloria Levin, Judy Schiffman, and Rita Sussman Ph.D. My friend, James Monaco, read and provided helpful comments on an early version of the first chapter. A special thanks goes to the members of my fourth-year class (2016), on "The Clinical Relevance of Neuroscience," at the Institute for Clinical Social Work for their responses to a version of my manuscript: Shalom Augenbaum, Cynthia Conner, Teresa Glaze-Shields, Robert Hilliker, Kacie Liput, Michelle Morales, Cassie McConn, Samantha Pryor, Jannira Roman, Danita Tanner. In particular, I want to thank Jannira Roman who has taken an active role in spreading my ideas to clinicians involved in providing services to military personnel.

I want to make special mention of the support that I have received from my editor, Steve Kuchuck.

Taylor & Francis, LLC has granted permission to republish the case of Pat that appears in Chapter 9, which originally appeared in Palombo, J. (2000). A disorder of the self in an adult with a nonverbal learning disability. In Goldberg (Ed.), *Progress in Self Psychology* (Vol. 16, Ch. 17, pp. 311–335). New York: Analytic Press.

As ever, during our 55 years of marriage, my wife, Dottie, has been a constant companion and a caring presence that has permitted me to spend long hours at my computer churning out pages for this manuscript. Her encouragement to have me return to the clinical application of my theoretical excursions has led to the strengthening of the underpinnings of this work.

Chapter 1

The neuropsychodynamic perspective[1]

As clinicians searching for a better understanding of our patients, we are caught in the unremitting flow of the hermeneutic circle through which we interpret and reinterpret the events to which our patients are exposed. However, as Whitehead (1967) maintained, as theory builders, we are like the airplane that takes off from the ground, takes flight into speculative thoughts and returns to the reality of the land from which we started (see also Mesle, 2008). We must ground our speculations in the scientific realism that provides assurance that we will not stray far from the experiences we are trying to explain. Even as we formulate hypotheses that will help us understand our patients' psychodynamics and plan interventions for their treatment, we must return to the data on which we base our speculations (Godfrey-Smith, 2003).

In psychoanalytic theory, the case study approach to theory-building has a long tradition beginning with Freud, who made it a central methodological anchor for his metapsychology. This work is in continuity with these efforts (cf. Kaplan-Solms & Solms, 2002). Cases such as those of Ryan, which I discuss in Chapter 3, present a puzzle that challenges our capacity to understand the patient's psychodynamics – that is, the mental processes that govern the functions of the self. The first challenge is that of *understanding our patients' experiences*, which always include the affect states associated with the events that took place at the time of their encoding (cf. Damasio, 1994, somatic marker hypothesis). Affects are the currency with which interpersonal transactions occur, whether through verbal or nonverbal modalities.

The feelings that often dominate many of these patients' lives are feelings of shame, which I describe as *the wall of shame*: a defensive wall behind which patients hide their feelings of embarrassment and humiliation associated with fears of the exposure of their self-deficit. Since they often have no awareness of the specific nature of their deficits, they attribute the reason for their actions to either ignorance or deficiencies in their personality. They blame themselves as others have criticized them. No matter how successful some are in their careers, they often feel that they are fraudulently deceiving others into thinking they are more competent than they are in reality. Deep down, they feel they have to hide the flaws in their personalities in order to keep up appearances. Although frequently found in patients with neuropsychological deficits, the experience of shame is not necessarily central to all patients. However, I highlight this experience because it is paradigmatic of the psychodynamics of such patients, and it provides an entry into the way they lead their lives.

A second challenge is that of *understanding the mental processes* through which patients integrate their experiences. This challenge involves not only gaining insight into the developmental factors that contributed to the formation of their personalities, but also to the influence of their endowment, their unique interpretations of the events to which they were exposed, and the milieu that they inhabit. In the case of Ryan, some of the questions we face (to which we must provide answers) are: How did his endowment, the strength and weakness of his neuropsychological givens, constrain the path of his development? What unique interpretations did he construe from his experiences? What were his experiences while growing up, and how did they contribute to his personality and his problems? What motivated him to behave as he did? How did the types of relationships he formed with his caregivers affect him, and how did the social context in which he grew up affect the trajectory of his development? How did the responses of those in his environment contribute to how he felt?

The conceptual problem

Historically, the psychodynamic literature has paid little attention to the contributions that neuropsychological problems make to patients' functioning and psychodynamics. Contributors to the literature have focused primarily on the effects of patients' early relationships or on the traumas from which they suffered. The treatment approaches employed seldom considered the possibility of the existence of neuropsychological deficits in those patients. The emergence of the neuropsychoanalysis movement, led by Mark Solms, has begun to fill in the void in this area (Kaplan-Solms

& Solms, 2002; Matto, Strolin-Goltzman, & Ballan, 2014; Solms, 2000, 2011; Solms & Turnbull, 2002).

Neuropsychological deficits may stem from impairments in functional areas of the brain, whose origins may be innate or acquired; in other words, they may be neurodevelopmental, neurocognitive, or caused by traumatic brain injuries or other insults. Those deficits that are innate may present as learning disorders such as dyslexia, attention-deficit/hyperactivity disorder, executive function disorders, and nonverbal learning disabilities.[2] Those that are acquired may stem from a much broader set of etiological factors, such as brain tumors, traumatic brain injuries, or histories of post-traumatic stress disorders (Van Der Kolk, 2014). These impairments often constrain patients' capacity to accommodate successfully to the context that they inhabit. I call the psychological functions associated with these deficits *adjunctive functions*.

The innate *adjunctive self-deficits*, at times, act as constraints that restrict or redirect the course of development, leading to unsuccessful accommodations. Often, individuals with these self-deficits confront situations in which demands are made of them that they cannot meet because they lack the necessary skills to be successful at the task that is required of them. Their subjective reactions are to feel embarrassment or shame at their sense of inadequacy, feelings that may be traumatic at times. Depending on how deeply those feelings affect them, they will bring to bear defenses, such as disavowal or dissociation, to deal with those feelings, building the wall of shame that I described earlier.

Individuals with neuropsychological impairments (i.e. adjunctive self-deficits) engage in a nonconscious active search for others to *complement* their sense of self and help them to restore their sense of self-cohesion. If that search is successful, as in the case of individuals who are able to find a partner or spouse who can fill in the missing functions, the relationship enhances their capacity to function and helps them to lead productive lives. If, however, their search does not bear fruit, then they become symptomatic and struggle to accommodate successfully to their context. It is then that some of them seek help from a therapist.

The conceptual problem that clinicians face is that of the formulation of a clinical theory that forms a coherent nucleus of ideas that addresses the problems of these patients. Such a theory must link the patients' mental processes with a set of interventions that is effective in bringing about changes that would enhance their capacity to regulate their feelings and to develop the skills that would permit them to function in the world they inhabit.

Whereas I draw on nonlinear dynamic systems theory as a metatheory to organize the data of patients' experiences, my clinical perspective is influenced by self psychology (Kohut, 1971, 1977, 1984), relational theory (Aron, 1996; Mitchell, 1988, 1995), and Fosshage (2003), who proposed a synthesis of self psychology and relational theory. The metatheory informs how we view the interrelationships among the neuropsychological deficits, the subjective experience of having the disorder, and the contributions of the environment to the mental processes (for a summary of this metatheory, see J. Palombo, 2013a, 2013b, In Press a, In Press b). As Fosshage (2011) stated:

> The paradigm shift from intrapsychic to intersubjective or relational theory and, more recently, to complexity or nonlinear dynamic systems theory has been nothing short of revolutionary in psychoanalysis. Its increased explanatory power of development and analytic interaction is contributing substantially to making psychoanalysis a growth-enhancing, effective treatment modality. Nonlinear dynamic systems theory is illuminating the intricate formative impact of experience that occurs within a context of multiple systems – individual, familial, ancestral, peer, community, cultural, national, and world systems.
>
> (p. 89)

In past publications, I focused on the specific psychodynamics associated with each learning disorder (J. Palombo, 1987, 1991, 1992, 1993, 1995, 2006). I noted that it was critical not to lump together all patients with learning disorders and to identify the major dysfunctions linked with each specific disorder. The treatment recommendations that I suggested were specific to the type of neuropsychological deficit from which the patient suffered.

In this work, I approach the task from a different view of the landscape. By taking a broad perspective, I attempt to explore the commonalities in these patients' psychodynamics and try to articulate the principles that govern the *processes* in all of their conditions. Through the application of an evolutionary perspective and a nonlinear dynamic systems view, my exploration leads me to a different understanding of these patients' neuropsychological deficits and their unsuccessful accommodations than was previously possible. This approach permits the development of a broad treatment framework that encompasses most dysfunctions associated with neuropsychological deficits while permitting clinicians to individualize each patient's unique psychodynamics and treatment interventions.

Whereas in this work I focus on the negative impact that the neuropsychological differences have on patients' functioning, some people survive the effects of their neuropsychological deficit and go on to be successful in their chosen careers. In fact, the presence of a deficit may remain undetected, either because the patient has learned to compensate for it or because the environment has not placed a demand on the person to demonstrate competence in this area. These individuals seldom come to therapy for those problems (for examples of individuals who were successful in spite of having a neuropsychological deficit, see www.businessinsider. com/ceo-learning-disabilities-2011-5).

At times, the capacity to compensate for neuropsychological deficits can act as a protective factor. Furthermore, since we may think of a deficit as a shortcoming in the resources required to accomplish a task, some people may succeed simply by virtue of choosing different career from than those that require abilities they do not possess. In other words, by using areas of strength, they achieve the goals they set for themselves. Finally, having caregivers or partners who complement the patients' neuropsychological deficits and/or having special talents can also protect people from developing psychological problems. It is, therefore, not true that every person burdened by a neuropsychological deficit is unsuccessful in overcoming her neuropsychological limitations. Having a neuropsychological deficit is not predictive of a person's capacity either to succeed or to fail to accommodate to the demands of the environment.

The data

In our explorations as clinicians, we always begin with and return to our patients' experiences as the data that provide an anchorage for our concepts and speculations. Simply defined, a human experience is a lived moment. Such moments enclose multiple elements that include the patients' affect states, the context within which the occurrence takes place, the meanings associated with those occurrences, and the memories that the events evoke. This is not meant to be an exhaustive list, since all human experience has multiple dimensions, some related to internal processes, such as hunger, thirst, and sexual arousal, and others related to external interchanges, such as the interplay of activities with others with whom one has established patterns of interconnectedness.

The data on which I build this framework come from my years of experience working with patients, children, adolescents, and adults with a variety of neurobehavioral and learning disorders. Over the years, I have documented the dramatic impact that learning disorders have on some patients' development, on their relationships to others and on other people's responses to them, and on their ability to be successful at the completion of the tasks that they undertake. These patients' neuropsychological differences had an impact not only on them but also on the entire milieu that they inhabit (J. Palombo, 1979, 1983, 1985, 1987, 1991, 1992, 1993, 1994, 1995, 1996, 2000, 2001, 2006, 2011; Palombo & Berenberg, 1997, 1999; Palombo & Feigon, 1984).

For some patients, the neuropsychological deficits limited their ability to cope with their environment and constrained their ability to form positive relationships, to respond appropriately to others, or to function in a school setting or in their jobs. For others, the neuropsychological deficits produced intense shame, as they felt that they could not be as successful as they wished. Although they realized that they were smart, they found themselves unable to demonstrate their competence in academic work or in their work settings. The disorder deeply affected their self-image. The net result was that their development took a different course than it would have taken had they not had a neuropsychological deficit (see Dawson & Guare, 2009; Orenstein, 1992, 2000; J. Palombo, 2011).

The extent to which their self-deficits affected these patients depended on many factors. Among these were the severity of their neuropsychological deficit, the demands and expectations made of them, their capacity to compensate for the disorder, the opportunities and resources available to them for the remediation of the disorder, and other people's responses to them, which in circular fashion affected how they reacted and responded to those reactions. Furthermore, the neuropsychological deficits were often transparent to them, as they were unaware of their deficits and failed to take into account the factors that initiated the derailment in the dialogue with others. Even if they became aware of their specific limitations, they had little realization of the contributions these made to their interactions with others. For these patients, their neuropsychological deficits became entwined with aspects of their personality traits that made it difficult to distinguish the specific source of their unsuccessful accommodations.

My experience treating these patients convinced me that a successful outcome often could only be obtained if all the resources available were brought to bear on behalf of the patients. That meant that having data from sources other than those they could provide during their session was essential to having a full understanding of their dynamics or to intervening successfully. Neuropsychological testing, for example, was often invaluable. Working with the parents of the children was a necessary adjunct; collaborative work with school settings or with partners complemented the work done individually with the patient. The neglect of any of these resources, while not necessarily detrimental to the treatment, always short-changed the patients because it did not provide the most comprehensive approach to benefit their condition.

The neuropsychodynamic perspective

Three major concepts serve as anchors for the neuropsychodynamic perspective, the concept of the *self as a complex adaptive system* (cf. S. R. Palombo, 2007), the concept of *self-deficits*, and the concept of *mind-sharing*. Each of these concepts is integral to the formulation of a clinical theory. Before addressing these concepts, I begin with some general comments on the methodology that informs this work: its evolutionary viewpoint and the nonlinear dynamic systems view of the self and its mental processes (In what follows, I will use the terms "nonlinear dynamic systems" and "dynamic systems" interchangeably).

Evolutionary viewpoint of the self as a complex adaptive system

By taking an evolutionary viewpoint as its point of departure, the neuropsychodynamic perspective places itself squarely within the framework of modern science (see Slavin & Kriegman, 1992). The view of the self as a complex adaptive system flows out of this evolutionary point of view. We have evolved as embodied beings who inhabit a social matrix that provides the opportunity for the growth that makes us human. The various elements of our neuropsychological makeup operate much as the DNA's nucleotides that combine and recombine to produce the more complex features of our psychological makeup (cf. Bagwell, 1999; Banathy, 2010; Edelman, 1992). This point of view proposes that all development emerges from the interaction between our environment and us. Our brains require exposure to external stimuli to grow and function. Slavin and Kriegman (1992) suggested, "Modern evolutionary biology can be used in a way that actually enhances our appreciation of the role of experience – both uniquely personal as well as cultural – in the growth and development of each individual psyche" (p. 2).

Part of our evolutionary heritage dictates the direction of our development as individuals. We are heirs to our ancestral gene pool. Our genome carries the potential for survival and adaptation or for abysmal failure to attain the goals we set for ourselves. Yet, our genes alone do not determine our lives; the contexts in which we are raised, as well our unique responses to the challenges we face, contribute to our capacity to realize or to fail in the goal of actualizing our potential.

The story of human evolution is the story of the survival of those who could adapt to the prevailing conditions they encountered. In describing how we became who we are, we must follow a path that more often than not led to cul-de-sacs, to wide-open spaces, or to the foot of seemingly insurmountable mountains. Often, our ingenuity, creativity, and adaptability permitted us to explore these expanses or overcome the obstacles they presented to us. Those who could conduct these explorations succeeded in opening frontiers for others. Those whose innate endowment limited their ability to accommodate successfully to their context faced challenges and constraints (cf. Bagwell, 1999; Banathy, 2010). Being less gifted, they confronted difficulties that threatened their survival. Such are the children, adolescents, and adults with neuropsychological deficits.

Adaptability represents the direction of the flow of change in the processes that occur as the infant and caregiver achieve a match in their interchanges such that the infant experiences greater coherence than previously existed. Edelman (1992) describes the *recognition process* as the process through which adaptation occurs:

> The notion of recognition is that there is a continual adaptive matching or fitting of elements in one physical domain through novelty occurring in elements of another, and matching occurs without prior instruction. An example is what occurs in the immune system.
>
> (p. 74)

Sander (1964, 1995) maintained that it is impossible to consider the infant in isolation from its context of caregivers. The process of *fitting together*, an integral part of the recognition process, requires that each member of the dyad modify itself and adjust to the other so as to arrive at the best state of coherence, continuity, and self-organization. Chess and Thomas (1986) introduced the concept of "goodness of fit" as a

> postulate that healthy functioning and development occurs when there is a goodness of fit . . . between the capacities and characteristics of the individual and the demands and expectations of the environment. . . . If, on the other hand, there is a poorness of fit between the individual and the environment, psychologic functioning is impaired, with the risk of behavior disorder development.
>
> (p. 12)

The processes involved in mindsharing, and the necessity to have others complement our sense of self, are in continuity with the evolutionary process of recognition and the psychological process of fitting together. From an evolutionary viewpoint, as social beings, others in our context provide us with the sustenance and support that we need to function successfully in our community. From a developmental perspective, being born as helpless creatures, the goodness of fit between our caregivers and us assures that we will have the opportunity to be launched into the world with the possibility of achieving our full potential.

The story of the development of patients with neuropsychological deficits parallels the history of our evolution. Each individual is born with capacities and limitations that control whether the path taken will be smooth and rewarding or whether obstacles will impede those individuals' capacities to find a safe haven. This work presents, in part, the experience of some of those individuals whose paths were filled with obstacles that made their lives more difficult than those who were more fortunate. Through the accidents of their genetic heritage, their unique responses to their self-deficits, and the environments that they inhabited, they were left without the means to traverse the paths they took as easily as others have. They stumbled and fell because their innate resources were inadequate to overcome the difficulties of the terrain they had to navigate. The limitations in their capacities to accommodate to their circumstances were insufficient to lead them to a successful endpoint in their journey. Their neuropsychological deficits contributed to those failures. For them, the search for complementary function to fill in their deficits became essential to their psychological survival.

Nonlinear dynamic systems view

In building the neuropsychodynamic perspective, I turn to *nonlinear dynamic systems theory* as the methodology that helps to organize the phenomena involved in human conduct (Coburn, 2000, 2009; Lichtenberg, Lachmann, & Fosshage, 2011; Seligman, 2005; Stolorow, 1997).

The application of dynamic systems theory to psychological and psychodynamic phenomena is a relatively recent development. These applications describe the processes that occur within organisms by providing models or analogs of an individual's psychological processes and functioning (Amadei & Bianchi, 2008; Beebe, Knoblauch, Rustin, & Sorter, 2005; Beebe, Lachmann, & Jaffe, 1997; Butz, 1997; Coburn, 2000, 2009; Cohler & Galatzer-Levy, 1988; Demos, 2007; Freedman, 2007; Galatzer-Levy, 1995, 2002, 2004; Ghent, 2002; Levin, 2003; Lichtenberg et al., 2011; Masterpasqua & Perna, 1997; M. L. Miller, 1999, 2004; S. R. Palombo, 1999; Piers, 2000; Piers, Muller, & Brent, 2007; Seligman, 2005; Shane, Shane, & Gales, 1997; Thelen, 2005; Thelen & Smith, 1996).

Freud's methodology suffered from a fundamental flaw because it was based on the Newtonian system of linear causality, as he clearly stated in the opening page of the *Project* (1895). Modern advances in the sciences argue that the concept of linear causality, while useful in providing some explanations, overlooks the complexity underlying the relationships among the processes that contribute to any set of feelings, thoughts, or behaviors. The processes that govern the functions of the components of the self *operate according to the laws of nonlinear causality.* Nonlinear causality is not deterministic; it manifests as reciprocal causality (i.e. the relationship between events is non-contiguous). The direction of change is non-deterministic. Among the factors that contribute to its complexity are its sensitivity to its initial conditions, the diversity of its components, its stability or instability, and its receptivity to inputs from others. Whereas we could determine retrospectively which factor was predominant as a contributor to a person's unsuccessful accommodations, we could not have prospectively forecast its significance (cf. M. L. Miller, 1999, pp. 355–379).

The concept of nonlinear causality highlights a theme on which I place heavy emphasis – that is, the presence of a neuropsychological deficit is not predictive of any specific outcome. The constrains that these self-deficits impose on a person may only lead us to speculate on the probability of the outcomes. This reminds me of my experiences, many years ago, interviewing families during the process of evaluating a child with a neuropsychological deficit for psychotherapy. All too often, I would hear from parents who were told by a professional they had consulted that their child, who had a learning disorder, would never make it to college because of the challenges the child faced. Hard experience taught me that such predictions were not only detrimental to the family and the child, but would ultimately be proved wrong. The path to a successful life is never linear, and the presence of challenges early in life does not mean that the neuropsychological limitations will inevitably lead to failure. Sander (2002) addresses this point, when he stated that

> [A] living system is described now as a nonlinear dynamic system, a system far from equilibrium (to use Prigogine's 1997 term) having features of sensitivity to initial conditions, the uncertainty of potential bifurcations, and an open-endedness of its trajectory. The nonlinear system perspective allows us to understand the way both the new and the creative, as well as the disorganizing and the destructive, can be potentials to the same system. Within such a framework, self-organizing, self-regulatory processes must be continuous at the hierarchy of levels of complexity to maintain the essential unity, or coherent wholeness, of the organism that is necessary for life to continue.
>
> (p. 16)

The self as a complex adaptive system

From a psychological point of view, the study of the self concerns the scientific study of a person's mental processes, their thoughts, feelings, and behaviors, and how internal processes and the environment affect them (see Crane & Hannibal, 2009). Using an evolutionary and nonlinear view, I conceptualize the self as a *complex adaptive system* (see J. Palombo, 2013a, 2013b, In Press a, In Press b). We may view the self from a developmental viewpoint or from a dynamic viewpoint – that is, as it presents in the here-and-now. The nonlinear dynamic approach challenges the traditional theories of development and seeks to correct these by substituting a view that depicts development as a continuous process rather than as dictated by sequential stages. I will propose that maturation consists of a movement from simple functional units to complex, hierarchically organizing processes. Furthermore, it will include changes that bring about greater differentiation and individuation than existed previously in the sense of self.

As a complex adaptive system, the self, as the person, is situated in a context and is in constant interaction with the various elements of that context. Schore (2014) indicated, "For most of the past century, science equated context with the organism's physical surround; this has now shifted to the social, relational environment" (p. 395). It is in the latter sense of the term that I use *context* in this work. Our interactions with others do not occur as isolated events; the context in which these occur is critical to understanding the meanings that people construe from their experiences. Furthermore, our social interactions and our emotional communication with others shape our relationships to others.

Self-deficits

Whereas neuropsychological deficits represent the impairment of one or more functional areas of the brain, from a dynamic systems perspective, self-deficits represent the failure of one of the system's components to function adequately in meeting the demands of the context in which it is situated. Such self-deficits must be understood as contributing to the system's failure to accommodate to the context. Furthermore, even as we consider the person as lacking the resources to deal with the challenges the context presents, a self-deficit also reflects the failure of the context to provide a complementary function that would enable the person to accommodate to that context.

In the discussion of self-deficits, I introduce the *levels-of-analysis perspective* as a useful heuristic for the organization of our data on the impact that neuropsychological deficits have on a person's experience and ability to function. I examine three domains of knowledge that address patients' experiences of their self-deficits: the *neuropsychological*, the *introspective*, and the *interpersonal* (J. Palombo, 2013b; Skurky, 1990; see also Emmons, 1995). The experiences associated with these domains form a system in which each domain affects the others and, in turn, is affected by the others.

The first domain is the *neuropsychological (biological) domain* (which I designate as L-I). In this domain, the focus is on patients' experiences of their neuropsychological strengths and weaknesses. These data provide the information necessary to interpret the initial conditions that shaped the person's early experiences and possibly the entire course of that person's lifespan. I define psychopathology as the unsuccessful accommodations that result *primarily* from these self-deficits. Such unsuccessful accommodations may manifest either the inability to perform a task or as anxieties that interfere with the person's ability to cope with the demands made by the context (cf. Brandchaft, Doctors, & Sorter, 2010).

The second domain is the *introspective (psychological) domain* (which I designate as L-II). In this domain, we access the person's inner world, which I will refer to as the *sense of self*, or to the experience of being a self or being a person. In this domain, the focus is on the impact of self-deficits on the systems' preferences or the values that shape the sense of self. The two preferences that I discuss are the preferences for *self-cohesion* and the preference for *self-understanding* (Kohut, 1977, 1984; Kohut & Wolf, 1978; J. Palombo, 1994, 1996, 2008b; Sander, 2002). I will explore how the presence of self-deficits affects patients' sense of self-cohesion and their self-understanding.

Finally, the third domain is the *interpersonal (social) domain* (which I designate as L-III). In this domain, the objects of study are the person's *modes of interactions with others*. Within this level of analysis, the attributes of patients' interactions with others are their *interconnectedness* and their *capacity to dialogue* with others.

The interplay among the three levels

The patient's psychodynamics incorporates themes from the three levels of analysis. By psychodynamics, in addition to the mental processes that govern the functions of the self, I refer to the nonconscious patterns of responses that patients encoded in procedural memory as a result of their experiences. The experiences of shame and humiliation that resulted from the exposure or fear of exposure of their self-deficits formed nuclei of narcissistic injuries, which triggered a set of defenses, whether disavowal or dissociation, to deal with the intense pain associated with these injuries. These experiences became attractors or nodal points around which patterns of thoughts, feelings, or behaviors were organized (see Harris, 2011).

Whereas each of the three levels of experience contributes to the totality of a patient's sense of self, the challenge for therapists is to determine which of the many factors supervene others or are major contributors to the patient's psychodynamics. For example, a severe neuropsychological deficit may override the patient's adaptability and capacity to learn from experience, as in the case of many patients with ADHD, where the negative consequences of their actions appear not to lead to a modification of their behaviors. In the case of patients on the spectrum, their deficits interfere with their adaptability and their capacity for relatedness. On the other hand, the greater a person's talents, the greater the possibility for creative productivity and for originality in the expression of their gift. Whether we think of Mozart, who composed his first symphony at the age of eight, or of Einstein, whose insights into the nature of space and time revolutionized our understanding of the universe, their gifts propelled their lives in the direction they took subsequently.

The nonverbal dialogue and mindsharing

In elaborating on the capacity to dialogue with others, I propose the concept of mindsharing as central to the nonverbal modes through which we communicate with others as well as interact with others. It is also the process involved in the search for complementarity – that is, for others to provide us with the functions that we are missing and us to provide others with similar functions. From an evolutionary viewpoint, Bowlby (1969) noted:

> [B]ecause . . . the survival of populations of higher species is dependent on the co-operation of individuals, much of the equipment of one individual is *complementary to that of another* of different age or sex in the same population. Behaviour patterns mediating attachment of young to adults are *complementary to those mediating care of young by adults*. . . .
>
> (p. 141, italics added)

Mindsharing is the process through which we are at one with other people's thoughts, feelings, and experiences. This process includes our capacity for empathy for other people and their ability for attunement to our mental states. As we will see, through mindsharing we provide others with psychological functions they require to maintain their self-cohesion, even as we, being interconnected to others, require them to provide similar functions for us. I call this process "providing complementary functions," a process through which we search for others to complement our sense of self.

The fact that we need others is not simply a reflection of our imperfections; our need is related to the social imperative to have others "be with" us. Others enhance our existence by their companionship, their presence, and the nurturance they provide us (Stern, 1983). For some patients with neuropsychological deficits, the negative view they have of themselves, as well as the critical responses they receive from others, will interfere with mindsharing processes and impair their capacity to maintain a sense of self-cohesion or an attachment to others.

We will find a useful application to the clinical setting of the processes that involve mindsharing. Whereas patients' psychodynamics provide a rendering of their mental states, mindsharing, through empathy, supplies the means through which we can vicariously introspect about their experiences. The psychodynamic statement is analogous to a road map that guides therapists and patients in the conduct of the therapeutic dialogue (J. Palombo, 2008a).

Restoring and healing the self

The therapeutic dyad forms a new complex adaptive system. The restoration and healing of the self are products of the dialogue between patients and therapists within the constraints set by the limitations that both participants bring to the process. The vehicle through which we conduct the dialogue is the process of mindsharing. From this perspective, treatment consists of the creation of a context within which patients can experience and share with a therapist their innermost longings for complementary functions that will then repair their self-deficits. For that to occur, they must be able to feel that we can hear the account they give of their experiences and they can receive some acknowledgment that the feeling associated with those experiences had validity within the context in which they occurred. Patients may be encouraged to be curious as to the origins of their self-deficits and must receive assurances that therapists will try to understand their significance. We may give them hope that relief will come through the experience of sharing their distress and that they may engage in the process of co-constructing a meaningful coherent narrative.

Whereas central to the therapeutic process is the concept of the dialogue as a change agent, we will see that there is no simple answer to the question of how changes occur in patients' psychodynamics. In view of the constraints that their self-deficits impose on some of these patients, understanding the effects of those self-deficits is insufficient to help restore the capacity for successful accommodations. For patients with neuropsychological deficits, an added set of interventions to traditional modes is often necessary. These may include didactic instruction, skill remediation, and referral for medication. Patients need tools that would help them bring about changes in their lives. I suggest that therapists can facilitate the acquisition of those tools by engaging the patients in a set of interactions that demonstrate their usefulness.

In contrast to the linear view of the therapeutic process as unfolding sequentially with a beginning, a middle, and a termination phase, I conceptualize the treatment process of patients with neuropsychological deficits as a *series of moments*. Moments in therapy are organizing events that capture the essence of the issues with which the patient is struggling at a given time during the process. These moments do not necessarily arrive sequentially but occur episodically. Moments occur when specific types of exchanges in the process between the therapist and patient are in the foreground of the interaction. By foreground, I mean periods during which the ebb and flow of the process are focused on a set of patterns that emerge in the transference. Such moments activate mindsharing responses by the therapist – that is, they evoke empathy or the desire to complement the patient's deficits. I conceptualize three types of moments: *concordant moments, complementary moments,* and *disjunctive moments* (cf. Racker, 1968, 1972).

During *concordant moments*, the foreground activities center on the establishment of a space in which the patient can be free to express her longing for complementary responses, while the therapist attunes himself to the nature of the patient's needs. I will suggest that the patient's expectations are found in what Ornstein (1986) called the "curative fantasy," whereas the therapist's responses are conveyed through what Spitz (1959) called the "diatrophic attitude." Therapists direct their efforts at understanding patients' experiences and creating a holding environment of safety. Once such an environment is established, the concordant moments recede into the background and the complementary moments come to the forefront.

During *complementary moments*, the patient reenacts within the transference the search for complementarity. The patient reveals the need for selfobject or adjunctive functions that would have been necessary to maintain a sense of self-cohesion. In the countertransference, the therapist may feel moved to respond to the patient's need for complementarity. As the patient's self-understanding develops, both therapists and patients work toward the co-construction of a narrative that incorporates elements of the patients' understanding of their experiences, the therapists' interpretations of what those meant, the factual knowledge acquired about the neuropsychological deficits themselves, and the effects these have had on the patients' life. A critical part of the process involves addressing the feelings of shame associated with having a deficit and the humiliations suffered by other people's criticism and disparagement of their behaviors, as well as dealing with the defenses engendered by these intense emotions. Through a recursive process in which the cycle of concordant, complementary, and disjunctive moments recurs, the therapist and the patient begin to modify their narratives and begin to co-construct a narrative that best fits all the information that is available to both.

Inevitably, *disjunctive moments* will occur because of ruptures in the process between therapists and patients (see Beebe & Lachmann, 2002, pp. 160–169; Beebe & Lachmann, 2014, p. 12; Schore, 2003, pp. 164–168). This will initiate the "rupture and repair" process. The ruptures will derail the dialogue. The resulting disjunction in the relationship will then come to the foreground. It will require immediate attention because of the disruption it causes in the treatment. Such disjunctions may result from the patient's fear of retraumatization or empathy failures. Both the therapist and the patient are participants in those disruptions. The process of their repair requires an examination of the contribution that each made to the disjunction and the extent to which these represent repetitions of the patient's dynamics. The successful repair of these ruptures may lead to a reorganization of the patients' dynamics, where greater differentiation and individuation occur, and more complex modes of relating to others than existed previously develops.

Summary

The central issue for clinicians who undertake the treatment of patients with neuropsychological deficits is that of understanding how they experience those deficits, how they process and integrate them, and what effects those deficits have on their developmental trajectory. The conceptual challenge we face in trying to answer these questions is that of proposing a framework through which we can account for the phenomena and the mental processes that accompany them. The data on which I build such a framework derives from the case material of patients with such deficits with whom I have worked for many years. This framework requires the introduction of an evolutionary viewpoint and a methodological shift to a nonlinear dynamic systems view of the relationship among phenomena.

By including neuropsychological deficits as contributors to the patient's symptoms, we are able to enlarge our view of the nature of these patients' psychodynamics. The concept of self-deficits, which some have criticized as politically incorrect and carrying some negative connotations, is meant to be descriptive and not judgmental. Its sense is no different from saying that someone has a fever or a parasitic infection. The introduction of the levels-of-analysis perspective – the neuropsychological, the introspective, and the interpersonal – describes the processes involved in patients' attempts at dealing with their self-deficits.

The interrelationship among the three domains of experience – the neuropsychological, the introspective, and the interpersonal – is an ever-changing process, whose course is unpredictable. Not only are the components deeply intertwined, but trying to untangle them, to tease them apart, leads to major challenges and may in fact lead to a distorted picture of the phenomena that contribute to the process. Therapists find themselves in the paradoxical position of trying to describe the process by focusing on one element and are misled into thinking that they have an understanding of what is occurring. On the other hand, trying to take into account all of the elements simultaneously is practically unfeasible. The balance lies in getting indications from the patients as to which factors were dominant in shaping their responses at different periods of time.

Mindsharing is the process through which complementarity occurs. Others in the patients' context respond to patients' self-deficits and are drawn to fill in the missing functions, a process that I call providing complementary functions. When such a complementarity is successful, the result is that the patient will be able to maintain a stable sense of self-cohesion.

The treatment process involves multiple modes of interaction between patients and therapists. These interactions, which involve explanations and interpretations, the relationship established between therapist and patient, and the patient's own proactive engagement, may become change agents.

The innovation to the understanding and treatment of patients with neuropsychological deficits that this work introduces is the emphasis on the interplay among the components of the domains of knowledge. We must consider not only the impact of the neuropsychological strengths and weaknesses on patients' development and ongoing accommodations to the circumstance that they confront, but also their unique interpretations of their experiences and the impact those deficits have on other individuals in the patients' context. The caregivers, teachers, and colleagues in the work environment will all have different interpretations that account for how patients think, feel, and behave. Based on those interpretations, some may have a negative and some a positive impact on the patient. Those responses will impinge on the patient, to which he or she will respond in turn. An added complexity will be the patient's own interpretation of and beliefs about the experiences to which he or she is exposed. These will contribute to the view of the world the patient forms. The circular interplay among these factors provides an initial set of conditions that require consideration during the assessment period and during the treatment.

Finally, I suggest that this framework is also applicable to acquired brain-based disorders, such as those caused by PTSD, traumatic brain injuries, brain lesions, the effects of radiation for brain tumors, and others. The clinical work and research necessary to test out its applicability to these conditions remains to be done.

Notes

1 In the 1990s, Laurence Miller (1991, 1992a, 1992b), a neuropsychologist, proposed in a series of papers, "A Neuropsychodynamic Model for Evaluation and Treatment," of patients with "organic" (i.e. neurological or neuropsychological) problems. His concerns were similar to mine in that he wished to integrate neuropsychological constructs with psychoanalytic theory. His proposals diverge from mine in two respects. The first is that he tied his model to ego psychology, and the second is that he did not integrate the data and processes that he discussed into a systems view. I have chosen to distinguish my approach from his by calling it a "perspective" rather than a model, because the

notion of a model implies a rigid framework into which the data and processes must fit, a view that is inconsistent with a systems approach.
2 For a more detailed discussion of learning disorders and these conditions, see Palombo (2001).

References

Amadei, G., & Bianchi, I. (Eds.). (2008). *Living systems, evolving consciousness, and the emerging person: A selection of papers from the life and work of Louis Sander*. New York: The Analytic Press.

Aron, L. (1996). *A meeting of minds: Mutuality in psychoanalysis*. New York: Routledge.

Bagwell, H. R. (1999). Integrative processing: A biological foundation for psychotherapy. *Psychiatry, 62*, 273–286.

Banathy, B. H. (2010). *Guided evolution of society: A systems view*. New York: Kluwer Academic/Plenum Publishers.

Beebe, B., Knoblauch, S., Rustin, J., & Sorter, D. (2005). Forms of intersubjectivity in infancy research and adult treatment: A systems view. In B. Beebe, S. Knoblauch, J. Rustin, & D. Sorter (Eds.), *Forms of intersubjectivity in infant research and adult treatment* (pp. 1–28). New York: Other Press.

Beebe, B., & Lachmann, F. M. (2002). *Infant research and adult treatment: Co-constructing interactions*. Hillsdale, NJ: The Analytic Press.

Beebe, B., & Lachmann, F. M. (2014). *The origins of attachment: Infant research and adult treatment*. New York: Routledge.

Beebe, B., Lachmann, F. M., & Jaffe, J. (1997). Mother-infant interactions structures and presymbolic self and object representations. *Psychoanalytic Dialogues, 7*, 133–182.

Bowlby, J. (1969). *Attachment and loss, Vol. I: Attachment*. New York: Basic Books.

Brandchaft, B., Doctors, S., & Sorter, D. (2010). *Toward an emancipatory psychoanalysis: Brandchaft's intersubjective view*. New York: Routledge.

Butz, M. R. (1997). *Chaos and complexity: Implications for psychological theory and practice*. New York: Taylor & Francis.

Chess, S., & Thomas, A. (1986). *Temperament in clinical practice*. New York: The Guilford Press.

Coburn, W. J. (2000). The organizing forces of contemporary psychoanalysis: Reflections on nonlinear dynamic systems theory. *Psychoanalytic Psychology, 17*, 750–770.

Coburn, W. J. (2009). Attitudes in psychoanalytic complexity: An alternative to postmodernism in psychoanalysis. In R. Frie & D. Orange (Eds.), *Beyond postmodernsim: New dimensions in clinical theory and practice* (pp. 183–200). New York: Routledge.

Cohler, B. J., & Galatzer-Levy, R. M. (1988). Self, meaning, and morale across the second half of life. In R. C. Nemiroff (Ed.), *Psychoanalytic perspectives on age and aging* (pp. 214–263). New York: Basic Books.

Crane, J., & Hannibal, J. (2009). *IB diploma programme: Psychology course companion*. New York: Oxford University Press.

Damasio, A. R. (1994). *Descartes' error: Emotion, reason, and the human brain*. New York: G.P. Putnam's Sons.

Dawson, P., & Guare, R. (2009). *Smart but scattered: The revolutionary "executive skills" approach to helping kids reach their potential*. New York: Guilford Press.

Demos, E. V. (2007). The dynamics of development. In C. Piers, J. P. Muller, & J. Brent (Eds.), *Self organizing complexity in psychological systems* (pp. 135–163). New York: Jason Aronson.

Edelman, G. M. (1992). *Bright air, brilliant fire: On the matter of the mind.* New York: Basic Books.

Emmons, R. A. (1995). Levels and domains in personality: An introduction. *Journal of Personality, 63*(3), 341–364.

Fosshage, J. L. (2003). Contextualizing self psychology and relational psychoanalysis: Bidirectional influence and proposed syntheses. *Contemporary Psychoanalysis, 39*(3), 411–447.

Fosshage, J. L. (2011). Development of individuality within a systems world. In R. Frie & W. J. Coburn (Eds.), *Persons in context: The challenge of individuality in theory and practice* (pp. 89–106). New York: Routledge.

Freedman, W. J. (2007). A biological theory of brain function and its relevance to psychoanalysis. In C. Piers, J. P. Muller, & J. Brent (Eds.), *Self-organizing complexity in psychological systems* (pp. 15–36). New York: Jason Aronson.

Freud, S. (1895). Project for a scientific psychology. In J. Strachey (Ed.), *Standard Edition* (Vol. 1, pp. 283–397). London: Hogarth Press.

Galatzer-Levy, R. M. (1995). Psychoanalysis and dynamical systems theory: Prediction and self similarity. *Journal of the American Psychoanalytic Association, 43*(4), 1085–1112.

Galatzer-Levy, R. M. (2002). Emergence. *Psychoanalytic Inquiry, 22,* 708–727.

Galatzer-Levy, R. M. (2004). Chaotic possibilities: Toward a new model of development. *International Journal of Psychoanalysis, 85,* 419–441.

Ghent, E. (2002). Wish, need, drive: Motive in the light of dynamic systems theory and Edelman's selectionist theory. *Psychoanalytic Dialogues, 12,* 763–808.

Godfrey-Smith, P. (2003). *An introduction to the philosophy of science: Theory and reality.* Chicago: University of Chicago Press.

Harris, A. E. (2011). Gender as a strange attractor: Discussion of the transgender symposium. *Psychoanalytic Dialogues, 21,* 230–238.

Kaplan-Solms, K., & Solms, M. (2002). *Clinical studies in neuro-psychoanalysis: An introduction to a depth neuropsychology* (2nd ed.). New York: Karnac.

Kohut, H. (1971). *The analysis of the self.* New York: International Universities Press.

Kohut, H. (1977). *The restoration of the self.* New York: International Universities Press.

Kohut, H. (1984). *How does analysis cure?* Chicago: The University of Chicago Press.

Kohut, H., & Wolf, E. S. (1978). The disorders of the self and their treatment: An outline. *International Journal of Psychoanalysis, 59,* 413–425.

Levin, F. M. (2003). Learning, development, and psychopathology: Applying chaos theory to psychoanalysis. In F. M. Levin (Ed.), *Psyche and brain: The biology of talking cures* (pp. 191–209). Madison, CT: International Universities Press.

Lichtenberg, J., Lachmann, F. M., & Fosshage, J. L. (2011). *Psychoanalysis and motivational systems: A new look.* New York: Routledge.

Masterpasqua, F., & Perna, P. A. (1997). *The psychological meaning of chaos: Translating theory into practice.* Washington, DC: American Psychological Association.

Matto, H. C., Strolin-Goltzman, J., & Ballan, M. S. (Eds.). (2014). *Neuroscience for social work.* New York: Springer.

Mesle, C. R. (2008). *Process-relational phylosophy: An introduction to Alfred North Whitehead.* West Conshohocken, PA: Templeton Press.

Miller, L. (1991). Psychotherapy of the brain-injured patient: Principles and practices. *The Journal of Cognitive Rehabilitation, 9*(2), 24–30.

Miller, L. (1992a). Cognitive rehabilitation, cognitive therapy, and cognitive style: Toward an integrative model of personality and psychotherapy. *The Journal of Cognitive Rehabilitation, 10*(1), 18–29.

Miller, L. (1992b). The primitive personality and the organic personality: A neuropsychodynamic model for evaluation and treatment. *Psychoanalytic Psychology, 9*(1), 93–109.

Miller, M. L. (1999). Chaos, complexity, and psychoanalysis. *Psychoanalytic Psychology, 16*, 355–379.

Miller, M. L. (2004). Dynamic systems and the therapeutic action of the analyst. In J. Reppen, J. Tucker, & M. A. Schulman (Eds.), *Way beyond Freud: Postmodern psychoanalysis observed* (pp. 132–155). London: Open Gate Press.

Mitchell, S. A. (1988). *Relational concepts in psychoanalysis: An integration.* Cambridge, MA: Harvard University Press.

Mitchell, S. A. (Ed.). (1995). *Self psychology after Kohut: A polylogue* (Vol. 5). Hillsdale, NJ: The Analytic Press.

Orenstein, M. (1992). Imprisoned intelligence: The discovery of undiagnosed learning disabilities in adults. A dissertation submitted to the faculty of the Institute for Clinical Social Work in Partial Fulfillment of the Degree of Doctor of Philosophy. Qualitative Study, Institute for Clinical Social Work, Chicago, IL.

Orenstein, M. (2000). *Smart but stuck: What every therapist needs to know about learning disabilities and imprisoned intelligence.* New York: The Hayworth Press.

Ornstein, A. (1986). Supportive psychotherapy: A contemporary view. *Clinical Social Work Journal, 14*(1), 14–30.

Palombo, J. (1979). Perceptual deficits and self-esteem in adolescence. *Clinical Social Work Journal, 7*(1), 34–61.

Palombo, J. (1983). Borderline conditions: A perspective from self psychology. *Clinical Social Work Journal, 11*(4), 323–338.

Palombo, J. (1985). The treatment of borderline neurocognitively impaired children: A perspective from self psychology. *Clinical Social Work Journal, 13*(2), 117–128.

Palombo, J. (1987). Selfobject transferences in the treatment of borderline neurocognitively impaired children. In J. S. Grotstein, M. F. Solomon, & J. A. Lang (Eds.), *The borderline patient* (pp. 317–346). Hillsdale, NJ: The Analytic Press.

Palombo, J. (1991). Neurocognitive differences, self-cohesion, and incoherent self-narratives. *Child & Adolescent Social Work Journal, 8*(6), 449–472.

Palombo, J. (1992). Learning disabilities in children: Developmental, diagnostic and treatment considerations. Paper presented at the Fourth National Health Policy Forum, Healthy Children 2000: Obstacles & Opportunities, April 24–25, 1992, Washington, DC.

Palombo, J. (1993). Neurocognitive Deficits, Developmental Distortions, and Incoherent Narratives. *Psychoanalytic Inquiry, 13*(1), 85–102.

Palombo, J. (1994). Incoherent self-narratives and disorders of the self in children with learning disabilities. *Smith College Studies in Social Work, 64*(2), 129–152.

Palombo, J. (1995). Psychodynamic and relational problems of children with nonverbal learning disabilities. In B. S. Mark & J. A. Incorvaia (Eds.), *The handbook of infant, child, and adolescent psychotherapy: A guide to diagnosis and treatment* (Vol. 1, pp. 147–176). Northvale, NJ: Jason Aronson.

Palombo, J. (1996). The diagnosis and treatment of children with nonverbal learning disabilities. *Child & Adolescent Social Work Journal, 13*(4), 311–332.

Palombo, J. (2000). A disorder of the self in an adult with a nonverbal learning disability. In A. Goldberg (Ed.), *Progress in self psychology* (Vol. 16, pp. 311–335). Hillsdale, NJ: The Analytic Press.

Palombo, J. (2001). *Learning disorders and disorders of the self in children and adolescents*. New York: W. W. Norton.

Palombo, J. (2006). *Nonverbal learning disabilities: A clinical perspective*. New York: W. W. Norton.

Palombo, J. (2008a). Mindsharing: Transitional objects and selfobjects as complementary functions. *Clinical Social Work Journal, 36*, 143–154.

Palombo, J. (2008b). Self psychology theory. In B. A. Thyer (Ed.), *Comprehensive handbook of social work and social welfare: Human behavior in the social environment* (Vol. 2, pp. 163–205). Hoboken, NJ: John Wiley & Sons.

Palombo, J. (2011). Executive function conditions and self-deficits. In N. H. Heller & A. Gitterman (Eds.), *Mental health and social problems: A social work perspective* (pp. 282–312). New York: Routledge.

Palombo, J. (2013a). The self as a complex adaptive system, part I: Complexity, metapsychology, and developmental theories. *Psychoanalytic Social Work, 20*(1), 1–25.

Palombo, J. (2013b). The self as a complex adaptive system, part II: Levels of analysis and the position of the observer. *Psychoanalytic Social Work, 20*(2), 115–133.

Palombo, J. (In Press a). The Self as a Complex Adaptive System Part III: A revised view of development. *Psychoanalytic Social Work*.

Palombo, J. (In Press b). The Self as a Complex Adaptive System Part IV: Making sense of the sense of self. *Psychoanalytic Social Work*.

Palombo, J., & Berenberg, A. H. (1997). Psychotherapy for children with nonverbal learning disabilities. In B. S. Mark & J. A. Incorvaia (Eds.), *The handbook of infant, child and adolescent psychotherapy: New direction in integrative treatment* (Vol. 2, pp. 25–68). Northvale, NJ: Jason Aronson.

Palombo, J., & Berenberg, A. H. (1999). Working with parents of children with nonverbal learning disabilities: A conceptual and intervention model. In J. A. Incorvia, B. S. Mark-Goldstein, & D. Tessmer (Eds.), *Understanding, diagnosing, and treating AD/HD in children and adolescents: An integrative approach* (pp. 389–441). Northvale, NJ: Jason Aronson.

Palombo, J., & Feigon, J. (1984). Borderline personality in childhood and its relationship to neurocognitive deficits. *Child & Adolescent Social Work Journal, 1*(1), 18–33.

Palombo, S. R. (1999). *The emergent ego: Complexity and coevolution in the psychoanalytic process*. Madison, CT: International Universities Press.

Palombo, S. R. (2007). Complexity theory as the parent science of psychoanalysis. In C. Piers, J. P. Muller, & J. Brent (Eds.), *Self-organizing complexity is psychological systems* (pp. 1–14). New York: Jason Aronson.

Piers, C. (2000). Character as self-organizing complexity. *Psychoanalysis and Contemporary Thought, 23*(1), 3–34.

Piers, C., Muller, J. P., & Brent, J. (Eds.). (2007). *Self-organizing complexity in psychological systems*. New York: Jason Aronson.

Racker, H. (1968). *Transference and countertransference*. New York: International Universities Press.

Racker, H. (1972). The meaning and uses of countertransference. *Psychoanalytic Quarterly, 41*, 487–506.

Sander, L. W. (1964). Adaptive relationships in early mother-child interaction. *Journal of the American Academy of Child & Adolescent Psychiatry, 3*(2), 231–264.

Sander, L. W. (1995). Identity and the experience of specificity in a process of recognition: Commentary on Seligman and Shanok. *Psychoanalytic Dialogues, 5*, 579–593.

Sander, L. W. (2002). Thinking differently: Principles of process in living systems and the specificity of being known. *Psychoanalytic Dialogues, 12*, 11–42.

Schore, A. N. (2003). *Affect regulation and the repair of the self.* New York: W.W. Norton.

Schore, A. N. (2014). The right brain is dominant in psychotherapy. *Psychotherapy, 51*(3), 388–397.

Seligman, S. (2005). Dynamic systems theories as a metaframework for psychoanalysis. *Psychoanalytic Dialogues, 15*(2), 285–325.

Shane, M., Shane, E., & Gales, M. (1997). *Intimate attachments: Toward a new self psychology.* New York: Guilford Press.

Skurky, T. A. (1990). *The levels of analysis paradigm: A model for individual and systemic therapy.* New York: Praeger.

Slavin, M. O., & Kriegman, D. (1992). *The adaptive design of the human psyche: Psychoanalysis, evolutionary biology, and the therapeutic process.* New York: The Guildford Press.

Solms, M. (2000). Preliminaries for an integration of psychoanalysis and neuroscience. *Annual of Psychoanalysis, 28*, 179–200.

Solms, M. (2011). What is neuropsychoanalysis? *Neuropsychoanalysis, 13*(2), 133–145.

Solms, M., & Turnbull, O. (2002). *The brain and the inner world: An introduction to the neuroscience of subjective experience.* New York: Other Press.

Spitz, R. A. (1959). Countertransference – Comments on its varying role in the analytic situation. *Journal of the American Psychoanalytic Association, 4*, 256–265.

Stern, D. N. (1983). The early development of schemas of self, other, and "self with other." In J. D. Lichtenberg & S. Kaplan (Eds.), *Reflections on self psychology* (pp. 49–84). Hillsdale, NJ: The Analytic Press.

Stolorow, R. D. (1997). Dynamic, dyadic, intersubjective systems: An evolving paradigm for psychoanalysis. *Psychoanalytic Psychology, 14*(3), 337–346.

Thelen, E. (2005). Dynamic systems theory and the complexity of change. *Psychoanalytic Dialogues, 15*(2), 255–284.

Thelen, E., & Smith, L. B. (1996). *A dynamic systems approach to the development of cognition and action.* Cambridge, MA: The MIT Press.

Van Der Kolk, B. A. (2014). *The body keeps the score: Brain, mind, and body in the healing of trauma.* New York: Viking.

Whitehead, A. N. (1967). *Science and the modern world: Lowell Lectures 1925.* New York: The Free Press.

Chapter 2

The self as a complex adaptive system

The concept of the self as a *complex adaptive system* (see J. Palombo, 2013a, 2013b, In Press a, In Press b) is a cornerstone of the *neuropsychodynamic perspective*. We may view the self as a complex adaptive system either from a *developmental viewpoint* (i.e. a historical viewpoint) or from a *dynamic viewpoint* (i.e. in its contemporaneous state). From a developmental viewpoint, the person is the product of her past; from a dynamic viewpoint, the person is a system of interactive components.

Obtaining a history of a patient's development during an evaluation may be enlightening, but alone it cannot give an understanding of the kind of integration the patient has achieved in his current adjustment. The patient's history may shed light on the meanings he or she derived from past experiences and how these affect the patient's current functioning. However, the history alone cannot account for the influence of events that occurred during the intervening years (see Wachtel, 2003).

The dynamic viewpoint focuses on the state of the self in the here-and-now, in its current relationships with others, and in its struggles with making experiences meaningful. While it provides a view of the self as the resultant of past experiences, the past is present in the here-and-now only as a shadow that may obscure or illuminate current meanings. Memories of past experiences are not fossilized artifacts that are recovered unchanged. They are recollections modified by their interrelationships with other experiences in the person's life. The two viewpoints, the developmental and the dynamic, while each is distinct from the other, are linked and intertwined with one another. Understanding our history is essential to understanding ourselves, but understanding ourselves also involves placing ourselves in the context of our present-day existence.

This chapter is divided into two sections. The first section is devoted to an examination of what we mean when we speak of the self as a complex adaptive system, which outlines the dynamic viewpoint. In this section, I introduce the levels-of-analysis perspective that permits the organization of the data of human experience. The second section summarizes the revised view of the development of the self (for a review of psychodynamic developmental theories, see Palombo, Bendicsen, & Koch, 2009), which outlines the developmental viewpoint.

The self as a complex adaptive system

The "self" is not an identifiable entity that is separable from the person; it consists of a set of experiences and psychological processes that form a person's subjectivity. As Sroufe reminds us, "For us, the unit of study is the whole person. It is the person that is accommodating, and the patterns we seek to assess are at the level of the person" (Sroufe, Egeland, Carlson, & Collins, 2005, p. 30). To speak directly of the self implies that there is an entity that can be defined and identified. Such a usage risks concretizing the self or positing it as a homunculus that is located within a person's psyche. To avoid this incoherence, the question we must ask is not "How do we define the self?" but rather "What do we mean when we speak of the self?" When using the term "self," I will be referring to what it means "to be a self," rather than what is the self (for a contrasting view, see Mitchell, 1991).

To be a self is to have the capacity to think, to feel, to learn, and to act. It means to be able to experience a sense of unity and cohesiveness to which individuals give expression through a coherent narrative that links the meanings of their experiences into a unified whole. This unified whole includes the past, the present, and the hopes for their future. Siegel (1999) refers to Alan Sroufe's definition of the self "as an internally organized cluster of attitudes, expectations, meanings, and feelings. In this view, the self emerges from an organized caregiving matrix that in part determines how the individual responds to and engages with or avoids the environment" (pp. 229–230).

To be a self also entails being more than the passive recipient of experiences (Stolorow & Atwood, 2016). To be a self is not to be a simple register or blank page on which experience is inscribed. We are also agents who act on our own behalf and who are capable of affecting others, being affected by others, and having an impact on the world around us through our actions. Our faculties and competencies filter and shape our experiences and give them a unique individuality that characterizes each person's response to an event. Some of these faculties and competencies are part of our "endowment." Each person's endowment is different and operates as a filter through which experiences register in a unique way for that person.

Furthermore, the self is not a static structure but a set of processes that are in continuous change. Unless interfered with, the direction of change during development is nonlinear. It progresses from the simple to the more complex at the three levels: the neurological, the psychological, and the social levels of organization. It moves on to an elaboration and transformation of psychological processes through its differentiation from others. Finally, it advances to the consolidation of the person's uniqueness and individuality. As Sander pointed out, "a wide range of research on both the animal and human levels . . . has revealed the singularity, the uniqueness of each newborn, each family system, and each individual's particular pathway of development" (Amadei & Bianchi, 2008, p. 167).

The self and its levels of analysis

To understand the self as a complex adaptive system requires that we examine the major components associated with the three domains of knowledge of the self as a system. At the neuropsychological level (L-I), I address the *diversity of the neuropsychological components*; at the introspective level (L-II), I discuss its *preferences*; and at the interpersonal level (L-III), I focus on the *modes of interaction among the components*. These components cannot be abstracted from the context that the person inhabits. Consequently, an understanding of the contribution of the context is an essential element of the complexity of the self. Furthermore, these components interact with each other to form clusters of processes that self-organize into stable patterns.

In considering the neuropsychological level (L-I), we will study the *diversity among each* individual's neuropsychological deficits. Included in the neuropsychological functions are the processes involved in cognition, in affect processing, and in social interaction and communication. The diversity in the innate givens of individuals with neuropsychological deficits contributes to how they experience the events to which they are exposed and how it shaped their responses to those events. Whether a child is born with ADHD or dyslexia, these will set constraints on his or her development. They will have an impact on the interaction among the components of the self and on relationships with others. Furthermore, depending on the type and severity of the self-deficit, the person's sense of self may be stable or unstable. The presence of a severe executive function disorder, when combined with an unsupportive environment, may be so destabilizing as to lead to chronic states of fragmentation. In other cases, the person may be resistant to change. In such cases, the system is closed to the reception of information or other interventions that may serve as change agents.

At the introspective level (L-II), two preferences guide the direction of the developmental process: the *preference for self-cohesion* versus fragmentation, and the preference for *self-understanding* that enhances the capacity to make the world intelligible to us (see Edelman, 1992; Emde, 1988; Stern, 1985).

The concept of *self-cohesion* is used descriptively to characterize a state of self-consolidation (Stolorow, Brandchaft, & Atwood, 1987). A sense of self-cohesion is fundamental to our psychological survival. It constitutes the totality of the person's experiences both conscious and unconscious and is an indicator of the individual's sense of stability or instability. At a subjective level, people experience the sense of self-cohesion as having a sense of agency, a sense of history, a sense of coherence, a sense of changing over time yet retaining their individuality, and a sense of privacy (see Stern, 1985, p. 229). The context, which supplies selfobject functions and adjunctive functions, permits individuals to feel whole. A set of positive affect states, such as feelings of well-being, wholeness, and vitality, are associated with the sense of self-cohesion. However, in patients with neuropsychological deficits, most often, affects of a negative valence associated with feelings of shame or inadequacy prevails and threaten their sense of self-cohesion.

The second preference that engages a person's sense of self is the preference for *self-understanding*. Self-understanding includes the hierarchies of meanings that individuals acquire from self-experience. The affect states that we bring to the events in our lives shape our experiences and our interpretations of the meanings of those experiences. Our self-understanding reflects the stability and integrity of the set of meanings that have organized those experiences into a system. Self-understanding may potentially open areas of the self that were sequestered and unavailable for successful accommodations. The self-narrative that we construct and through which we integrate the meanings of our experiences supplements our efforts at self-understanding. Although we do not necessarily construct these narratives consciously, they find expression in the fragments of autobiographical statements through which we give expression to them.

In patients with neuropsychological deficits, the impact of the neuropsychological strengths and weaknesses will impose constraint on the path their development will take. Along with those constraints, their capacity to accommodate to the demands made of them will determine whether they can maintain a sense of self-cohesion. Furthermore, since such patients are rarely aware of the fact that they have a brain dysfunction, their responses to other people's labeling of their actions will bias their self-understanding and their failures to live up to their own expectations. These patients' self-narratives often reflect the failure to integrate the origins of their self-deficits, as those are often transparent to them.

At the interpersonal level (L-III), the *modes of interaction with others*, I discuss our interactions with others through our interpersonal relationships and through the dialogue in which we engage with them. I conceptualize the nature of people's interactions with others as our *interconnectedness*. The context in which we live anchors our interconnectedness. This context interpenetrates our experiences.

Attachment theory provides a neurobiological underpinning for the bond that infants form with their caregivers (Schore, 1994, 2000, 2003, 2005). The *relational patterns* that we bring to our interactions with others as well as the type of *attachment* that we form with them define our interconnectedness with others. We are also in communication with others in the environment, whose inputs constitute change agents that may transform or modify internal processes. I will refer to these exchanges between people as a *dialogue*. We may then think of the dialogue between caregivers and infants as a *developmental dialogue* and the interchanges between therapists and patients as a *therapeutic dialogue*.

For patients with neuropsychological deficits, a pattern of reciprocal and circular interchanges among the patient, the deficits, and the context is the hallmark of the interactions with others. For them, if a mismatch exists between the competencies or abilities they bring to the context and environment's demands, the conditions may be analogous, from the point of view of the recognition process, to the deficits representing the wrong key to the lock that would open the door to a successful accommodation. As we will see, patients with a neuropsychological deficit evoke responses from others around them that are different from the responses that a person without such a disorder evokes. Nevertheless, that is only the beginning of a complex set of interactions. The person responds to those responses in ways that often heighten the sense of difference. These responses lead to further responses that, at times, reinforce the vicious cycle of negative interactions. Even if the responses from the context are positive, a set of circular interactions may be unavoidable. The presence of the neuropsychological deficit inevitably alters the course of the person's development.

Another major element in this level of analysis is the human capacity for *dialogue*. The capacity to communicate at a cognitive and emotional level is vital to our ability to function in social contexts. I focus on the dialogue as the prototypical experience that we have in connecting with others. The domain of *communication* is central to all interactions within systems. All social interactions occur within a context that imbues those interactions with communicative acts, both verbal and nonverbal, cognitive and affective. Through verbal and nonverbal language, we convey our feelings and thoughts to others who attempt to grasp not just what we say, but also what we intend to convey. Affect and cognition are closely entwined and provide insight into the forces that motivate individuals. Affective communication and affect processing are integral to all social relationships.

For patients with neuropsychological deficits, the interaction with others and other people's responses to them, which in a circular way produce a set of new responses, coalesce into patterns that uniquely contribute to their identities. The extent to which their ability to dialogue with others, whether verbal or nonverbal, is constrained will make it possible for them either to maintain a sense of a connectedness with others or to lapse into solitary isolation.

The controversy in psychoanalytic theories as to whether a one-person or a two-person psychology presents a more valid view of psychological functioning deserves much more extended treatment than can be given here (Aron, 1990; Stolorow, 1997). Elsewhere, I stated that the bifurcation between the two positions reflects the insistence that only one perspective from which to view psychological phenomena is tenable or that more than one perspective cannot be held simultaneously. Proponents of the two-person view deny the validity of any other perspective. Whereas theoretical purity may dictate such a view, it does not account for the complexity of the observed phenomena and for the existence of other perspectives. I suggest that the levels-of-analysis methodology combined with the nonlinear dynamic systems perspective offers a possible resolution to the false polarity of whether a two-person psychology has greater validity than a one-person psychology. This point of view suggests that each position has validity depending on the level of analysis from which investigators examine the phenomena. The controversy stems from a failure to specify the levels of analysis from which the data for the theory are derived and the failure to take into account the fact that the associated field of observation requires that the observer stand on a platform that is itself part of a dynamic system (J. Palombo, 2013b).

Changed perspective on developmental theories

Since the appearance of Stern's (1985) landmark book *The Interpersonal World of the Infant*, a quiet upheaval has occurred in our understanding of infants' development. Traditional psychoanalytic theories of infancy have been slowly and systematically undermined. The charts of infant development have been radically redrawn. The integration of the new evidence from developmental psychology has led to a different prospective view of the infant as contrasted with the old reconstructed view (see Palombo, Bendicsen, & Koch, 2009). Contributing to this upheaval have been the attempts to integrate the findings from neuroscience into psychoanalytic theories, in particular, the integration of the insights gained in our understanding of the processes involved in attachment, the role of memory function in structuring relational patterns (Lyons-Ruth, 1998, 1999), and the effects of trauma, such as abuse and neglect, on children's lives (Fonagy, 2000, 2001, 2005; Fonagy & Target, 2002; Schore, 2000, 2001a, 2001b, 2002, 2005; Siegel, 1999; Van Der Kolk, 2014).

Trends that contributed to the revised views of development

Three broad trends have contributed to the revolution that has taken place in our thinking about development in recent years. The *first trend*, led by Bowlby (1969, 1973, 1980) and Stern (1985), revised traditional theories of development by replacing the data sets of the old theories with those based on the newer findings from infancy. Cozolino (2006, 2010, 2014), Schore (1994, 1997a, 1997b), Siegel (1999), and Palombo (Palombo,

Bendicsen, & Koch, 2009) led the *second trend*. Each of these authors sought to integrate the findings from the neurosciences into psychoanalytic or psychodynamic theory. Schore and Siegel chose attachment theory into which to incorporate the brain functions associated with the right orbitofrontal region as critical to the development of the capacity for self-regulation. Cozolino offered a broad framework for a neurobiological basis for interpersonal relationships. Palombo (1991, 1996, 2001a, 2006) focused on the integration of the effects of neuropsychological deficits, such as learning disorders, into a psychodynamic clinical theory. The contributors to the *third trend* were Sander (Amadei & Bianchi, 2008; Sander, 1980, 2002, 2008b), Thelen (2005) and Tronick (2007). Each broke new ground through the application of a nonlinear dynamic view of development to our understanding of human psychology.

The contributions of Bowlby and Stern

Bowlby's (1969, 1973, 1980) attachment theory held a problematic place in the history of psychoanalytic developmental theories because of his initial ostracism from the psychoanalytic community. It gained broad acceptance by developmental psychologists who conducted numerous studies to support its findings (Sroufe et al., 2005). In recent years, it has found increasing acceptance by psychoanalysts through the work of Fonagy (2001, 2005) and Lyons-Ruth (1998, 1999), who have integrated its findings into a psychoanalytic framework.

Bowlby's major contribution was to place developmental theory into the mainstream of the scientific paradigm. Borrowing from Konrad Lorenz's ethological findings and taking an evolutionary viewpoint, he proposed that attachment was a species-specific behavioral pattern that infants manifest in the service of survival. Infants seek shelter from predators by forming a secure bond with their caregivers. Separation from the caregiver leads to a characteristic set of sequential patterns that manifest through external behaviors and that accompany internal experiences.

In the initial phase of separation, children display a pattern of protest that reflects separation anxiety. Next, children manifest despair that denotes the process of grief and mourning. Finally, they become detached from the environment as a defense against the intolerable psychic pain with which they are flooded. Caregivers respond to the infants' communications (i.e. cries and calls) by reestablishing the attachment through reunion.

Bowlby's theory was met with an outcry of criticism by Anna Freud (1960) and others in the psychoanalytic community (Schur, 1960; Spitz, 1960), who claimed that the theory dealt more with behavioral aspect of attachment than with its intrapsychic effects. Bowlby's response was two-fold. First, he pointed to the data from Harlow and others that contradicted the claim that object relations were based on "need satisfaction," which he disparagingly called the "cup-board theory" of attachment. Second, he borrowed from cognitive psychology the concept of "internal working models" to reinforce his claim that he did address the children's psychodynamics. He proposed that internal working models are cognitive maps that children construct of themselves, of others, and of the interactions among both.

The relationship with the caregiver, which consists of affective interchanges between mothers and infants, is critical to the infant's survival. The quality of the caregiver's responses to the infant's needs determines whether continued growth can occur (see Palombo, Bendicsen, & Koch, 2009, p. xxxix). Attachment theory emphasizes the quality of the caregiver's relationship to the infant as determining the type of attachment the infant will form. The innate need drives the infant to seek proximity to the caregiver and not the infant's psychological nutritional needs.

In his landmark book, *The Interpersonal World of the Infant*, Stern (1985) elaborated a new theory of the subjectivity of the infant that is based both on the data collected by developmental theorists and the data from the clinical setting with which psychoanalysts are most familiar. Beebe (1982) and Demos (1984, 1988, 2007) each made their own significant contributions through their research on infants. The result has been a radically different view of infancy from the one accepted traditionally.

Stern proposed that development may be conceptualized as occurring along four domains, each of which is initiated at a different period but continues through the lifespan. The first domain of the emergent self begins at around birth through the second month. Its characteristics are that the infant's sense of self comes into being. The second domain has its ascendency between the second and seventh month, when the core sense of self begins to form. It heralds the beginning of the infant's social interactions, which through the social smile and vocalization lead to the formation of the sense of agency, the sense of self-coherence, self-affectivity, and self-history. In the third domain, which begins at 7 months and has its apex at 15 months, the subjective sense of self emerges. Infants discover that they have minds; they become aware of the affective responses, which the caregivers' affect attunement makes possible. The verbal sense of self emerges in the fourth domain with the onset of language acquisition between 15 and 30 months. In this domain, language acquisition provides a major impetus for separation and individuation. With it comes the capacity to represent events mentally and encode them in long-term memory. Stern saw language acquisition as causing a breach between infants' earlier preverbal experiences because they become reinterpreted and lead to a slippage between the personal world and the external world. Following the publication of his book, Stern added a fifth domain, that of the narrative sense of self, which occurs between 30 and 48 months. During this period, infants construct stories that serve to explain what is happening to them. They then weave these stories into autobiographical narratives that lend coherence to their lives (cf. Palombo, Bendicsen, & Koch, 2009, pp. 243–256).

Whereas Stern largely based his earlier work on empirical findings from the research that he conducted or with which he was familiar, following his participation in the Boston Change Process Study Group (2010), he shifted his position to a relational and social constructivist view of the therapeutic process. This position became problematic to the efforts to integrate the neurosciences and psychoanalysis. As he stated, "There are past events that radically influence the present, not by actively shaping it in an ongoing fashion, but rather by imposing initial constraints and degrees of freedom on what are possible experience. These constraints include neurophysiological alternations that were irreversibly fixed early in development due to sensitive/critical periods, trauma, and conflict." He follows this view with the puzzling statement: "This past is no longer an active influence. It is a past only in the historical sense or the narrative sense, when viewed from the outside. *Phenomenologically it does not exist and never will exist*" (Stern, 2004, p. 206, italics added).

Schore, Cozolino, and Palombo

Contributing to the second trend are the attempts at integrating attachment theory and the finding from the neuroscience within a psychodynamic framework. The work of Schore on the neuropsychological foundations of attachment provided a strong impetus to further exploration of the contributions that brain functions make to development (Schore, 2001a, 2001b, 2012; Siegel, 1999). In his first book, Schore (1994) provided an ontogenetic view of the neurobiology of subjectivity and intersubjectivity. In subsequent works, he elaborated on the neurobiological processes involved in infants' attachment to their caregivers. He postulated that attachment is a regulatory theory, whose brain mechanisms are understandable in light of the findings of current neuroscience. The process that is central to infant development is the capacity for affect regulation. He stated: "A fundamental theme of the current paradigm shift in conceptualizations of human infancy is articulated in the principle that learning how to communicate emotional states is an essential developmental process" (Schore, 2012, p. 230). Through the modulated interchanges between the caregivers' right brain functions and the infants' right orbital frontal region, the maturation of the region permits the infant to auto-regulate affect states and function independently.

During the first year, limbic circuits emerge in the sequential progression, from the amygdala to the anterior cingulate to the insula and finally to the orbital frontal region. As a result of attachment experiences, the system enters a critical period of maturation in the last quarter of the first year. The orbital prefrontal cortex is a convergence zone where the cortex and subcortex meet. It is the only cortical structure with direct connections to the hypothalamus, the amygdala, and the reticular formation in the brain stem that regulates arousal. Through these connections, it can modulate instinctual behaviors. However, because it contains neurons that process face and voice information, this system can appraise changes in the external environment, especially the social object-related environment.

Due to its connections, at the orbital frontal level, cortically processed information concerning the external environment is integrated with subcortically processed information regarding the internal visceral environment. The orbital frontal cortex is involved in critical human functions, such as social adjustment and the control of mood, drive, and responsibility, traits that are crucial in defining the "personality" of an individual.

The orbital frontal system, the "senior executive" of the social-emotional brain, is especially expanded in the right cortex and its role as an executive of the limbic arousal; it acts in the capacity of an executive control function for the entire right brain. For the rest of the lifespan, the right brain plays a superior role in the regulation of fundamental physiological and endocrinological functions whose primary control centers are located in subcortical regions of the brain. The infant's capacity to cope with stress correlates with certain maternal behaviors, but the attachment relationship directly shapes the maturation of the infant's right brain stress coping system that acts at levels beneath awareness.

Building a bridge between Bowlby's theory and the neurobiological underpinnings of attachment, Schore proposed that the right brain stores an internal working model of the attachment relationship that encodes strategies of affect regulation and maintains basic regulation and positive affect even in the face of environmental challenge. These unconscious processes are stored in the right cerebral non-declarative-procedural memory (Schore, 2001b).

Cozolino (2014) did not address directly issues of development but undertook the task of describing the neurobiological processes involved in social relationships and attachment that occur in the social brain. Drawing an analogy between brain function at the neuronal synaptic level, he outlines the functions of the "social synapse."

The *social synapse* is the space between us – a spaced filled with seen and unseen messages and the medium through which we are combined into larger organisms such as families, tribes, societies, and the human species as a whole. Because our experience as individual selves is lived at the border of this synapse and because so much communication occurs below conscious awareness, this linkage is mostly invisible to us (p. xv, italics in original).

In his book, richly illustrated with clinical examples, Cozolino outlines the set of brain structures involved in our interactions with others. These structures include the cortical and subcortical structures, the integrated networks of the basal forebrain and the default mode network, the sensory, motor, and affective systems, and the regulatory networks. Through a detailed description of the functions of the structures and their substructures, he documented the contribution that each makes to our humanity and social behavior. The significance of his contributions along with those of Solms (2011) and the neuropsychoanalysis movement is that they further the agenda of establishing an association rather than a correlation between neural processes and mental processes.

Long before these contributors to neuropsychoanalysis made their impressive progress in the project of integrating the findings of neuroscience and psychoanalysis, beginning in 1979, I became aware of the complexities of the etiologies of dysfunctional states that result from learning disorders (J. Palombo, 1979, 1992, 1995, 1996, 2001a, 2001b, 2006). My efforts were directed at integrating concepts from self psychology with the neuropsychological deficits found in children with learning disorders. My goal was to modify treatment interventions to make them effective in working with this population (e.g., J. Palombo, 2011).

Development and nonlinear dynamic theory

A major early contributor to the third trend was Sander (Amadei & Bianchi, 2008; Sander, 1962, 1964, 1985, 1998, 2000, 2002, 2008a, 2008c), who began to apply the methodology of nonlinear dynamic systems theory to infant observation and to a psychoanalytic developmental theory as early as 1954. Sander, influenced by Bertalanffy (1972) and Weiss (1945), sought to expand psychoanalytic theory with the inclusion of research on infants. He applied the principles of systems theory, permitting him to include biological as well as environmental factors into his conceptual framework. This trend highlights the shift away from the view that the source of all psychopathology stems from the "endogenous" (i.e. repression of drives or drive derivatives) to appreciate the place of the "exogenous" (i.e. external trauma-based factors) (Howell & Itzkowitz, 2016, p. 29).

In two seminal papers that are richly rewarding to read, Sander (2000, 2002) summarized his views on development. He began by proposing that our understanding of mental health requires the integration of the data from multiple disciplines, such as biology, neuroscience, psychology, anthropology, and others, a proposal that I consider critical to placing developmental theories within the disciplinary matrix (cf. Kuhn, 1970) that encompasses the knowledge acquired by the scientific community.

Sander (2000) viewed development as occurring within an evolutionary context that for human beings reaches its apex with the organization of consciousness and self-awareness. The task of a developmental theory is to trace the processes that lead an infant as a biological being to a self that has the capacity for self-reflection. Among the initial conditions involved in the traversal of that path are the infant's experiences that sculpt brain development. Critical to those experiences is the specificity of fit between the infant and its caregiving environment, while appreciating the wide diversity of child-rearing procedures. He identifies the "recognition"[1] process as an essential contributor to the facilitation of the "fittedness" (i.e. fitting together) between infant and caregiver. The recognition process, as we have seen, is an evolutionary construct through which adaptation occurs. When an infant experiences a caregiver's positive response as addressing a specific affect state, the infant feels recognized, that its caregivers have satisfactorily met its needs. At such moments, shared awareness occurs and the infant feels capable of affecting its environment. By seven to nine months, a sense of agency emerges that lays the groundwork for the infant's capacity to be a self-initializing agent and to affect the context by its actions. These processes engender the coherence of the system, that is, the coordination of the component parts of the self into a functional whole occurs, which result in higher hierarchical levels of mental organization and complexity (Sander, 2000, 2002).

Schore (1994) was also an early proponent of the application of nonlinear dynamic systems theory to development, as was Siegel (1999), who in a critical chapter of his book extended attachment theory by introducing concepts from complexity theory to our understanding of states of mind. He outlined some of the processes through which the self-system emerges as a result of the self-organization and adaptability to environmental changes. Internal and external constraints direct the trajectory of the individual's development. He stated:

> Complexity theory suggests that self organization allows the system to adapt to environmental changes through the movement of its states towards increasingly complex configurations. Moving with a balance of flexibility and continuity, the system emerges within the internal and external constraints that define the trajectory of state changes. Internal constraints include the strength distribution of synaptic connections within neural pathways, external constraints include social experiences that the two and emotional communication between people. By regulating these internal and external constraints, the self system evolves through an emerging set of self states that have cohesion in continuity within themselves.
>
> (p. 238)

Through the application of *nonlinear dynamic systems theories* and a *complexity view* to human development, we may link data about neuropsychological, psychological, and social aspects of human functioning into an organizing framework. Such a framework would provide an inclusive, comprehensive, and coherent account of the self as a *complex adaptive system*. This trend is consistent with the broad acceptance of evolutionary theory as a bulwark of our understanding of our capacity to adapt and to survive. In their work, Beebe and Lachmann (2002, 2014) provide an excellent example of the integration of findings from infant research with an interactive system's model for the treatment of patients.

As we have seen, the principles these theories articulate provide a guide to the processes involved in the changes that occur within and these among components of human psychological functioning. When applied to human conduct they provide a powerful tool, a metatheory, through which we can cross traditional disciplinary lines and integrate knowledge acquired by different disciplines into a broad, inclusive panorama of human beings as biological, psychological, and social beings.

A revised view of development

In the revised view, development occurs not in stages but through a set of processes, such as self-regulation (Schore, 1994), self-organization, values, and biases that govern its direction, heightened affect states, and the desire for coherence, all of which contribute to the capacity to accommodate the context that we inhabit. We can best understand human development through an analysis of the processes that govern the self as a complex adaptive system (Lansing, 2003; J. Palombo, 2013a, 2013b, in Press a, in Press b). Masterpasqua (1997, pp. 23–33) describes some characteristics of complex adaptive systems from a developmental perspective. First, the elements of such systems are not centrally controlled; what emerges is the result of the interactions among the elements. This means that, among other factors, no central mechanism directs the phases or stages of development. Second, the elements of the system are responsive to the internal or external context in which the system exists. The significance of this characteristic is that during development, human beings respond to their internal states and to the external environment in which they live. A communication system exists among the internal components and between the system and its environment, which affects what goes on within the system. Third, a set of patterns forms a map of the interactions between the context and its environment such that the map acts as a guide to future interactions. Finally, complex adaptive systems, as living systems, are open systems that are dynamically, continuously changing and reorganizing themselves. There is no single path to the trajectory of development, but many alternative paths.

Advocates of developmental theories based on nonlinear causality propose a continuous construction model. Masterpasqua (1997) quotes Zeanah as stating that "patterns of subjective experience and patterns of relating to others are derived from past relationship experiences that are continuously operating in the present" (p. 35). Self-organization and emergent properties are characteristics of such systems. For example, one might interpret Spitz's (1965) Organizers: the *smiling response*, which emerges at 2 to 3 months; *stranger anxiety*, which becomes evident at around 8 months; and *negation*, which occurs at around 18 months, as evidence of such a self-organizing principle.

The new perspective suggests that we may characterize growth as the unfolding of the innate maturational patterns in interaction with the environment (cf. Weiss, 1945). It represents an ongoing series of changes in the direction of higher levels of organization. It connotes the emergence of something new within something old and a progression in which a succession of changes occurs in an orderly manner. The new emergent organization recursively reworks the old, providing continuity in the succession of organizational states. The progression may include temporary states of instability, thus presenting an ebb and flow that may be rhythmic and characteristic for any given infant.

Consistent with this view, the neuropsychodynamic perspective proposes that all development is contingent on the interaction between our environment and us. Our brains require exposure to external stimuli to grow and function. Both endowment and the environment impose constraints on the extent to which we can develop and mature. Innate differences may constrain the extent to which we can achieve in our environment, and, in turn, the unavailability of resources in our environment may impose constraints on how we mature. All development occurs within a social context to which each infant is exposed. Infants are born within a context from which they are inseparable. The caregiving environment endows each child's actions with meaning. Yet, the context alone does not determine the nature of a child's experience; the child's endowment and the unique interpretation the child brings to those experiences also influence those experiences. Adaptability brings together all of the elements at play within the system into an integrated, organized, and coherent experience.

From a biological perspective, we may also view the self as becoming progressively differentiated from less developed or immature on to more developed or mature states. The more mature, the more complex is the state of its organization. The process occurs epigenetically – that is, the self develops hierarchically while preserving traits from prior states. These traits have their origin in the heritable components carried genetically by the person. Similarly, from a psychological perspective, maturation entails three sets of interacting processes: those that lead to more *complex levels of organization*, those that enhance *differentiation* from others, and those that strengthen the person's *individuality* (see Weiss, 1945).

From simple to complex

During development, the movement from simple to more complex levels of organization, which is closely linked to the process of adaptation, is activated by the system's self-organizing functions (Amadei & Bianchi, 2008; Piers, Muller, & Brent, 2007). While the concept of growth gives a holistic view of development, we may identify components within this whole as playing significant roles. These components appear marshaled together in a way that permits their orderly unfolding. In the same way that the genetic code encased in the fertilized egg determines the direction of fetal development, a similar process exists for psychological development. An example is the elaboration of self-understanding that occurs during development. As we accrue experiences, mature in our cognitive capacities, learn from our exposure to the world, and acquire an enhanced capacity for self-reflection, our self-understanding as well as our understanding of our relationships to others grows in sophistication and complexity. We also develop a greater appreciation of the complex world that we inhabit. Self-organization occurs at multiple, hierarchical levels, at the level of brain function, at the psychological level, and at the social level.

At the biological level, the brain is an example of a self-organizing system (Edelman, 1992). As Perry (Perry, Pollard, Blakley, Baker, & Vigilante, 1995) maintained:

> The brain is not a "single" system. It is constituted of many interacting and interconnected systems organized in a specific hierarchy with the most complex (cortex) and the least complex (brainstem) on the bottom. Different parts of the brain, different "systems" in the brain

mediate different functions (e.g., the cortex mediates thinking, the brainstem/midbrain mediate state of arousal).

(p. 290)

At the psychological level, the sense of self is ever in transition from one state to the next, moving from less complex to more complex states of self-organization. It is capable of continuous self-organization around attractors. It is ever-changing, ever in flux, and in interaction with others. Yet, we remain identifiable as being the same person in spite of the many changes through which we go as we age. Our capacity for a Theory of Mind, which emerges at around age 4, provides us not only with a sense of privacy but also with the ability to realize that others have beliefs, desires, intentions, and motives that are distinct from ours. The contribution of attractors and the maturation of cognitive functions lead to emergent properties that in conjunction with other functions increase the level of organization and build on hierarchical modules that enhance our capacity to deal with increasingly more complex tasks.

At the social level, we may speak in many ways about our relationship to the social context that we inhabit. To be a person means always to be *embedded in a context*, which we may call the universe or environment that the person inhabits. To be a person is to be a member of a human community. Each of us is born into a community that gives meaning to our existence and to which we contribute by our existence. The community represents the context of others with whom we are connected and with whom we communicate. The community provides a physical, social, cultural, and psychological *context* in which we develop. We bring to the social context a set of biological givens that shape our responses to others and other people's responses to us. Our sense of self is constituted from our experiences and from the explanations that we give ourselves about those experiences. However, our interconnectedness also sets constraints on our abilities to function independently from others. In fact, without others, our existence would be in jeopardy (cf. Coburn, 2011; Fosshage, 2011; Frie, 2002; Lachmann, 2011).

The social context, which represents the environment of evolutionary adaptedness, also provides a set of *complementary functions* necessary for the development of our sense of self and for the movement to higher levels of organization. As stated earlier, the fit between a person's competencies and the environment's requirements is like a lock and a key, the lock being the environment and the key being the individual's capacities; unless a match exists, they cannot unlock the door. When applied to children's development, the concept of "fit" describes the conditions in which a communicative link with caregivers exists through which the child can mature. Depending on the child's temperament, parents attune themselves and resonate with the inner states of their infants; they organize themselves to complement the infant's psychic needs and become translators of the infant's nonverbal messages. In a variety of areas, their psychic functions compensate for those the child is too immature to perform. The harmony created from birth through these efforts provides a hospitable environment in which the infant can thrive. It includes an active, though nonconscious, molding of the parent to the infant. Thus, parents and children harmoniously adapt to each other, creating an interaction in which each partner responsively cues the other so that no disruption need occur. When successful, this interaction has the appearance of a joyous engagement in which maternal bliss accompanies the infants' smile. These conditions permit the processes involved in reaching higher hierarchical levels of psychological organization to occur within the child.

Differentiation

Differentiation occurs at multiple levels. It is observable at the neurophysiological level in the brain changes that occur through maturation, at the psychological level in the complexity of our capacity to process thoughts and feelings, and at the social level in the entangled relationships that we develop with others. As an example of our differentiation from others, I highlight our sense of agency and the unique capacity we have, as persons, to control our thoughts and actions, which stem from the subjective conviction that we as agents are actors in our daily lives, all of which differentiate us from others.

Several authors have addressed the issue of the sense of agency (Frie, 2008a, 2008b). Stern (1985) maintained that to have a sense of agency is to be the locus of activity, whereas Kohut (1977) referred to the self as "the center of initiative" (p. 99), which emerges from the sense of self-cohesion. Sander (2002) attributed the development of the sense of agency as emerging at the moment an infant becomes conscious that its cry can evoke a response from another. He called this process the capacity for self-activation. He proposed that the ontogeny of the sense of agency is found in "the motivation to act as directed by the desire to attain the goal." He stated: "In the human, the experience of a sense of validity of one's self-as-agent in one's own self-regulation and self-organization is an essential feature of mental health" (2000, p. 7). Others, such as Stolorow, reject the idea that individuals have a sense of agency as based on the confusion created by failing to distinguish between a one-person and a two-person psychology. He believed that a sense of agency can only exist in an "isolated mind" (see Frie, 2002, p. 668).

The sense of agency is associated with the capacity to effect changes in ourselves and in the context that we inhabit. We associate it with the experience of being effective as agents of change and the experience that Basch (1980) called the feeling of competence. The loss of the sense of agency is critical to our understanding of some patient's inability to accommodate to the context. When that occurs, they feel hopeless, unable to control their lives, and keep enacting old patterns. Our understanding of psychopathology accounts for this loss of control over one's life; it attempts to explain how it is that self-deficits deprive patients of the ability for purposive behavior.

The sense of agency is therefore not only critical to the conduct of our lives, but it also serves as a change agent in the therapeutic setting: "[T]he notion of the person as agent of change is undeniably central to the clinical work of psychoanalysis. . . ." (Frie, 2002, p. 659). The broader implications of having a sense of agency plays out during the therapeutic process, where we expect patients to undertake changes in old patterns as well as in other areas of their lives. This view – of patients taking charge of their lives in an effort to effect changes in themselves – is in contrast to the position that insight and interpretation are the only mutative factors in therapy. This reminds me of a patient I saw early in my career who had achieved great insight into the conflicts that buffeted her life. At one point, she stopped her train of thoughts and, looking puzzled, said, "I certainly understand myself, the way my childhood contributed to my problems, and the motives for my thoughts and actions, but that does not seem to help me make any changes in my life." What she lacked was the ability to act in order to make the changes to undo some of the effects of her old patterns of relating. I contributed to her helplessness with the belief that understanding alone should have been enough to produce a positive outcome.

Ultimately, differentiation results in, among other experiences, the joyous encounters with life's challenges, the consolidation of the self in adolescence, the ambitious pursuit of an ideal in adulthood, the creative generativity of maturity, the sense of being an independent center of initiative, and the possessor of a coherent narrative. Finally, the harmony, firmness, and vitality of the sense of self will reflect the motives and interpretation of events that people bring to their lives. Each developmental step includes an integration of the parts into a whole that is more than the sum of its parts.

Our sense of agency as therapists is no less important. It finds expression not only in our capacity to be authentic with our patients but also in our belief that we can be effective as change agents. We not only expect patients to be proactive on their own behalf and to take ownership of their feelings, thoughts, and behaviors but we contribute to the process by effecting changes in ourselves because of what we learn from our patients.

Individuation

The uniqueness of each individual challenges us to explain how it is that each person retains her individuality even as each is in a continuous state of flux. As mentioned earlier, the sense of self is ever in transition from one state to the next. It is in continuous self-organization around attractor states. The central enigma we face is how to delineate our individuality without particularizing our separateness. "We are not separable from others, but we are distinguishable from others" (Colapietro, 1989). We live in a context of which we are an integral part. The context becomes part of us even as we lend parts of ourselves to others within our context. What makes it possible for us to retain a sense of individuality is that we do not sink into a morass that merges us into the rest of humanity. Lines of demarcation exist that make us distinguishable from each other. We each have a sense of agency, a history; each of us follows a separate developmental path. Like the river that keeps flowing, whose waters are never the same, yet it remains recognizable as the existing body of water, so it is with our sense of self. It is ever-changing, ever in flux, and always interacting with others. Yet as persons, we remain identifiable by others.

Each person is an *individual* that is distinct from others, although not separable from others. Beyond our attachment to others, we are entwined with others who provide us with complementary functions, such as selfobject and adjunctive functions, even as we provide them with similar functions. As social beings, isolation from others deprives us of the psychological nourishment that we need to survive. Each infant creates its own unique organization contingent on its initial conditions and the dynamic interactions among those conditions and its environment; it cannot survive alone (Sander, 1995).

Our individuality, our uniqueness, is an emergent property of the interactions among the components of the self: "Each person's life has its own patterns" (Sander, 2002, p. 12). Contributing to that uniqueness are factors that stem from our neuropsychological endowment. The diversity of our endowment, in interaction with the environment in which we grew up and currently inhabit, contributes to our uniqueness and our individuality. From an introspective perspective, each of us has a history, and each of us has followed a separate developmental path that contributes to the sense of self-cohesion that we experience. Our history provides a sense of continuity that permits us to develop a coherent autobiographical account of the events in our lives.

For patients with neuropsychological deficits, the uniqueness of their profile's strengths and weaknesses reflects their individuality. What this means is that their needs for complementary functions are as varied as are their self-deficits. Their individuality is therefore intimately tied to their interconnectedness to others (Fosshage, 2009; Frie & Coburn, 2011; VanDerHeide & Coburn, 2009).

Summary

Human development and the psychological phenomena that accompany maturation are best understood as complex adaptive systems (Lansing, 2003). The two views of the self as a complex adaptive system, the developmental and dynamic views, complement each other and enrich our understanding of our mental processes. From a developmental perspective, we understand maturation to consist of the increasing complexity that results from the self-organizing processes involved in the integration of experience. From a dynamic perspective, we define the self as a system constituted of a neuropsychological dimension that delineates the person's neuropsychological strengths and weaknesses, an introspective dimension that provides a window into the person's subjectivity and an interpersonal dimension that tells us about the person's interconnectedness with others and the dialogue we conduct with others. The term *self* encompasses all of these three dimensions.

The importance of an evolutionary viewpoint of the self is that it enlarges our understanding of the adaptive processes in which we engage to attain the goals we set for ourselves. Central to adaptation is the recognition process or the process through which we try to match our abilities to best fit the context we inhabit. Whereas, at times, it is possible for us to modify that context to achieve our goals, at other times we must modify ourselves to attain those goals. The complementary functions that others provide us and that we provide to others are central to our functions as social beings and are continuous with the recognition process that is part of our evolutionary heritage.

Three major trends have influenced the revised view of development: first, the replacement of traditional theories by the data from attachment theory and findings from infancy research; second, the attempt to integrate the findings from the neurosciences into psychoanalytic theory; and third, the application of the methodology of nonlinear dynamic theory to the revised views of development. The effect of these modifications of developmental theory led to the proposal that maturation of the person involves three sets of processes: the movement from simple to complex levels of organization, the differentiation of its functions, and the development of the person's uniqueness.

Finally, the *context that we inhabit* is an inextricable part of our interactions with others. Even though we are always embedded in this social context, this does not mean that we lose our individuality or sense of agency. We are distinct from others because of our neuropsychological makeup, our histories, and our relationships. However, that does not necessarily mean that we are therefore separable from others. Our capacity to exercise our sense of agency and volition permits us to express our individuality within the constraints imposed by our natural abilities and the social environment.

We are all situated in contexts that contribute to how we develop, who we are, and what we become. The communities in which we are raised define, in part, the meanings of our experiences. Caregivers convey to each child a view of the world, a shared vision of the reality to which the child is exposed. Just as the context lends an imprint to children's experiences, they in turn interpret those experiences through the lens of their neuropsychological strengths and weaknesses. Children are neither born with a blank slate, upon whom experiences are inscribed, nor are they entirely the creators of the reality to which they are exposed. Individuals contribute their share to the final vision of the world to which they arrive.

In summary, the value of this approach to understanding psychological phenomena as applied to individuals with neuropsychological deficits is twofold: It discredits old ways of thinking and it opens the door to new insights into psychological processes that guide their development.

Note

1 Sander assigns a different sense to the term *recognition* than does Edelman (1992). For Amadei and Bianchi (2008), recognition "gives ascendency to a new level of awareness in negotiating adaptation for both mother and toddler" (p. 97). It includes the "realization that another can be aware of what one is aware of within oneself, that is a shared awareness" (p. 97). This concept is closer to Fonagy's concept of mentalization (Fonagy, Gergely, Jurist, & Target, 2002), whereas Edelman (1992) considers it part of the evolutionary adaptive process.

References

Amadei, G., & Bianchi, I. (Eds.). (2008). *Living systems, evolving consicousness, and the emerging person: A selection of papers from the life and work of Louis Sander*. New York: The Analytic Press.

Aron, L. (1990). One-person and two-person psychologies and the method of psychoanalysis. *Psychoanalytic Psychology*, 7, 475–485.

Basch, M. F. (1980). *Doing psychotherapy*. New York: Basic Books.

Beebe, B. (1982). Micro-timing in mother-infant communication. In M. Key (Ed.), *Nonverbal communication today: Current research* (pp. 168–195). New York: Mouton.

Beebe, B., & Lachmann, F. M. (2002). *Infant research and adult treatment: Co-constructing interactions*. Mahwah, NJ: The Analytic Press.

Beebe, B., & Lachmann, F. M. (2014). *The origins of attachment: Infant research and adult treatment*. New York: Routledge.

Bertalanffy, L. V. (1972). The history and status of general systems theory. *The Academy of Management Journal*, 15(4), 407–426.

Boston Change Process Study Group. (2010). *Change in psychotherapy: A unifying paradigm*. New York: W. W. Norton.

Bowlby, J. (1969). *Attachment and loss, volume I: Attachment*. New York: Basic Books.

Bowlby, J. (1973). *Attachment and loss, volume II: Separation, anxiety and danger*. New York: Basic Books.

Bowlby, J. (1980). *Attachment and loss, volume III: Loss: Sadness and depression*. New York: Basic Books.

Coburn, W. J. (2011). Reflections on the challenges of individuality. In R. Frie & W. J. Coburn (Eds.), *Persons in context: The challenge of individuality in theory and practice* (pp. 121–145). New York: Routledge.

Colapietro, V. M. (1989). *Pierce's approach to the Self: A semiotic perspective on human subjectivity*. Albany, NY: State University of New York Press.

Cozolino, L. (2006). *The neuroscience of human relationships: Attachment in the developing social brain*. New York: W. W. Norton.

Cozolino, L. (2010). *The neuroscience of psychotherapy* (2nd ed.). New York: W. W. Norton.

Cozolino, L. (2014). *The neuroscience of human relationships: Attachment in the developing social brain* (2nd ed.). New York: W. W. Norton.

Demos, E. V. (1984). Empathy and affect: Reflections on infant experience. In M. B. J. Lichtenberg & D. Silver (Eds.), *Empathy II* (pp. 9–34). Hillsdale, NJ: The Analytic Press.

Demos, E. V. (1988). Affect and the development of the self: A new frontier. In A. Goldberg (Ed.), *Frontiers in self psychology* (Vol. 3, pp. 27–54). Hillsdale, NJ: The Analytic Press.

Demos, E. V. (2007). The dynamics of development. In C. Piers, J. P. Muller, & J. Brent (Eds.), *Self organizing complexity in psychological systems* (pp. 135–163). New York: Jason Aronson.

Edelman, G. M. (1992). *Bright air, brilliant fire: On the matter of the mind*. New York: Basic Books.

Emde, R. N. (1988). Introduction: Reflections on mothering and on reexperiencing the early relationship experience. *Infant Mental Health Journal, 9*(1), 4–9.

Fonagy, P. (2000). Attachment and borderline personality disorder. *Journal of the American Psychoanalytic Association, 48*(4), 129–146.

Fonagy, P. (2001). *Attachment theory and psychoanalysis*. New York: Other Press.

Fonagy, P. (2005). Attachment, trauma and psychoanalysis: When psychoanalysis meets neuroscience. Paper presented at the IPA 44th Conference on Trauma: Developments in Psychoanalysis, Rio de Janeiro.

Fonagy, P., Gergely, G., Jurist, E. L., & Target, M. (2002). *Affect regulation, mentalization, and the development of the self*. New York: Other Press.

Fonagy, P., & Target, M. (2002). Early intevention and the development of self-regulation. *Psychoanalytic Inquiry, 22*(3), 307–335.

Fosshage, J. L. (2009). Some key features in the evolution of self psychology and psychoanalysis. In N. VanDerHeide & W. J. Coburn (Eds.), *Self and systems: Explorations in contemporary self psychology* (Annals of the New York Academy of Sciences ed., Vol. 1159, pp. 1–18). Boston, MA: Blackwell.

Fosshage, J. L. (2011). Development of individuality within a systems world. In R. Frie & W. J. Coburn (Eds.), *Persons in context: The challenge of individuality in theory and practice* (pp. 89–106). New York: Routledge.

Freud, A. (1960). Discussion of Dr. John Bowlby's paper. *The Psychoanalytic Study of the Child, 15*, 53–62.

Frie, R. (2002). Modernism or postmodernism? Biswanger, Sullivan, and the problem of agency in contemporary psychoanalysis. *Contemporary Psychoanalysis, 36*, 635–673.

Frie, R. (Ed.). (2008a). *Psychological agency: Theory, practice, and culture*. Cambridge, MA: The MIT Press.

Frie, R. (2008b). Introduction: The situated nature of psychological agency. In R. Frie (Ed.), *Psychological agency: Theory, practice, and culture* (pp. 1–32). Cambridge, MA: The MIT Press.

Frie, R., & Coburn, W. J. (2011). Introduction: Experiencing context. In R. Frie & W. J. Coburn (Eds.), *Persons in context: The challenge of individuality in theory and practice* (pp. xv–xxx). New York: Routledge.

Howell, E. F., & Itzkowitz, S. (2016). From trauma-analysis to psycho-analysis and back. In E. F. Howell & S. Itzkowitz (Eds.), *The dissociative mind in psychoanalysis: Understanding and working with trauma* (pp. 20–32). New York: Routledge.

Kohut, H. (1977). *The restoration of the self.* New York: International Universities Press.

Kuhn, T. S. (1970). Reflections on my critics. In I. Lakatos & A. Musgrave (Eds.), *Criticism and the growth of knowledge* (pp. 231–278). Cambridge: Cambridge University Press.

Lachmann, F. M. (2011). Development of individuality within a systems world. In R. Frie & W. J. Coburn (Eds.), *Persons in context: The challenge of individuality in theory and practice* (pp. 107–117). New York: Routledge.

Lansing, J. S. (2003). Complex adaptive systems. *Annual Review of Anthropology, 32,* 183–204.

Lyons-Ruth, K. (1998). Implicit relational knowing: Its role in development and psychoanalytic treatment. *Infant Mental Health Journal, 19*(3), 282–289.

Lyons-Ruth, K. (1999). The two-person unconscious: Intersubjective dialogue, enactive relationsal representation, and the emergence of new forms of relational organization. *Psychoanalytic Inquiry, 19*(4), 576–617.

Masterpasqua, F. (1997). Toward a dynamical developmental understanding of disorder. In F. Masterpasqua & P. A. Perna (Eds.), *The psychological meaning of chaos: Translating theory into practice* (pp. 23–40). Washington, DC: American Psychological Association.

Mitchell, S. A. (1991). Contemporary perspectives on self: Toward an integration. *Psychoanalytic Dialogues, 1,* 121–147.

Palombo, J. (1979). Perceptual deficits and self-esteem in adolescence. *Clinical Social Work Journal, 7*(1), 34–61.

Palombo, J. (1991). Neurocognitive differences, self-cohesion, and incoherent self-narratives. *Child & Adolescent Social Work Journal, 8*(6), 449–472.

Palombo, J. (1992). Learning disabilities in children: Developmental, diagnostic and treatment considerations. Paper presented at the Fourth National Health Policy Forum, Healthy Children 2000: Obstacles & Opportunities, April 24–25, 1992, Washington, DC.

Palombo, J. (1995). Psychodynamic and relational problems of children with nonverbal learning disabilities. In B. S. Mark & J. A. Incorvaia (Eds.), *The handbook of infant, child, and adolescent psychotherapy: A guide to diagnosis and treatment* (Vol. 1, pp. 147–176). Northvale, NJ: Jason Aronson.

Palombo, J. (1996). The diagnosis and treatment of children with nonverbal learning disabilities. *Child & Adolescent Social Work Journal, 13*(4), 311–332.

Palombo, J. (2001a). *Learning disorders and disorders of the self in children and adolescents.* New York: W. W. Norton.

Palombo, J. (2001b). The therapeutic process with children with learning disorders. *Psychoanalytic Social Work, 8*(3/4), 143–168.

Palombo, J. (2006). *Nonverbal learning disabilities: A clinical perspective.* New York: W. W. Norton.

Palombo, J. (2011). Executive function conditions and self-deficits. In N. H. Heller & A. Gitterman (Eds.), *Mental health and social problems: A social work perspective* (pp. 282–312). New York: Routledge.

Palombo, J. (2013a). The self as a complex adaptive system, part I: Complexity, metapsychology, and developmental theories. *Psychoanalytic Social Work*, 20(1), 1–25.

Palombo, J. (2013b). The self as a complex adaptive system, part II: Levels of analysis and the position of the observer. *Psychoanalytic Social Work*, 20(2), 115–133.

Palombo, J. (In Press a). The Self as a Complex Adaptive System Part III: A revised view of development. *Psychoanalytic Social Work*.

Palombo, J. (In Press b). The Self as a Complex Adaptive System Part IV: Making sense of the sense of self. *Psychoanalytic Social Work*.

Palombo, J., Bendicsen, H., & Koch, B. (2009). *Guide to psychoanalytic developmental theories*. New York: Springer.

Perry, B. D., Pollard, R. A., Blakley, T. L., Baker, W. L., & Vigilante, D. (1995). Childhood trauma, the neurobiology of adaptation, and "use-dependent" development of the brain: How "states" become "traits." *Infant Mental Health Journal*, 16(4), 271–291.

Piers, C., Muller, J. P., & Brent, J. (Eds.). (2007). *Self-orgnanizing complexity in psychological systems*. New York: Jason Aronson.

Sander, L. W. (1962). Issues in early mother-child interaction. *Journal of the American Academy of Child & Adolescent Psychiatry*, 1(1), 141–166.

Sander, L. W. (1964). Adaptive relationships in early mother-child interaction. *Journal of the American Academy of Child & Adolescent Psychiatry*, 3(2), 231–264.

Sander, L. W. (1980). New knowledge about the infant from current research: Implications for psychoanalysis. *Journal of the American Psychoanalytic Association*, 28(1), 181–197.

Sander, L. W. (1985). Toward a logic of organization in psychobiological development. In H. Klar & L. J. Siever (Eds.), *Biologic Response Styles: Clinical Implications* (pp. 21–36). Washington, DC: American Psychiatric press.

Sander, L. W. (1995). Identity and the experience of specificity in a process of recognition: Commentary on Seligman and Shanok. *Psychoanalytic Dialogues*, 5, 579–593.

Sander, L. W. (1998). Intervention that effect change in psychotherapy: A model based on infant research. *Infant Mental Health Journal*, 19(3), 280–281.

Sander, L. W. (2000). Where are we going in the field of infant mental health? *Infant Mental Health Journal*, 21, 5–20.

Sander, L. W. (2002). Thinking differently: Principles of process in living systems and the specificy of being known. *Psychoanalytic Dialogues*, 12, 11–42.

Sander, L. W. (2008a). The event-structure of regulation in the neonate-caregiver system as a biological background for early organization of psychic structure. In G. Amadei & I. Bianchi (Eds.), *Living systems, evolving consicousness, and the emerging person: A selection of papers from the life and work of Louis Sander* (pp. 153–166). New York: The Analytic Press.

Sander, L. W. (2008b). Investigation of the infant and its caregiving environment as a biological system. In G. Amadei & I. Bianchi (Eds.), *Living systems, evolving consicousness, and the emerging person: A selection of papers from the life and work of Louis Sander* (pp. 115–138). New York: The Analytic Press.

Sander, L. W. (2008c). Paradox and resolution: From the beginning. In G. Amadei & I. Bianchi (Eds.), *Living systems, evolving consicousness, and the emerging person: A selection of papers from the life and work of Louis Sander* (pp. 167–176). New York: The Analytic Press.

Schore, A. N. (1994). *Affect regulation and the origin of the self: The neurobiology of emotional development*. Hillsdale, NJ: Lawrence Earlbaum.

Schore, A. N. (1997a). A century after Freud's *Project*: Is a rapprochement between psychoanalysis and neurobiology at hand? *Journal of the American Psychoanalytic Association, 45*(3), 807–840.

Schore, A. N. (1997b). Interdisciplinary developmental research as a source of clinical models. In M. Moskowitz, C. Monk, C. Kaye, & S. J. Ellman (Eds.), *The neuronbiological and developmental basis for psychotherapeutic intervention* (pp. 1–72). Northdale, NJ: Jason Aronson.

Schore, A. N. (2000). Attachment and the regulation of the right brain. *Attachment and Human Development, 2*(1), 23–47.

Schore, A. N. (2001a). Effects of a secure attachment relationship on right brain development, affect regulation, and infant mental health. *Infant Mental Health Journal, 22*(1/2), 7–66.

Schore, A. N. (2001b). Minds in the making: Attachment, the self-organizing brain, and developmentally-oriented psychoanalytic psychotherapy. *British Journal of Psychotherapy, 17*(3), 299–328.

Schore, A. N. (2002). Advances in neuropsychoanalysis, attachment theory, and trauma research: Implications for self psychology. *Psychoanalytic Inquiry, 22*(3), 433–484.

Schore, A. N. (2003). Minds in the making: Attachment, the self-organizing brain, and developmentally-oriented psychoanalytic psychotherapy. In J. Corrigall & H. Wilkinson (Eds.), *Revolutionary connections: Psychotherapy and neuroscience* (pp. 7–51). London: Karnac.

Schore, A. N. (2005). Attachment, affect regulation, and the developing right brain: Linking developmental neuroscience to pediatric. *Pediatrics in Review, 26*(6), 204–217.

Schore, A. N. (2012). *The science of the art of psychotherapy*. New York: W. W. Norton.

Schur, M. (1960). Discussion of Dr. John Bowlby's paper. *The Psychoanalytic Study of the Child, 15*, 63–84.

Siegel, D. J. (1999). *The developing mind: Toward a neurobiology of interpersonal experience*. New York: Guilford Press.

Solms, M. (2011). What is neuropsychoanalysis? *Neuropsychoanalysis, 13*(2), 133–145.

Spitz, R. (1960). Discussion of Dr. John Bowlby's paper. *The Psychoanalytic Study of the Child, 15*, 85–208.

Spitz, R. A. (1965). *The first year of life: A psychoanalytic study of normal and deviant development of object relations*. New York: International Universities Press.

Sroufe, L. A., Egeland, B., Carlson, E. A., & Collins, W. A. (2005). *The development of the person: The Minnesota study of risk and adaptation from birth to adulthood*. New York: Guilford Press.

Stern, D. N. (1985). *The interpersonal world of the infant*. New York: Basic Books.

Stern, D. N. (2004). *The present moment in psychotherapy and everyday life*. New York: W. W. Norton.

Stolorow, R. S. (1997). Principles of dynamic systems, intersubjectivity, and the obsolete distinction between one-person and two-person psychologies: A meeting of minds: Mutuality in psychoanalysis by Lewis Aron. *Psychoanalytic Dialogues, 7*, 859–868.

Stolorow, R. D., & Atwood, G. E. (2016). Experiencing selfhood in not "a self." *International Journal of Psychoanalytic Self Psychology, 11*(2), 183–187.

Stolorow, R. D., Brandchaft, B., & Atwood, G. E. (1987). *Psychoanalytic treatment: An intersubjective approach*. Hillsdale, NJ: The Analytic Press.

Thelen, E. (2005). Dynamic systems theory and the complexity of change. *Psychoanalytic Dialogues, 15*(2), 255–284.

Tronick, E. Z. (2007). *The neurobehavioral and social-emotional development of infants and children*. New York: W. W. Norton.

VanDerHeide, N., & Coburn, W. J. (Eds.). (2009). *Self systems: Exploration in comtemporary self psychology*. Boston: Blackwell.

Van Der Kolk, B. A. (2014). *The body keeps the score: Brain, mind, and body in the healing of trauma*. New York: Viking.

Wachtel, P. L. (2003). The surface and the depths: The metaphor of depth in psychoanalysis and the ways in which it can mislead. *Contemporary Psychoanalysis, 39*, 5–26.

Weiss, P. (1945). The problem of specificity in growth and development. *Yale Journal of Biology and Medicine, 19*(3), 235–278.

Chapter 3

Self-deficits
The neuropsychological domain (L-I)

The first domain is the neuropsychological (biological) domain, which I designate as L-I, and focuses on *patients' experience of their neuropsychological strengths and weaknesses* – that is, their experience of the profile of their brain functions as obtained through a neuropsychological assessment. Each person is endowed with a set of competencies that include (among others) cognitive faculties, skills, and talents (cf. Kohut, 1991), the capacity to process affect states including the capacity for self-regulation, and the ability to form attachments and to engage in a dialogue with others.

However, considerable variability may exist in any individual's profile, with deviation from the norm in specific areas of functioning. Neuropsychological deficits consist of impairments in functional areas of the brain that may be due to neurodevelopmental or neurocognitive factors or they may also result from acquired insults, such as traumatic brain injuries or psychological trauma. However, while the latter may bear similarities to innate deficits, they require separate treatment. I will refer to these as *neuropsychological self-deficits*. These data provide the information necessary to interpret the initial conditions that shaped each person's early experiences and possibly the entire course of that person's lifespan.

I will propose a definition of psychopathology as *the unsuccessful accommodations to the patient's context that result primarily from these self-deficits*. Such unsuccessful accommodations may manifest either as the inability to perform a task, or as anxieties that interfere with the person's ability to cope with the demands made by the context (cf. Brandchaft, Doctors, & Sorter, 2010). That is, both the self-deficits, as part of the person's functional impairment, and the context's failure to provide for the missing function contribute the person's unsuccessful accommodations. The combination reflects the system's failure.

Since the primary focus of this work is on neuropsychological deficits, I focus in this chapter on self-deficits in the neuropsychological domain (L-I). In the chapters that follow, I discuss the impact of these neuropsychological deficits on patients' experiences as they manifest in the introspective domain (L-II). I then deal with the effects of these deficits on patients' interactions and relationships with others, as displayed in the interpersonal domain (L-III). Even though this sequential presentation may appear to do violence to a systems' view, I will allude to the interplay among the three domains and the components of the three domains as I discuss each domain.

A nonlinear dynamic systems view of neuropsychological deficit

The proposal to extend the concept of *self-deficits* from its original usage in self psychology to the domain of neuropsychological deficits originated from my work with children with learning disabilities. For self psychology, deficits result from the repeated frustrations associated with an environment that individuals experienced as unresponsive to their needs (i.e. empathy failures) that led to selfobject deficits. The deficits denote the absence of the development of psychological functions that enhance the capacity for self-cohesion. Evidence for the absence of those functions appears in the anxiety generated by the threat to the individual's sense of self-cohesion and the longings for missing selfobject functions (Kohut, 1971, 1977, 1984; J. Palombo, 2008). It is important to keep in mind that in referring to "longings," I am using the term metaphorically, as the driving motivational factor at play is the system's preference for self-cohesion rather than some sort of independent drive to seek the missing functions.

I suggest the existence of a different type of self-deficit, which I call *adjunctive deficits*, that are associated with innate neuropsychological functions (J. Palombo, 2011), which are associated with impairments in functional areas of the brain. Adjunctive deficits may occur in one or more of the brain's functional units, such as impairments in cognitive, affective, or social domains.

Self-deficits may therefore result either from factors related to nurture (i.e. selfobject function) or from those related to our endowment (i.e. adjunctive functions). Selfobject deficits result from an environment that is unresponsive to the person's emotional needs, whereas adjunctive deficits are due to innate factors.

Neuropsychological deficits, such as specific learning disorders associated with dyslexia, ADHD, executive function disorders, or nonverbal learning disabilities, represent an impairment in a functional area of one or more components of the brain as a system. For neuropsychologists, deficits in functional areas of the brain are regarded as occurring when a person's test scores on normed instruments appear at the low end of a normal distribution curve for the functions being tested. There is a large repertoire of neuropsychological function that includes, among others, the *cognitive domain*: sensory, perceptual, motor, attentional, memory, executive functions, and receptive, expressive, and language processing. In the *social and emotional domains*, we have the capacities for verbal and nonverbal communication and the ability to be in touch with, to regulate, and communicate affect states. In the *interpersonal domain*, we find aptitude for social connectedness and social interactions, including types of attachment. This incomplete catalogue of functions serves to underscore the complexity of the task of attempting to identify the part each function plays (see Lezak, Howieson, & Loring, 2004).

From a dynamic systems perspective, it is important to remember that such neuropsychological deficits do not represent absolute impairments in the person's sense of self, but rather they reflect a system's failure to accommodate a specific context. We may say that the person lacks the resources necessary to deal with the challenges the context presents, even as the context fails to provide the necessary complementary function for the person to successfully accommodate the context. Although such dysfunctions have reverberations throughout the system, they seldom have predictable outcomes. At times, they may set constraints on the individual's ability to accommodate the context and to accomplish the goals they set for themselves. For example, ADHD as a disorder that reflects a deficit in the capacity for self-regulation and may set constraints on a person's capacity for intimacy in a relationship, because of the person's diminished tolerance to stay connected to positive affect states. The individuals' specific psychodynamics determine the outcomes.

From a nonlinear dynamic systems perspective, the neuropsychological deficits become focal points around which the self-organization of patients' psychodynamics and lived experiences occurs. These experiences produce what we may call an "attractor" around which patterns of responses become organized. An attractor is a mental function that has become an organizer of experience. The nucleus of an attractor is an experience or set of experiences that has left an imprint because of the special meaning attributed to it by the person. This imprint consists of a set of conscious or nonconscious memories that were encoded at the time of the occurrence of the experience. These then exert a "gravitational pull" that leads to the accrual of patterns of responses that become habitual. These patterns lead the person to anticipate that similar outcomes will ensue whenever confronted with experiences that recall the original ones. I call these attractors "adventitious organizers" because they opportunistically bring together factors that may or may not be related to each other, forming enduring patterns of responses or interactions that become encoded either in declarative or non-declarative memory. These attractors also become entwined with other personality factors, such as temperamental variabilities, genetic predispositions, innate capacities for self-regulation, and others.

In other words, if we think of the experience of a patient with ADHD, the presence of such a disorder (i.e. self-deficit) will affect many of that person's day-to-day activities. The repetition of positive and negative experience will cluster together into a pattern that becomes habitual for that person. This pattern will then form a template around which other experiences will accrue, thus forming an "attractor" or an organizer of future experiences. These patterns are encoded in implicit memory and serve as ways in which the person will respond to situations that evoke any aspect of the original experiences. The result is that for patients, these patterns become traits that distinguish them from others. They compare themselves to others, viewing their differences as something to conceal and of which they should be ashamed. These feelings constrain their capacity to meet the demands and challenges that the context imposes on them or to accommodate to them.

When we consider individuals with neuropsychological deficits, we note not only the differences in the severity of their deficits but also the coexistence of other conditions that contribute to that uniqueness. For example, a patient's nonverbal learning disability can coexist with exceptional sensory or motor problems or with musical gifts that receive great recognition. In addition, environmental variability, such as having been raised by a single parent, having multiple siblings, being a minority, or suffering poverty, abuse, or neglect, will each add to the uniqueness of the person.

Individuals' neurobehavioral deficits filter their experiences. The resulting meanings they draw from the events they encounter impose a further level of complexity on their development (J. Palombo, 2001). Some have to hide parts of themselves from others; they have to be constantly vigilant to the possibility of the exposure of their self-deficits and live with the convictions that they are leading fraudulent lives. Since most often they are unaware of the nature of these deficits, they will seek to explain to themselves the reasons for the disruptions in their relationships to others. They will construct explanations to integrate their life experiences. Some of these explanations will become themes in this self-narrative that will shape their expectations of how others might respond to them.

Diversity as variability in patients' endowment

Endowment is constituted, among other factors, of the biological correlates of behaviors, brain process, neurotransmitters, hormones, and behavioral genetics. In what follows, I will use the term *innate* in the sense that Damasio defined and use it interchangeably with the term *endowment*. According to Damasio (1994),

> [W]hen I use the word innate (literally, present at birth), I am not excluding a role for environment and learning in determination of the structure or pattern of activity. Nor am I excluding the potential for adjustments brought by experience. I am using innate in the sense that William James used "pre-set," to refer to structures or patterns that are largely but not exclusively determine by the genome, and that are available to newborns to achieve homeostatic regulation.
>
> (p. 109)

To be a self is to be in possession of faculties and competencies with which each person is endowed at birth. Each person is born with a set of neuropsychological strengths and weaknesses that are distinctive for that person. Each person is endowed with different capacities for cognition, perception, affectivity, memory, motor function, and linguistic and other abilities. In addition, each person's endowment includes the capacity to feel, to think, to learn, and to act, the capacity to generate and interpret signs, the capacity for self-awareness, self-criticism, and self-control, and the capacity for attachment to others. As Milner and her colleagues (Milner, Squire, & Kandel, 1998) stated: "Recent work on plasticity in the sensory cortices has introduced the idea that the structure of the brain, even in the sensory cortex, is unique to each individual and dependent on each individual's experiential history" (p. 463).

While this view may seem to exaggerate the differences among people, it highlights the uniqueness of each person, his individuality, and his distinctiveness from everyone else. The importance of insisting on these differences is that from a dynamic systems perspective, we are focusing on the diversity among the processes that govern the internal workings of the components. Sander (1995) referred to *specificity* as the uniqueness of a system's attributes; that is, individuals bring particular sets of givens to the context that are then matched by a particular set of responses by another. Specificity of fittedness (matching) leads to a unique process of interaction between a mother and her infant, such that the uniqueness of a mother's interactions with her infant leads to specific adaptive patterns in the infant (cf. Weiss, 1945).

Luria (1973) introduced the concept of functional units of brain processes. He maintained that mental functions are the products of complex systems, the component parts of which may be distributed throughout the structures of the brain. Disturbance in any of the component parts causes the entire functional system to malfunction. Functions are distributed widely among networks of brain structures; each structure contributes a particular component to the dynamics of the system as a whole (see also Solms & Turnbull, 2002).

As exemplars of mental functions, I deal with three domains: the cognitive, the affective, and the social. Among the functions associated with the *cognitive domain* are memory functions, attentional capacities, executive functions, and receptive, expressive, and language processing capacities. Included in the *affective domain* are the ability for emotional communication and, for the evaluation of self-states, and the capacity for self-regulation. The *social domain* includes the broad range of abilities involved in the capacity for social interactions and social communication. From a dynamic systems perspective, I will refer to these mental functions as *adjunctive functions* to the sense of self and will draw a parallel between these functions and selfobject functions. As we will see, much as others complement a person's sense of self by providing selfobject functions, so it is with adjunctive functions.

Endowment and environment

As complex adaptive systems, individuals respond differently to events to which they are exposed, and every relationship that a person has is embedded in a context that is different from every other person. Endowment cannot be isolated from the context in which the person emerges, which also contributes to the uniqueness of the person's experience. Alone, it does not define all of the person's experiences. We must also take into account the interpenetration of the context into the person's experiences (Pally, 1997). Environmental variability interacts with genetic variability. For some, genetic structures set constraints, while environmental factors influence gene expression and behavior. For others, their capacities, environmental variability, and learning have a more complex role. Basic biological capacities are necessary but not sufficient conditions for individual learning. The learning steps that lead to symbolic thought are embedded in cultural learning processes, not in the structure of the genes. Culture is necessary for the development of higher levels of symbolic and reflective skills.

The context and endowment act as filters of experience much as a prism breaks up light into different colors of the spectrum (see J. Palombo, 2001, p. 28). The material out of which the prism is made has a refractive index that affects the colors that emerge. For patients with cognitive or affective deficits, some events will appear highlighted while others will appear nonexistent. A different analogy is that of a color-blind person who fails to see certain colors of the spectrum. A patient with a neuropsychological deficit will fail to "see" some events or will process them differently from peers. For such a person, the information she needs will be missing, much as for the color-blind person, or the information she receives will be discordant from that received by her peers.

Environment is to endowment as the context is to that person's competencies. The two dimensions must be paired inseparably for a coherent understanding to emerge. Each in isolation is a meaningless abstraction. Since brain development is contingent upon stimuli that the environment must provide, the context in which the child matures is an essential contributor to the trajectory that the infant's development will take (J. Palombo, 2001, 2006). The context within which people perform a task and the resources (competencies) they bring to the task determine whether they will be successful. These competencies and capacities constitute the initial conditions that determine how well the person will perform.

The complementarity between one's endowment and the environment may explain how the environment either can mitigate the impact of poor endowment, or at the other extreme, may act as a destructive force that overwhelms the person. A benign environment can compensate for the limitations set by one's endowment and good endowment may help overcome the deleterious effects of some terrible environments.

In summary, the spectrum of strengths and weaknesses, the diversity in the types of components, and the differences within these components constitute the system's initial conditions. Each contributes to the uniqueness of the individual, which we designate as a phenotype. Those differences determine the trajectory of each person's development. For example, for a child with a neuropsychological deficit, the severity of the disorder may range from mild to severe. If we also include the fact that there are different types of dyslexia, ADHD, or executive function disorder, we conclude that the diversity of the system's components contributes not only to the uniqueness of the patients' unsuccessful accommodations but also to the overall personality style the patient presents. Consequently, each patient will be unlike any other patient with a similar disorder because each person will experience the presence of these differences in endowment differently.

The diversity among the system's components becomes a set of nondiscrete variables that contribute to the complexity of the individual's experience and determine the extent to which that individual can accommodate successfully to the context. Individual variations in competencies and capacities may impose constraints on a person's capacity to complete a task successfully, but these constraints are also responsive to information gained from within or outside the organism. They make up a system within the larger self-system. Demos (2007) stated that competencies are "continually elaborated over time in dynamic, creative, and highly idiosyncratic ways" (p. 140). The responses of the caregivers and other factors in the environment also mediate them.

Self-deficits and unsuccessful accommodations

An account from an evolutionary viewpoint that is consistent with systems theory proposes that psychopathology reflects a system's dysfunction. It suggests that a failure has occurred in the coordination of the components of the system or in the integration of their functions in a synchronous manner. Under those circumstances, self-deficits may compromise or may destabilize an individual's sense of self. On the other hand, a person's capacity to accommodate the deficits may lead to unusual success in a career path. Charles Schwab, who started an extremely successful investment firm, has acknowledged having dyslexia that was unrecognized until the diagnosis of his son (Shaywitz, 2003).[1]

In our attempts to link specific self-deficits with specific outcomes, the danger we face is that of reintroducing a linear causal relationship between the two. From a dynamic systems perspective, understanding psychopathology is not to be found in the genesis of the problem alone but also in the relationship that specific components of the self have to each other in the here-and-now and to the context that it inhabits. That is, it is in the relationship of the parts to the whole that the greatest relevance exists. Zeanah and his associates have suggested the concept of "Continuous Construction" to conceptualize this view of psychopathology (Morton & Frith, 1995; Zeanah, Anders, Seifer, & Stern, 1989). In a sense, we can conceive of psychopathology as reflective of the system's dysfunction, a breakdown in an individual's capacity to accommodate successfully the context that the person inhabits. For patients with neuropsychological deficits, the central dynamic that interferes with the smooth coordination of these components is that constellation of experiences of shame around which adventitious attractors were formed and the defensive wall of shame that patients construct.

Unsuccessful accommodations, therefore, represent failures in the match between the patients' capacity to find the resources to maintain their self-cohesion and their environment's responses to their needs. Specific self-deficits may constrain the self as a system and lead to unsuccessful accommodations. Such self-deficits may limit the system's capacity for self-organization and accommodation or they may make it impervious to internal or external feedback. Unsuccessful accommodation may manifest either as overt signs, such as the inability to perform a task, or as subjective experiences, such as anxieties that interfere with the person's ability to cope with the demands made by the context they inhabit or as disturbance in their relationships to others.

In self psychology, the concept of "fragmentation" was used to characterize states that result from severe narcissistic injuries. Used descriptively, the concept may be said to designate the loss of self-cohesion, a state of disorganization that leads patients to fail to cope with the circumstances with which they are faced. From a dynamic systems perspective, the term may be said to refer to the state of the self in which experiences have become decontextualized and essentially have lost their meanings. Such episodes, whether transient or permanent, result in patients' inability to accommodate successfully to their context.

Neuropsychological deficits may produce such episodes and may opportunistically (adventitiously) become attractors for patterns of self-organization that result in unsuccessful accommodations. These patterns result from the nonlinear processes that initiate them, which include affects, the context in which they occur, and the responses from others to the patients' actions. Depending on the specific type of neuropsychological deficit, these emergent patterns may interfere with the capacity for self-cohesion.

Other ways in which adjunctive deficits may instigate such states of disorganization are through the disorganizing effect of overstimulation. The capacity for self-control and self-discipline is not just a requirement that society expects of its members; it extends to the optimal state for the person to retain a sense of inner organization. A patient whose excitement is not modulated by proper responses from others may continue to crave excitement at the cost of integrating experiences to which they are exposed. Since excitement often feeds on itself, some patients will have great difficulty maintaining self-cohesion and may soon fragment. However, patients often experience other people's failure to provide the function of modulation and containment as a willful frustration of their urgent needs. By not having the required response, the patient ends up enraged at others, resulting in the loss of self-cohesion.

The experience of having self-deficits need not always constrain or compromise individuals' capacity to fit successfully to their context. No simple linear correlation exists between self-deficits and failures in accommodations. *The principle we derive from this is that whereas the presence of a set of unsuccessful accommodations may indicate the presence of a self-deficits, the presence of a self-deficit is not necessarily predictive of an unsuccessful accommodation as its outcome.* We may retrospectively identify the neuropsychological deficit that led to a disturbance in the sense of self, but we cannot assume that a neuropsychological deficit will invariably lead to a disruption of the continuity of the sense of self.

Neuropsychological deficits and development

As we have seen, personality development is epigenetic – that is, the prior set of processes contribute to those that follow. These processes are also sensitive to initial conditions: the context, the point in time at which processes take place, and the related processes that occur at that point. Elements in the initial conditions constrain the developmental process that provides a set of limitations to what a person may hope to achieve. Since there is a continual matching between elements in the phenotype and elements of the context, the elements of the phenotype automatically (without prior instruction) will either enhance or inhibit the further unfolding of habitual patterns of interaction (Sander, 1983). Another way to think about this is that we cannot predict the unpredictable. However, the constraints under which systems operate can set the parameters within which they must function.

The concept of initial conditions, as an example of the application of nonlinear dynamic systems thinking to psychological phenomena, enriches our understanding of the effects of neuropsychological deficits on the trajectory of development. Among the initial conditions that determine patients' subjective response to their self-deficits and their reactions to the environments they inhabit are their specific neuropsychological strengths and weaknesses as reflected in the variability of their endowment. From the perspective of nonlinear dynamics, an important characteristic of the system's sensitivity to its initial conditions is that small differences in those conditions can have large effects of what occurs subsequently. This phenomenon, called the "butterfly effect," proposes that a butterfly flapping its wings in Argentina can produce a tornado in Texas (see Gleick, 1987, pp. 20–23).

For example, the presence of what may appear as a small atypical neuropsychological weakness, such as a lack of small motor coordination, may redirect a child's development in ways that we could not anticipate. The implication for us is that the small differences that obtain during the early years of a child's development can lead to large differences later in life. Similarly, when applied to the clinical setting, the differences in the therapeutic dyad will create conditions that will make the treatment process unique to that dyad.

The emphasis on the application of this way of thinking is to highlight the reconceptualization of the psychodynamics that results. We may conceive of the processes that occur in the self as a system to include the self-organization of the person's experience around attractors, such as neuropsychological deficits, the emergence of either higher levels of complexity of organization or of the entrenchment of dysfunctional patterns that resist modification. Either outcome is possible depending on the interaction among the components.

The interaction among endowment, experience, and context represents inputs, whether verbal, nonverbal, or through mindsharing, that may enhance or inhibit the epigenetic flow of development. The person may become capable of self-regulation and self-righting as he or she reaches a homeostatic state of stable instability. The direction of change, however, is nondeterministic. A set of values and preferences act as guiding principles under which the processes operate. It is important to remember that the interactions vary with the age of the person, the social and cultural context, as well as the person's cognitive capacities. Finally, the severity of the neurocognitive weaknesses or deficit will be more influential in determining the course of development than the introspective or interpersonal.

In past publications (J. Palombo, 1992, 1995, 2001, 2006), I attempted to provide some common developmental paths taken by children with neuropsychological deficits; the assumption was that each set of neuropsychological deficits was organized around specific patterns of interactions or psychodynamics. The new insights gained by the nonlinear dynamic perspective lead to an enrichment of this view. As we have seen, development does not follow a linear path, no central patterns guide its course, and in a closed system, we cannot define its trajectory with great specificity. We can understand the developmental variability that we encounter in children with these specific neuropsychological deficits only by taking into account the initial conditions that exist at any given moment in the person's life, the diversity in the neuropsychological deficit within a given specific type of disorder, and the social context in which the person exists. Any generalization that we make represents a macro view that is modifiable once we examine the individual closely.

The presence of a neuropsychological deficit inevitably alters the course of a person's development. In this viewpoint, the emphasis is on the processes that determine the trajectory taken by the unfolding organism. Since development always occurs within the context of caregivers, understanding the processes that take place between children and their caregivers become central to this viewpoint. Caregivers provide functions that sustain their children's capacity to accommodate to the demands made of them by the environment. Mindsharing, in part, consists of those complementary functions the caregivers provide.

Summary

Self-deficits are dysfunctional elements in one or more components of a system. I defined psychopathology as an unsuccessful accommodation in which a mismatch occurred between a person's self-deficits and the context's capacity to provide complementary functions that would permit the person to maintain a sense of self-cohesion. In individuals with neuropsychological deficits, which I call adjunctive deficits, self-deficits may produce unsuccessful accommodations, or they may act as catalysts that enhance the system's capacity to meet day-to-day challenges. Their presence therefore is not necessarily predictive of an unsuccessful accommodation.

Among the initial conditions of the self as a complex adaptive system is the uniqueness of each individual, and the diversity among individuals is due to differences in endowment, to the environment in which they develop, and to the trajectory of their development. Furthermore, variations within these components, which occur as a spectrum of strengths and weaknesses, and the diversity in the types of components and the differences within these components, all contribute to the uniqueness of each individual, which we designate as phenotypes. For example, for a child with a neuropsychological deficit, we stipulate the specific disorder that affects the child (e.g., dyslexia, ADHD, executive function disorder, or other). We must then indicate the severity of the disorder, which may range from mild to severe. Finally, we include the fact that there are different types of dyslexia, ADHD, or executive function disorder. Consequently, that child will be unlike other patients with a similar disorder.

The relationship between unsuccessful accommodations and neuropsychological deficits varies with the specific disorder, the complementary functions the context provides, and the point during the child's development when these functions are necessary. The relationship is fluid and varies as the context changes and the child develops. The relationship between disorders of the self and neuropsychological deficits varies with the specific disorder. While it is possible to conjecture, based on clinical experience, that some neuropsychological deficits may be specifically associated with specific psychodynamics that accompany disorders of the self, upon closer inspection, a different view may be obtained.

Patients' psychodynamics are tied closely to their development and the initial conditions as these unfolded during their lifespan. The nonlinear dynamics view posits that at each point during the person's life, factors enter in to affect the system's organization. Consequently, the psychodynamics of each person will be as variable and unique as their DNA. We can only hypothesize which of the many variables had the greatest impact and have to be mindful to avoid simplistic linear explanations that attempt to establish correlations between a deficit and a subsequent outcome.

Finally, the relationship between childhood unsuccessful accommodations and adult disturbances remain largely unexplored because we have not conducted longitudinal systematic studies. We cannot point to clear linkages between what occurs in childhood and the outcome in adulthood. Conversely, however, the adult manifestations of unsuccessful accommodations bear no resemblance to their childhood counterpart.

Clinical presentation: Ryan

Ryan's case illustrates many of the phenomena and dynamics discussed in the preceding and subsequent chapters. Most of all, the case demonstrates the complex interaction among his neuropsychological deficits, his understanding or lack of understanding of the nature of those deficits, the impact they had on how he felt about himself, and how those deficits affected his interactions with others and other people's responses to him.

Ryan was a 42-year-old man, currently divorced, employed in a supervisory position in a large merchandising store. The referring psychologist had diagnosed an executive function disorder,[2] ADHD, and a mild nonverbal learning disability.[3] He also referred him to a psychiatrist for medication. The psychiatrist placed him on Prozac. The psychologist explained to the patient that he made the referral to me because of my experience in dealing with the effects of learning disabilities on personality development. The psychologist thought the patient needed to understand the ways in which his executive function disorder and ADHD affected his career and how the nonverbal learning disability contributed to the disrupted relationships that he has had over the years.

Ryan presented as a casually dressed, unassuming man who related deferentially and compliantly. His movements were quick and his gestures had a disjointed, spastic quality. He often sat on the edge of the chair, speaking in rapid-fire, staccato fashion. A disconcerting feature to his manner of relating was the turn-taking aspect of our dialogue. He would relate an event and pause, looking at me for a response. However, before I could say a word, he would continue his account elaborating on what he had been talking about. This pattern repeated itself to the point where I doubted whether he wished to hear my comments or questions. However, midway into a session, he would stop, mildly irritated, saying, "But you haven't said anything! What are you thinking?" I would again mobilize myself to make an empathic comment, but even as I clearly indicated that I had a response for him, he would be off to discussing something else.

Background and history

I gathered the following information on Ryan over several sessions of this once-a-week therapy: He grew up in an upper-middle-class suburb in Madison. His father was a successful attorney. His mother was a stay-at-home mom. He was the youngest of a sibship of four. Being the only boy in the family, he was doted upon during his younger years. As he grew older, his behavior became more difficult to manage, and his school performance did not meet his parents' expectation. School was difficult for him from first grade on. Teachers attributed the lack of success to his failure to exert himself and to his not making an effort to direct his attention to assigned tasks. He was always starting projects that he never finished. He recalled being constantly active, although he could not channel his energies into any single direction. Since he was not well coordinated, sports never provided a good outlet for him. He remembered always having a circle of friends, all of whom were high achievers. While they included him in their group, he always felt himself to be an outsider.

By the time he reached high school, his parents had concluded that he had no bent for academic work. They encouraged him to prepare himself in a career in sales where he might use his skill in relationships to be successful. They understood his reluctance to go to college, since he felt it would not benefit him and he would probably not make the grade. However, upon graduating from high school, he did enroll in a junior college, taking four years to complete the two years of work.

Interestingly, in contrast to other youngsters with ADHD, he never had an interest in experimenting with drugs or using alcohol. During those years, his impulsivity and poor judgment got him into many difficulties from which his parents had to extricate him. He got into several car accidents purely because he was inattentive or impulsive. His goal throughout high school and later was to have a girlfriend, a goal he pursued obsessively. On one occasion in high school, he became interested in a girl who initially responded to him but soon lost interest. The narcissistic injury was intolerable; he found himself calling her repeatedly from 10 to 20 times an evening. When she did not respond, he began following her around. Her parents became alarmed and eventually notified the police. In spite of the intervention of the police, who warned him to stay away from the girl, he would impulsively go up to her in the hallways in school and beg to start a conversation with her. Finally, the school authorities had to institute a monitoring system to ensure that he kept away from her.

Life after junior college remained difficult. He lived at home but had few friends, as his former friends were all away at college. Even during the summers when they returned, they were less tolerant of him. He felt isolated, frustrated, and bewildered by their reactions. He dated episodically, some of these relationships lasted a few months, and often the girlfriends quickly ended the relationship.

Eventually, at age 25, he met a woman who seemed tolerant of his idiosyncrasies and of the storms in the relationship resulting from his erratic behavior and impulsivity. They married and soon had a child. During this period, he found employment easily. These jobs were exclusively in sales. He presented well, and impressed his employers by the appearance he made initially in his interviews. They felt he had potential for managerial responsibilities. He would begin work and was soon in trouble. His executive function disorder and poor social skills would often get in the way of his performance. In addition, his poor attention span would lead him to get distracted from tasks that they assigned him. He would often begin a task only to be distracted by another, by the time he remembered to return to the initial task, deadlines would have passed. To make matters worse, he would hide the unfinished work in order not to appear irresponsible. Inevitably, things would catch up with him; he would be warned and finally fired.

In time, the relationship with his wife deteriorated. At first, it appears that she had enjoyed his lifestyle, interpreting his impulsivity as creative spontaneity. She found being around him to be fun and exciting. As problems piled up and crisis followed crisis, she became impatient with him. She no longer perceived his impulsivity as childlike enthusiasm but as endangering the family's stability. This manifested itself in his erratic driving patterns. As she became more critical of him, his sense of injury grew to resentment of her. He was finally enraged at her. These outbursts were frightening and threatening to her. The first time he hit her, she picked up and left with their child. However, she soon returned after he promised that there would never be a recurrence of this abuse. The relationship continued to be stormy, eventually deteriorated, and another incident of abuse occurred. This time, although he felt devastated by what he had done, his wife resolved to divorce him. The dissolution of the marriage took some years.

During the time of the separation, he began an affair with a woman. That relationship lasted several years, although they never lived together. However, she insisted that she would remain in the relationship only if he got help for his emotional instability. They had a brief period of couples therapy, but he did not find that experience particularly helpful. Employment continued to be a problem, but he was always able to make a reasonable living. Finally, after he was fired again, he felt that his work options were running out in Madison. He resolved to move to make a new start in the Chicago area. His girlfriend, however, was not prepared to make the move. Since his attachment to her was tenuous, he felt little pain at the thought of leaving her. He took the first offer that came his way, once more this was a sales position that led to a managerial track.

In his new surroundings, however, history began to repeat itself. Feeling adrift at the age of 41, his work options were narrowing again. He began dating a psychologist, who suggested that he obtain psychological testing and now encouraged him to enter treatment. By then, he had diagnosed himself as having ADD but hesitated to take medication. He had struggled to take care of his problems alone but found that he could not manage them. He still had no inkling regarding his executive function disorder or the role it played in his underachievement or of the way in which his nonverbal learning disability contributed to his poor social judgment and the disruptions in his relationships.

Initial diagnostic formulation and recommendation

The referring source had spoken to him of me in such high terms that the patient looked to me as an expert in learning disorders who could soon help him get his life in order. To accomplish this, he felt that I would give him advice and guidance. He wanted concrete ways to deal with his impulsivity, to help him not get distracted, and above all to keep his current job. The initial transference was a ready-made idealizing transference. At this point, he gave little evidence of a capacity to be self-reflective to address the underlying feeling and narcissistic injuries that motivated some of his behaviors.

My initial responses to these requests were to say that I would be happy to give him advice, but first I needed to get to know him and to understand specifically how his executive function disorder had affected his life and how his nonverbal learning disability and ADHD had served to disrupt his relationships. I found it difficult to be empathic because of the intense pressure I experienced to respond to these requests. My own impulse was to plunge in and tell him what to do. I also knew that if I went in that direction the therapy would be derailed. On the other hand, I had to find a way to convey that I understood his predicament. From experience, I found that initially giving a general explanation regarding the impact of these disabilities on patients' development conveys a sense that I know what they are feeling and that down the road there would be ways of dealing with the difficulties. However, I also knew from my experience with patients with these types of learning disorders that at some point he would need to learn specific skills to compensate for his self-deficits. Understanding alone was insufficient to helping him avoid the failures in accommodation.

I recommended twice-a-week therapy. However, because of financial constraints, we settled on once-a-week sessions.

Initial phase of treatment

Over a period of several sessions, since he seemed unready to address the underlying feelings that motivated his conduct, I started by giving him general explanations regarding the nature of his problems. I felt that he needed a cognitive understanding of the ways in which his neuropsychological deficits contributed to his problems before we could work through the psychological impact that they had on his overall functioning and relationships to others. I explained to him that from my experience, the types of deficits the neuropsychologist had diagnosed greatly affected people's self-esteem. I first focused on the nonverbal learning disability, stating that people with this disorder have an intense desire for a relationship but that often they cannot sustain the relationship because of poor social skills and an inability to negotiate differences that arise between people. This leaves the person feeling inadequate while desirous of making a good impression on people. It also makes the person unable to experience the kind of closeness that they wish to have with others. Often, this results in their feeling that they are playing out a role rather than being genuinely themselves. They also fear that once people will get to know them they will realize how incompetent they believe themselves to be.

In addition, I informed him that his ADD causes two sets of problems. On the one hand, the neurological aspect of his drivenness contributes greatly to his impulsivity and inattention. Just as important was the accompanying "psychological problem," that of not being able to regulate his feelings generally, and not being able to soothe himself or use others who are available to soothe him. As a result, he feels that he often cannot control himself, and he feels buffeted by feelings instead of being in charge of them. I said that I realized that he had tried to compensate either by using others to help contain his feelings or by trying to be more disciplined, but these efforts did not work. I finally added that it was important not to forget the role played by his executive function disorder in his underachievement. I commented that he seemed to have the potential for higher positions than he had held but that his executive function disorder must have interfered with his attaining those positions.

It took considerable patience on his part to hear me through when I gave him these formulations, which I gave in simple language over a period of weeks. While I sometimes feared that these explanations would overwhelm him, I hoped that he would feel relieved by understanding the reasons for some of his difficulties. I also hoped that he would experience my empathy as finally feeling understood. Ryan, however, while seeming to wish to integrate what I was saying, would interrupt me after every sentence. He had a thousand questions. While eager to absorb what I was saying, he seemed to wish to put his entire life together in one fell swoop. In addition, the tension between his wish to understand, which required him to restrain himself, and his impulse to interrupt was almost unbearable. He often sat at the edge of his chair nodding in approval, while raising his hand in a motion to interrupt me to ask a question. At the end of each session, it was necessary for me to take a few extra minutes to satisfy his curiosity, so that he could leave feeling that I understood his situation well.

From my perspective, I felt a parallel tension to his but at a different level. I saw Ryan's predicament as twofold. On the one hand, I struggled to make sense of the incoherence of his self-narrative. On the other hand, I felt an urgency to help him with the task of developing ways to regulate himself by dealing with the feelings of shame that were deeply buried and to develop better coping skills in relationships by dealing with the injuries that he felt he suffered in how others treated him. Whereas the deficit in self-regulation reflected both his ADHD and the absence of selfobject functions, the difficulties in coping with relationships had much more complex roots. His neuropsychological deficits limited his ability to process social cues. During his early years, they impaired his ability to learn from others and to gain through maturation what others learned through their interactions with others.

Treatment process

While we spent a lot of time trying to reinterpret Ryan's history in light of what we now understood about him, the initial focus of the treatment was to help him with his unregulated feelings and to develop some insight into the ways in which his inability to process social situations disrupted his relationships. The task of acquiring the skills to deal with his circumstances had to come later. In particular, we spent time on the embarrassment brought on by his actions, the feelings of shame associated with his inability to control himself, and his puzzlement as to what drove him to behave as he did.

He brought in innumerable instances of how he lost control, got furious at another driver, acted impulsively at work, or lost his temper on the phone while talking to his parents. For my part, I sought to convey to him a sense of calm understanding that I hoped he could experience as soothing. In the positive idealizing transference, he saw me as benignly in control of myself, able to deal with stormy feelings in a quiet but effective fashion, and displaying a sense of competence that he overtly admired. He would comment that I was "so civilized!" Whereas he considered his behavior as coarse and unpolished, I became a soothing selfobject and someone with whom to identify. As we talked about the events in his life, he remembered many examples, past and present, of the anxious excitement he would feel, the way it clouded his judgment and led him to act out. He would say that he often thought about how he experiences me especially after leaving a session. He wishes he could carry the calmness and strength he gains from the sessions into his life. The following are three vignettes from sessions that illustrate our work together.

Six months into his therapy he came to a session agitated. An incident had occurred, which was typical for him. He wished he could have handled it differently. During his lunch hour, his manager asked him to cover the switchboard because they were short-staffed. Although he had never done that, he felt confident that he could operate it with no problems. As phone calls came in, he routed them to the appropriate people, all the while he struggled with the excitement generated by this new activity. He was having great fun. Then a phone call came in for the store manager. He paged the manager but got no response. Not knowing how to evaluate the urgency of the call, he felt great pressure to get the manager to the phone. He placed the caller on hold but described himself as almost in a panic. He impulsively left the office and switchboard to go in search of the manager. As he walked around the store looking for the manager, a customer stopped him with a question. His attention was diverted from his goal and now he set out to problem-solve with the customer. Half an hour later, his boss came looking for him, furious that he had left the switchboard unattended. Instead of admitting his error and apologizing, he struggled with his rage at his boss but was able to contain it. Instead, he gave a lame excuse that he was helping the customer.

Meanwhile, he felt humiliated. He had goofed again and felt shattered. The incident had a devastating effect on his self-esteem. He felt like a total fool. His shame was unbearable. He wished he could hide and never show himself again at work. Facing his boss was as painful as being caught masturbating in public. When he was operating the switchboard, he had fantasies of having others appreciate and compliment him for the good job he had done. He so wished for recognition and approval. Instead, what he got was contempt and derision.

We explored the meanings of this experience to him. First, the new activity was a departure from the routine to which he used at work, so that he was unprepared to deal with the excitement of "playing with a new toy!" Many feelings and associations came to mind around that. What stood out were the many times as a young child when a fun game would be spoiled because he got out of control, or became over excited and his parents screamed at him. He rarely had a chance to have good clean fun without something bad happening. His rage at the failure to get the proper response overshadowed his longings for comfort and soothing. His rage covered his underlying feelings of inadequacy and incompetence.

My responses to both these sets of feelings were to be empathic with his pain. When I commented, I said that I recognized this as lifelong themes that had followed him through the years. These themes had organized many of his responses. I continued by saying that he had missed aspects of childhood experiences that people value and retain with them as adults, experiences that people treasure and turn to time when in pain. He did not have such a store of experiences. This left him with the deep longings for responses that would heal these old wounds. At a later session, when he was not in as much pain, I returned to these incidents and expanded on his longings. I spoke of how a child feels when held and comforted by an admired caregiver, of the sense of security and contentment that results. I added that in addition, he missed another set of experiences, which are just as critical: the experiences of having someone praise him for a job well done, of being given the unconditional approval that only a parent can give. Ryan was touched by these words and almost became tearful, but the feelings were too powerful for him. He quickly moved on to ask what he could do about that now. He cannot keep going back to what he had missed as a child. I responded that it was true that our understanding alone is insufficient to heal him. What we hope is healing in therapy is the experience of having someone who gives him the kind of understanding he so deeply needs, but who also can help him not feel alone with the feelings. Sharing his pain with someone is itself consoling. He no longer felt the sense of isolation and alienation that he had felt previously.

Another incident Ryan brought in dealt with the effects of his executive function disorder. Over the course of several sessions, he spoke of an assignment given to him at work to write a weekly report on the status of his section. To help him, his boss had given him copies of prior reports to use as models. His manager also gave him a simple outline to follow. All he needed to do was write two pages describing the activities for which he was responsible. Determined to succeed, he took home the reports he had been given. He felt that he needed a quiet place to concentrate. His first attempt at reading these reports found him falling asleep on the couch before he came to the end of the first page. It was less that he was tired than that the task of reading exhausted him. He renewed his efforts and found a report that was six pages long. He fantasied impressing his boss by producing one just as long, if not longer. Meanwhile, the deadline that had been set for him to turn in his first report had passed. He obsessively read the outline trying to integrate how to approach the task. At times, his distractibility interfered. At times, he simply procrastinated avoiding a task that was so difficult and painful to him. His boss soon realized that he was having difficulties and offered to help him. The boss in fact wrote the first report for him, trying to reduce the pressure Ryan felt.

As the weeks went by, Ryan brought to the sessions the reports he had written. He had developed some stilted sentences to fill the blanks under each section of the outline. They were just informative enough for his boss to rewrite a more respectable report. However, Ryan would then make simple mistakes, such as skipping sections altogether, or misreading information he had to include in the report. The reports were inadequate. At this point, I felt it necessary to intervene by providing him with an example of the skills that were necessary for him to complete the task. The process took a didactic turn as I instructed him on how to develop an outline, how to select the major points to include under each heading, and how to refrain from including tangential or irrelevant items. Our efforts were undermined by the fact that he stated, "Very often, once I leave your office, I forget everything we talked about!" These interactions highlighted to both of us the extent to which his executive dysfunction impaired his capacity to organize his thoughts and the reports he had to write. We deferred referral to a learning specialist who could help him with these difficulties to a later point when he was more ready psychologically to benefit from such interventions.

The final incident involved his relationship with his girlfriend, which had deteriorated to the point where she decided to break up with him. He was devastated but resolved to rebuild the relationship. He pursued her relentlessly, but she would have none of it. Eventually, she was so enraged at him that she reported him to the police for stalking her. A court issued an order enjoining him to stay away from her. However, he violated the order and ended up in court. The judge required him to take a six-week course for sex offenders. Once again, he felt humiliated. We struggled with his puzzlement as to why the relationship had been unsuccessful and with his bewilderment that she would have reported him and taken him to court. He felt that they had gotten along well, that she understood his shortcomings and was willing to accept them. However, when we tried to explore how he understood her needs in the relationship, he was totally in the dark. He had never thought of a relationship as one in which he could reciprocate her feelings for him. What emerged was his desperation for closeness. His longings were so intense that they overshadowed his judgment. In pursuing her, he was merely expressing his need for her and his hope that she would understand his longings to be with her. He found it difficult to see that his actions had been inappropriate. While I wished to bring in some of the dysfunctional elements of his interactions between us, I feared that he would take such transference interpretations as criticism that would be more embarrassing than helpful. We were only able to establish that in his intense desire for a relationship he was blind to the effects that he and his personality quirks had on those with whom he sought to be close.

After about a year-and-a-half in treatment, Ryan was offered a job out of town. Since he was eager to extricate himself from his current situation, he resolved that he needed to move out of state and accepted the offer. Ryan felt that he had understood much of what had occurred to him while growing up and was occurring in relationships with others in the present. He had gained a sufficient understanding of his self-deficits to help him integrate some of his dysfunctional experiences. This understanding was helpful to him in containing the erosive effects of his failures, although it did not serve to boost his self-esteem. In addition, with the help of his medication, he learned to titrate his responses, containing his impulsivity. He learned to regulate the fluctuations in his self-states to a degree but realized that modifying the longstanding patterns would require considerable ongoing effort. We agreed that he would be in touch with me for a referral should problems arise in the city to which he was moving. I did not hear from him again.

Ryan's psychodynamics

By psychodynamics, I refer to mental processes that govern the function of the self and to the nonconscious patterns of responses that patients encoded in procedural memory as a result of their experiences. The experiences of shame and humiliation that resulted from the exposure or fear of exposure of their self-deficits formed nuclei of narcissistic injuries, which triggered a set of defenses, whether disavowal or dissociation, to deal with the intense pain associated with these injuries. These experiences became attractors or nodal points around which patterns of thoughts, feelings, or behaviors were organized. However, psychodynamics are seldom monothematic; often, aspects of the patients' personality as well as other contributors are entwined with those of the self-deficits. It is also important not to think of such psychodynamics as simply dwelling within individuals in isolation from others or the social context. From a dynamic systems perspective, they are part of the complex of interactions among the neuropsychological, the introspective, and the interpersonal domains of experience.

The formulation of the patient's psychodynamics[4] is an essential prelude to the beginning of treatment. It serves as the provisional guide to an understanding of the patient's experience. To understand the patient's psychodynamics fully requires that we go beyond what the patient tells us. The data for the formulation derives from several sources. Neuropsychological assessments, for example, when available, add considerably to our insight into the patient's strengths and weaknesses. In the case of school-aged children and adolescents, we must also digest information from psychological, reports from speech and language pathologists, occupational therapists, and school personnel, as well as information about the family's dynamics, the patient's relationship with siblings and peers, and much other relevant data that may enhance our view of the factors that contributed to the patient's self-state.

The second source is the patients' reports of their subjective experiences, their thoughts and feelings, many of which are related to their self-deficits. However, any psychodynamic formulation is constrained by the fact that it describes the conditions present at the time the data are collected and the context in which it is obtained. In fact, the formulation constitutes an interpretation diagnosticians make of the material available and is subject to change over time. However, the notion that we can only rely on the patient's reports to understand them seriously underestimates the importance of these other sources of information. True empathic understanding cannot be achieved in many cases in the absence of such information. In fact, I believe that a danger exists of seriously misunderstanding both the patient's self-state and the motives for the thoughts and behavior in the absence of such information.

The profile that follows presents a model for the formulation of a patient's dynamics. It is intended both as a demonstration of the application of the constructs discussed in the previous chapters and an illustration of the futility of trying to assign simple linear explanations to the thoughts, feelings, and behaviors that some patients present to clinicians. In years past, when therapists were wedded to a more linear view of causality, they propose a single factor, such as the learning disorder or "the mother's psychopathology," as causing the patient's problems; all other contributors were either overlooked or their effects were minimized. This "parent blaming" posture has not only caused much distress to parents who see themselves as victimized, but has also led to an incorrect understanding of the forces at work in the case.

From a developmental viewpoint, Ryan was born with a set of conditions that played an increasingly significant role in the development of his personality. These included adjunctive deficits in his capacity for self-regulation related to his ADHD, the ability to sequence and organize his thinking and activities associated with his executive function disorder, and his aptitude to decode social signs connected with his nonverbal learning disability.

The warmth and attention he received from his doting family in the early years appear to have mitigated the effects of his neuropsychological deficits. The attentional problems did not manifest as problematic until middle school. He surmounted his executive function disorder, probably with the family's assistance. His poor social judgment and his desperation for a close relationship emerged full-blown when he began to stalk the young woman in whom he became interested while in high school. Not only did each of these deficits set constraints on his life and career choices, but they also re-entered recursively to affect his functioning at different periods of his life. They periodically caused crises with which he had to cope.

A major dynamic that organized his relationships was the search for others to complement his deficits. Ryan was intent on finding a relationship with a woman with whom he could be close. However, he was not always successful in finding a match that complemented his weakness and permitted him to accommodate to situations. In many ways, he could not find others who could provide selfobject functions and adjunctive functions for him. Had he been fortunate enough to find someone who could have provided such functions, he could have remained cohesive and made successful accommodations to whatever tasks he confronted.

Diversity in his endowment

His basic endowments presented a unique configuration of elements that were diverse in the sense that they were unlike those of any other person. They represented filters through which he processed his experiences. Furthermore, the diversity of environments that he confronted contributed to the uniqueness of his interactions with them. The results of his neuropsychological assessment reflect the diversity of factors that were involved. A summary of the findings are as follows:

Ryan's overall intellectual functioning on the test placed him in the average rate of functioning. His Full Scale IQ was 108, his Verbal IQ was 120, and his Performance IQ was 96. The 24-point discrepancy between the Verbal IQ and the Performance IQ is significant and generally (but not always) indicative of a nonverbal learning disability. On a standard memory test, his score was in the low average range. Whereas his performance in verbal memory was low average, his visual memory and his delayed recall were in the borderline range. These results indicated the existence of problems with working memory, which are often associated with attentional and executive function difficulties. He had difficulties in organization, self-monitoring, self-regulation, and effective performance in the completion of tasks. These deficits were offset, to a degree, by his ability to conform to external structure when it was present. These difficulties, in tandem with his attentional problems, indicated the presence of an executive function disorder. Clinical indicators pointed to deficits in the ability for sustained attention and high levels of distractibility and impulsivity. His receptive and expressive language skills were in the high average range. His score in reading comprehension, word accuracy was in the low average range. His written language and spelling scores were in the borderline range. His capacity for higher order cognitive function, for problem solving, concept formation, hypothesis testing, understanding cause-effect, and appreciating incongruities were in the low average range.

Ryan presented as moderately depressed. He manifested evidence of having suffered multiple injuries to his sense of self over the years. These injuries seriously compromised his self-esteem. His capacity to modulate his affect states was impaired due to his hypersensitivity to criticism. He responded with irritation or rage when he experienced that an area of vulnerability was endangered. Furthermore, his nonverbal learning disability led to an interference is his ability to decode other people's affect states and to monitor his own emotional reactions. The result was that his capacity for self-cohesion was unstable, leading to periods of fragmentation.

Preferences and biases: Self-cohesion and self-understanding

We may use the terms *self-cohesion* and *fragmentation* to describe the stability or instability of Ryan's sense of self. In many ways, he retained a sense of self-cohesion for prolonged periods. Ryan often appeared to be living at the "edge of chaos." We may use that expression to describe the instability of his sense of self and its propensity to fragmentation. In large part, his executive function disorder, which manifested in chronic disorganization in his daily life and in his approach to problem solving, contributed to this instability.

In spite of lurching from job to job and relationship to relationship, he avoided crises by either fleeing problematic situations or being rescued by his parents or others. The two episodes of losing control of himself and assaulting his wife represent times when he probably fragmented. The injuries he suffered from her constant criticism eroded his self-esteem to the point where they became intolerable. Her departure was devastating. However, he could recover by quickly finding someone else to replace her.

Ryan initially exhibited little capacity for self-reflection or introspection. He was more action-oriented and limited in the capacity for self-examination and self-understanding. Given that, he had little insight into the effects of his neuropsychological deficits on his day-to-day functioning and on his relationship. He presented a disjointed, fragmented self-narrative that lacked internal coherence.

His limited capacity for introspection and self-reflection prevented him from the kind of self-examination that might have helped him compensate for his shortcomings. He appeared to be in the dark as to the motives that drove his conduct. His efforts to find others to provide the missing functions were haphazard and unguided by any understanding of what he needed. Consequently, he attributed his failures to forces outside of him; he misinterpreted events or found them bewildering. In spite of these constraints, he was nevertheless able for periods of time to find companions and to be self-supporting.

Modes of interaction with others

Ryan demonstrated an impaired capacity to interpret social situations and to draw correct inferences from other people's communication. He seemed limited in his ability to read other people's intentions or empathize with their feeling states. This impairment extended to the domain of emotional communication. It resulted in an inability to process his own and other people's feeling states.

In his interactions with others, the intensity of his desire for a relationship drove him to pursue women who clearly indicated they were not interested in him. Yet, he pursued them to the point where they had to appeal to outside interventions to curb his pursuit of them. Although he desired intensely to be involved with the person, his action had the opposite effect. His obtuseness and lack of tact resulted in their distancing themselves from him. In some respects, some of his habitual patterns of interaction had become encapsulated and resistant to change. His difficulties with organization and his ADHD, his impaired capacity to self-regulate, which manifested as impulsivity, continued to contribute to the disruptions in many aspects of his functioning through most of his life. This pattern represented a closed system that was impermeable to modification except through medication. Having no awareness of his nonverbal learning disability and the part it played in his inability to sustain a job for reasonable periods of time, he could not modify his behavior to make better accommodations to situations. The repetitive nature of these patterns indicated their rigidity and lack of flexibility and their impermeability to inputs from others.

Furthermore, he had little understanding of the effects for his behavior. His response was to feel criticized and to be the object of their disapproval. Feeling misunderstood reinforced some of his negative behaviors as he sought to justify his actions. The circular loop created by this pattern became an organizer of his experiences and his behaviors. Some patients who manifest this pattern of behavior at times are mistakenly described as having developed an "oppositional/defiant" attitude toward others. These problems were compounded by the fact that others in his environment often failed to understand the causes for his behavior. They interpreted it as lack of self-control and as a willful exercise of contrariness.

Processes that guided his functioning

From a developmental viewpoint, Ryan failed to find the requisite selfobject and adjunctive functions not because the parents did not or could not provide them, but probably because the neurological deficits defeated the parents' efforts at providing the functions. These deficits constituted the initial conditions that set the course of his development and periodically reentered into his life as he confronted tasks that required functions he did not possess. As a result, his ability to benefit from the feedback that others provided was limited and aspects of his development became impermeable to change. The rigid patterns that he brought to interactions with others eventually led to crises and a period of fragmentation.

What stands out about Ryan's history is how much he relied, during his youth, on the energies associated with his ADHD to deal with his anxiety and possibly with his underlying depressive feelings. He valued the excitement and pleasure he obtained from his impulsive behaviors over the dullness of day-to-day activities. When he could no longer evoke the affect states associated with this preferred state of arousal, he confronted a void that led him to lapse into depression. This preferred patterned, at times, served to help engage others into shared activities; however, it also served as a barrier to the development of deeper and more meaningful relationships.

His ADHD and nonverbal learning disabilities were the primary attractors that served to organize his experiences. The attractors led to "scripts" through which he interpreted other people's responses, leading to expectations that were not consonant with how others responded to him. The persistence of his impulsivity gives evidence of an inability to control his behavior that compelled him to respond as he did in spite of his awareness that what he did was self-destructive.

In Ryan's case, whereas he continued to grow older, the level of his social and emotional maturity did not keep pace with his chronological age. He continued to carry forward some of the dysfunctional patterns that were formed during his early years and seemed not to benefit from the lessons learned from hard experience. The consequence was that until he got into therapy and could become more self-reflective, the early patterns remained dominant. The ongoing reorganization of his personality, both as a result of his maturation and of his experiences, carried over unchanged patterns from his past. Experience-dependent brain regions that contributed to this reorganization did not benefit from the exposure to new experiences. When confronted with novel or complex social situations, his responses were stereotypic and immature. As a result, he felt isolated, experiencing loneliness that aggravated his depression. We may best characterize the type of attachment that Ryan manifested as Type A: Anxious/Avoidant, although, at times, it bordered on Type D: Disorganized/Disoriented.

Treatment outcome

The only point in his life that may be interpreted as representing the emergence of a change agent that had the potential of bringing about greater integration occurred when his last girlfriend, who was a psychologist, insisted on his getting tested and on his entering into therapy. The steps that he took gave promise of a set of life-changing experiences.

The fact that he could benefit from the short-term therapeutic experience suggests that he retained a level of flexibility that permitted him to make changes that had long-term beneficial effects on his overall functioning and on how he felt about himself. The role of medication contributed to his ability to benefit from what the therapy offered and to the gains that he made in his daily life. He was also able to be more introspective and to process interpretations. However, the constraints set by his neuropsychological disabilities limited the extent to which he could successfully accommodate to his environment.

As treatment progressed, Ryan gained a measure of understanding of his neuropsychological strength and weakness and of the impact that these had on his overall functioning. These explanations gave him an opportunity to reflect on his thoughts, feelings, and behaviors. To some extent, his understanding led to the modification of some of his behaviors. However, he continued to have limited insight into the processes involved in forming an intimate relationship and the ability to engage in mindsharing with others. His level of integration moved him in the direction of growth, but the process was interrupted before the full resumption of the developmental progression and the attainment of greater complexity. His sense of self-cohesion was partially enhanced and self-understanding led to a more coherent self-narrative than formerly existed.

Notes

1 Each year, the Lab School of Washington, DC, honors distinguished individuals who have been successful in spite of their learning disorder. Among those who have received the award are: Cher, Tom Cruise, Henry Winkler, Tracey Gold, Magic Johnson, Daniel Stern, Susan Butcher, Fannie Flagg, Vince Vaughn, Don Coryell, Billy Bob Thornton, and Danny Glover (see www.wikipedia.org/wiki/Lab_School_of_Washington#Awards).

2 Executive function disorders involve a complex set of deficits that include difficulties in the initiation, conception, and implementation of a plan. These difficulties include the inability to manage time, to organize resources, to self-monitor and self-regulate, and to translate a plan into productive activity that ensures its completion. ADHD is frequently associated with this condition, although the actual rate of its coexistence is unknown. Some of the symptoms of ADHD, such as impulsivity and inattention, may be present; however, unlike ADHD, the symptoms associated with executive function disorders do not respond to stimulant medication (Anderson, 2008).
3 A nonverbal learning disability (NLD) is a developmental brain-based disorder that constrains a person's capacity to perceive, express, and understand nonverbal (nonlinguistic) signs. The disorder generally manifests as a pattern of impaired functioning in the nonverbal domains with higher functioning in the verbal domain. The neuropsychological deficits associated with this disorder constrain people's capacity to function in academic, social, emotional, or vocational domains, and lead to a heterogeneous set of neurobehavioral symptoms. The brain dysfunctions affect their behaviors, their social interactions, their feelings about themselves and others, and their emerging personality (J. Palombo, 2006).
4 When considering the psychodynamics of any given individual, while many processes may be active in conjunction with the components we discussed, the problem we face is that of trying to keep track of them simultaneously. In practice, such a task would be extremely cumbersome, and perhaps lead to unnecessary repetition and even confusion. In returning to the case of Ryan, for purposes of illustration, I provide a formulation of his psychodynamics that attempts to include most of the components and identified by the neuropsychological evaluation.

References

Anderson, P. J. (2008). Towards a developmental model of executive eunction. In V. Anderson, R. Jacobs, & P. J. Anderson (Eds.), *Executive functions and the frontal lobes: A lifespan perspective* (pp. 3–21). New York: Taylor & Francis.

Brandchaft, B., Doctors, S., & Sorter, D. (2010). *Toward an emancipatory psychoanalysis: Brandchaft's intersubjective view.* New York: Routledge.

Damasio, A. R. (1994). *Descartes' error: Emotion, reason, and the human brain.* New York: G. P. Putnam's Sons.

Demos, E. V. (2007). The dynamics of development. In C. Piers, J. P. Muller, & J. Brent (Eds.), *Self organizing complexity in psychological systems* (pp. 135–163). New York: Jason Aronson.

Gleick, J. (1987). *Chaos: Making a new science.* New York: Viking.

Kohut, H. (1971). *The analysis of the self.* New York: International Universities Press.

Kohut, H. (1977). *The restoration of the self.* New York: International Universities Press.

Kohut, H. (1984). *How does analysis cure?* Chicago: The University of Chicago Press.

Kohut, H. (1991). Four basic concepts in self psychology (1979). In P. H. Ornstein (Ed.), *The search for the Self: Selected writings of Heing Kohut: 1978–1981* (Vol. 4, pp. 447–470). Madison, CT: International Universities Press.

Lezak, M. D., Howieson, D. B., & Loring, D. W. (2004). *Neuropsychological assessment* (4th ed.). New York: Oxford University Press.

Luria, A. R. (1973). *The working brain: An introduction to neuropsychology.* New York: Basic Books.

Milner, B., Squire, L. R., & Kandel, E. R. (1998). Cognitive neuroscience and the study of memory. *Neuron, 20,* 445–468.

Morton, J., & Frith, U. (1995). Causal modeling: A structural approach to developmental psychopathology. In D. Cicchetti & D. J. Cohen (Eds.), *Manual of developmental psychopathology* (pp. 357–390). New York: Wiley.

Pally, R. (1997). How brain development is shaped by genetic and environmental factors. *International Journal of Psychoanalysis, 78*, 587–593.

Palombo, J. (1992). Learning disabilities in children: Developmental, diagnostic and treatment considerations. Paper presented at the Fourth National Health Policy Forum, Healthy Children 2000: Obstacles & Opportunities, April 24–25, 1992, Washington, DC.

Palombo, J. (1995). Psychodynamic and relational problems of children with nonverbal learning disabilities. In B. S. Mark & J. A. Incorvaia (Eds.), *The handbook of infant, child, and adolescent psychotherapy: A guide to diagnosis and treatment* (Vol. 1, pp. 147–176). Northvale, NJ: Jason Aronson.

Palombo, J. (2001). *Learning disorders and disorders of the self in children and adolescents*. New York: W. W. Norton.

Palombo, J. (2006). *Nonverbal learning disabilities: A clinical perspective*. New York: W. W. Norton.

Palombo, J. (2008). Self psychology theory. In B. A. Thyer (Ed.), *Comprehensive handbook of social work and social welfare: Human behavior in the social environment* (Vol. 2, pp. 163–205). Hoboken, NJ: John Wiley & Sons.

Palombo, J. (2011). Executive function conditions and self-deficits. In N. H. Heller & A. Gitterman (Eds.), *Mental health and social problems: A social work perspective* (pp. 282–312). New York: Routledge.

Sander, L. W. (1983). To begin with: Reflections on ontogeny. In J. D. K. Lichtenberg (Ed.), *Reflections on self psychology* (pp. 85–104). New Jersey: The Analytic Press.

Sander, L. W. (1995). Identity and the experience of specificity in a process of recognition: Commentary on Seligman and Shanok. *Psychoanalytic Dialogues, 5*, 579–593.

Shaywitz, S. (2003). *Overcoming dyslexia: A new and complete acience-based program for reading problems at any level*. New York: Vintage Books.

Solms, M., & Turnbull, O. (2002). *The brain and the inner world: An introduction to the neuroscience of subjective experience*. New York: Other Press.

Weiss, P. (1945). The problem of specificity in growth and development. *Yale Journal of Biology and Medicine, 19*(3), 235–278.

Zeanah, C. H., Anders, T. F., Seifer, R., & Stern, D. N. (1989). Implications of research on infant development for psychodynamic theory and practice. *Journal of the American Academy of Child & Adolescent Psychiatry, 28*(5), 657–668.

Chapter 4

Self-deficits
The introspective domain (L-II)

The second domain to which I give consideration is the *introspective (psychological) domain* (L-II). As stated earlier, in this domain, we access the person's inner world, to which I will refer as the *sense of self*, or to *the experience of being a self or being a person* (see Chapter 2). In this domain, the focus is on the impact of self-deficits on the systems' preferences or the values that shape the sense of self. This is not to say that we view the person's experiences as isolated from the impact of the presence of neuropsychological deficits or the responses of others in that person's context. From a dynamic systems perspective, each of those makes its own unique contribution to person's view of themselves.

The presence of neuropsychological deficits leaves its own mark on patients' subjective experiences. From the introspective perspective, we can note that these deficits have a bearing on patients' self-cohesion and their self-understanding. In this chapter, the questions we try to answer are: What impact does the presence of neuropsychological deficits have on the patients' capacity to retain a stable sense of self-cohesion? How do patients integrate the meaning of having such deficits into their view of themselves, and how do these meanings structure their self-narratives?

Two preferences

In the introspective domain, the concern is with the person's sense of self or the *experience* of being a self; we are attempting to describe people's inner world, their subjectivity. Through introspection, we access an individual's affective states and the meanings they have construed from their experiences. Within the introspective domain, one gateway to understanding the impact of self-deficits on the sense of self is through an examination of two of the system's preferences: the preference for *self-cohesion* and for *self-understanding*. As human beings, these two psychological preferences shape our sense of self and act as simple rules that guide the organization of the person's lived experiences. These self-organizing functions produce the subjective experience of *self-cohesion*, and the processes that lead to *a self-narrative*, an understanding that need not be conscious.

The sense of self-cohesion is a concept borrowed from self-psychology that acquires new meaning in this context. Demos (2007) stated that one of the most basic human biases is that "[p]sychic coherence and organization is better than noncoherence, a bias in which the vicissitudes of affects play a central role" (p. 141). The experience of self-cohesion provides a measure of the person's stability and capacity to tolerate adversity. It may also reflect the system's openness to communication with others and the readiness to modify feelings, thoughts, and behaviors that permit the integration of associated experiences. Positive affective valences accompany this experience, which include feelings of well-being, of vitality, and of competence (Sander, 2008).

The second preference is the activity of self-understanding (Kohut, 1977, 1984; Kohut & Wolf, 1978; J. Palombo, 1994, 1996, 2008; Sander, 2002). Self-understanding includes the hierarchies of meanings that acquire coherence and derives from the person's conscious, unconscious, and nonconscious experiences. This preference results in the establishment of a coherent personal and/or shared set of meanings. The structure associated with this self-understanding is the self-narrative, which is an account that we give ourselves to make sense of, among other things, our history, our desires, our goals, and ambitions, a result that may produce a feeling of satisfaction through the insights obtained from knowing ourselves.

I distinguish *cohesion* from *coherence* as distinct emergent properties of the self. Cohesion is associated with the *subjective experience* of competence, vitality, wholeness, and integrity, whereas coherence is the *product of the understanding* we achieve of ourselves through which we feel that we have made sense of an experience or set of experiences. A complex interrelationship exists between self-cohesion and self-understanding. Self-understanding may enhance the experience of self-cohesion, whereas self-cohesion may not necessarily accompany self-understanding. In other words, insight into our troubles may help us maintain our integrity in the face of adversity, whereas our understanding the depth of our depression may not diminish our feelings of despair. If we do not feel cohesive, we may have difficulty integrating what is happening in our lives into our self-understanding; if we do not understand what is happening to us, our self-cohesion may be threatened (J. Palombo, 2001b).

From the perspective of the self as a complex adaptive system, both preferences are context-dependent and never attained in isolation from that context. The presence or absence of selfobject or adjunctive functions that complement our sense of self may constrain or enhance the effects of neuropsychological deficits. For patients with neuropsychological deficits, the major impairments in this domain are the interference with the capacity for self-cohesion or with the acquisition of a self-narrative. In these patients, the fear of the loss of self-cohesion or disturbances in self-understanding may be associated with the loss of the meaning of self-experiences and confusion as to the motives for their actions.

Self-cohesion

A primary motive that engages a person's sense of self as a complex adaptive system is the positive affect states associated with self-cohesion, often experienced as positive self-esteem. The sense of self-cohesion is fundamental to our psychological survival. Self-cohesion is an essential attribute of the sense of self that contributes to the experience of individuality and continuity in space and time.

When used descriptively, the concept of self-cohesion characterizes a state of self-consolidation (Stolorow, Brandchaft, & Atwood, 1987). From the perspective of the self as a complex adaptive system, self-cohesion is an attribute that denotes the stability of the person's sense of self and the capacity to withstand adversity. At an introspective level, feelings of positive self-regard, a sense of pride and self-confidence, and a feeling of being connected to others within the larger community accompany self-cohesion. To these, we may add the attributes of Stern's (1985) domain of the core sense of self: having a sense of agency, a sense of historical continuity, a sense of coherence, and a sense of privacy. For Stern, to have a *sense of agency* is to be a locus of activity, power, and control, to have the capacity to give expression to intentionality, an attribute of the self that Kohut (1977) called being the "center of initiative" (p. 99). For Sander (2002), the sense of agency refers to the capacity for the initiation of self-organization, self-regulation, and for making self-correcting moves.

Self-cohesion is context-dependent, as it requires selfobject functions and adjunctive functions to sustain it. The maintenance of the capacity for self-cohesion depends on the availability of others who provide these functions in the ever-changing flow of daily life. Isolation from others or loss of contact endangers the sense of self and threatens the loss of this capacity.

However, self-cohesion is not a static state but a dynamic state that represents the organizing capacities that are at play to synthesize and integrate self-experiences. Maintaining self-cohesion does not involve striving for a stable homoeostatic state. It is a dynamic, active expression of the continual movement from destabilization to re-stabilization, a characteristic of individuals who can endure psychological stresses or narcissistic injuries without suffering from fragmentation. This characteristic attests to the fact that such individuals have sufficient resiliency, endurance, and strength to tolerate insults without major psychological sequela (Frie, 2009; Frie & Orange, 2009). During the life cycle, patients can maintain a sense of cohesion because of the success they have had in synthesizing new experiences into old ones, in reworking old experiences by reinterpreting them in light of new ones, and in maintaining a level of attachment to those who provide selfobject functions (J. Palombo, 1990).

Affects, self-experience, and self-cohesion

The Darwinian perspective on affects focuses on the function of emotions in the context of their evolutionary development. Contemporary affect theories, such as that of Panksepp (1998, 2001), lend support to and build on Tomkins' theory of affect (Tomkins, 1962, 1963, 1991, 1992), which follows Darwin's studies of affect (Darwin, 1998). LeDoux suggested that affects have been retained by human beings because of their survival value in eliciting a response from caregivers (Bowlby, 1969; LeDoux, 1996; Solms & Turnbull, 2002). They are a separate inherited program for responding to stimuli. Developmentally, affective communication is a basic language that begins in infancy. Affects are the primary nonverbal medium of communication between infants and caregivers. They act as powerful motives to sustain the attachment between infants and their caregivers. The infant's cry serves as a sign to the caregiver and is a signal to which the caregiver responds (Bowlby, 1969).

Damasio (1994) maintained that body changes are an integral part of emotion, which he called somatic markers, that serve as a form of communication to oneself. These body changes play a crucial role in reasoning and adaptive problem solving. Solms and Turnbull (2002) follow Panksepp in maintaining that "emotion is an internally direct sensory modality that provides information about the current state of the body self, as opposed to the state of the object world" (pp. 105–106). It is an internally directed perceptual modality, which permits the perception of the state of the subject not of the object world.

The experiences of shame and humiliation that often punctuate the lives of individuals with neuropsychological deficits present a threat to their sense of self-cohesion. Shame, one of the categorical affects that Tomkins (1963) identified, is a response to other people's judgments and disapproval but may also be evoked by one's own experience of not living up to one's expectations by saying, "I am embarrassed because I have failed!" For Tomkins, shame is a highly toxic affect, whose aim is to reduce facial communication. It is activated by the "incomplete reduction of interest or joy" (p. 123); "It does not matter whether the humiliated one has been shamed by derisive laughter or whether he mocks himself. In either event he feels himself naked, defeated, lacking in dignity or worth" (p. 118).

For Schore (1994), shame is a painful affect state that reflects the transition from high levels of sympathetic arousal to parasympathetic low energy states. It is part of the developmental socialization process in that it serves an "essential task of socioemotional development" (p. 240). The prolongation of the state of shame in children without an attuned and timely intervention interferes with the development of the capacity for self-regulation and hence with the attachment that the child forms with the caregivers.

Cozolino (2014) distinguishes "appropriate shame" from "core shame." The first is linked to the socialization process of children, through which they go when their "primitive, uncivilized, animalistic instincts" are curbed (p. 281). Core shame is an experience of the individual being "fundamentally defective, worthless, and unlovable, the polar opposite of self-esteem" (p. 282). It is associated with the freeze response that reflects the autonomic system's shift from sympathetic arousal to parasympathetic inhibition. The repeated repair from the state of shame that children experience from parents who are attuned to their responses contributes to the development of the capacity for self-regulation and the restoration of a positive relationship with the parents. On the other hand, the chronic failure of such reparative efforts leads to depression, low self-esteem, hostility, and other symptoms that undermine the sense of self.

Morrison (1994) presented a view of the development of the experience of shame from a self psychology perspective. He suggests that shame results from the misattunements and unresponsiveness of the providers of selfobject functions. In a recent contribution, DeYoung (2015) presents a "relational/neurobiological" view for understanding and treating the chronic shame from which some patients suffer. Her thesis is that "[s]hame is an experience of one's felt sense of self disintegrating in relation to a dysregulating other" (p. xiii). She proposes the use of Schore's affect regulation theory as the framework with which to understand the establishment of the patterns of shame in patients.

For most patients with neuropsychological deficits, shame is a central organizer of their psychodynamics. They have long histories of feeling embarrassed and humiliated because of their shortcomings. From their early years, misunderstandings of the reasons for their behaviors contaminated the socialization process. When confronted with tasks they could not accomplish because of their deficits, they were accused of being lazy, not trying hard enough, being oppositional, or simply being stupid. In the face of such assaults, some felt confused and incorporated those criticisms into a view of themselves, with devastating effects on their self-esteem. They instituted defenses behind which to conceal their presumed ineptitude and the shame associated with those judgments.

Others rejected those depictions and fought back, but only to define themselves negatively as to what they were not rather than with a positive sense of identity. As we will see from the description of their psychodynamics, most bear the scars of these experiences as manifested in the defenses they use to help salvage what they could of their sense of self. Those experiences often have a profound effect on patients' sense of self-cohesion.

The loss of self-cohesion

The loss of self-cohesion is a common condition for patients with neuropsychological deficits. They find themselves unable to maintain the experience of inner organization and self-continuity. They are possessed by anxiety, defenses against anxiety, and a variety of symptoms. Anxiety is both an indicator of an unstable sense of self-cohesion and a contributor to it. A threat to self-cohesion activates defenses that represent attempts at self-rescue. Disorders of self-cohesion may result from self-critical attitudes that patients develop in comparing themselves with others. They may also result when patients cannot avail themselves of the complementary functions that caregivers can provide or when those functions are not available to them. Depending on the stability or instability of the patients' sense of self-cohesion, the support they receive from others in their community, and the subjective meaning of the injury, two types of defenses are characteristic of their psychodynamics: *disavowal* or *dissociation*. These defenses serve to organize the patients' experience and provide a measure of stability to their sense of self-cohesion.

Disavowal

Since early childhood, patients with neuropsychological deficits have often been the object of criticism, ridicule, or bullying. They were perceived as inept, unmotivated, or simply stupid. In addition, by comparing themselves to others, they found confirmation for some of those depictions of their behaviors. Unaware of the causes for their conduct, they blamed themselves or responded with rage at those who were critical of them. If the injuries they suffered were experienced as narcissistic wounds, some patients responded with *disavowal*.

In disavowal, the affect states are partitioned off from their cognitive contents, which the left hemisphere processes, so that patients disregard the meaning of the message but act on the feelings generated by the circumstances. For example, when an adult with dyslexia is asked to read a speech before an audience, the anticipation of such an undertaking evokes considerable anxiety, but also humiliation at not being able to perform the task. The initial process involves the activation of the autonomic system's flight/flight response. However, soon the hypoarousal activates the parasympathetic system leading to the institution of a defense to protect against fragmentation. The person now disavows the consequences of his actions, and feelings of grandiosity or omnipotence are evoked in an attempt at self-rescue. These feelings may lead him either to make a mockery of the task or through some theatrical performance to avoid it. The inappropriate public display displaces the audience's attention away from that person's deficit while preserving his self-cohesion.

The common psychodynamics in such cases are that the narcissistic injury becomes the nodal point around which a set of experiences are organized as a pattern of expectations. The patient is sensitized to any situation that arouses familiar feelings, which in turn triggers the defenses that the patient has used habitually. The configuration of patterns and defenses become a trait (i.e. an attractor) that provides some stability to the sense of self-cohesion. However, the stability it provides also becomes problematic as patients hold on to it with rigidity; the patterns become almost impermeable to change. Furthermore, as a stable pattern, patients nonconsciously apply it indiscriminately to situations that feel threatening. Consequently, the rigidity of the patterns compromises their capacity to accommodate successfully to situations. Their relationships suffer, as does their ability to respond to demands made of them.

Disavowal: Josh

Josh was a 17-year-old high school junior with severe dyslexia that interfered with his ability to perform academically. He felt chronically narcissistically injured by his being required to perform tasks that he was unable to complete. He dreaded having teachers call on him in class to give reports and oral presentations. In therapy, he revealed his intense longing for affirmation and admiration. Whereas his parents attempted to provide these for him, he diminished their value, insisting that it was more important that he receive these from teachers and peers than from those who cared for him.

One day during the second year of therapy, he came to a session excitedly asking the therapist to assist in the plan he had conceived. He began by asking the therapist how much it would cost to rent a helicopter. The therapist responded that he had no idea, but not wishing to inhibit the patient's momentum, said that they could easily get the information from looking it up on the Web. He then asked what Josh had in mind.

Josh stated that he had a plan for the weekend homecoming football game that would "blow everyone out of the water!" He would rent a helicopter and land it on the football field just before the game was about to start. He would then kidnap the quarterback of the visiting team and fly off. This would make it possible for the home team to win the game easily. He would get credited for the triumph. Josh gave this account with the conviction that he had every intention of carrying it out.

The therapist burst out laughing, saying, "What a great idea! Wouldn't that be great fun if you could do it!" They went on to fantasize about the reaction of his peers, who would look on him as the hero, while the adults would be appalled by the ill-conceived and outlandish conduct. Josh needed the therapist's admiration for the creativity displayed in conceiving the plan. The experience provided him with a temporary respite for his discordant and unstable sense of self, which he could use as a template in the future to repair his fragmented sense of self.

Josh's plan clearly illustrates his disavowal of the unreality of his scheme. He presented it as a well-thought-out series of steps that he could implement given the resources that he could muster. The underlying motive was the need for admiration and recognition for which he was starved. The therapist's response indirectly provided this much-needed selfobject function.

By the end of the session, it was evident that the entire exercise was restorative for Josh, whose fantasy was in the service of salvaging a sense of well-being. There was no need for the therapist to point out the dangers or the irresponsibility of the plan. Had he done that, not only would he have injured Josh, but also he would have repeated the multiple narcissistic injuries that he had suffered.

Dissociation

In recent years, we have seen a significant increase in the literature on dissociation, much of which has focused on highlighting the long-neglected contribution of Pierre Janet (1907/2012). A major point made by many of these contributors to the literature is that although Freud initially subscribed to the view that sexual abuse was the primary cause of the hysterical symptoms that his patients manifested, he later turned away from an exogenous cause to an endogenous drive-related factor. He was led to attribute the primary defense as that of repression rather than dissociation (Howell & Itzkowitz, 2016a, 2016b; van der Hart, 2016). Some of these authors emphasize the suppressed contribution to the psychoanalytic literature made by Ferenczi (Hainer, 2016).

Patients respond with *dissociation* if they feel the assault to be of traumatic proportions (Van Der Kolk, 2014). As Bromberg (2011) described the experience:

> Sudden shame, a threat equal to that of fear, signals that the self is or is about to be violated, and the mind-brain triggers dissociation in order to prevent a recurrence of the original affective tsunami. Shame that is linked to trauma is a horrifying unanticipated sense of exposure as no longer the self that one has been.
>
> (p. 23)

Dissociation then results when the fragility of the sense of self and the circumstances in which the event occurs does not permit a response other than conservation/withdrawal (Bromberg, 2003; Janet, 1907/2012; Ogden, 2009; Schore, 2003). Schore defines dissociation:

> Neurobiologically, dissociation reflects the inability of the right brain cortical-subcortical implicit self-system to recognize and process the perception of external stimuli (exteroceptive information coming from the relational environment) and on a moment-to-moment basis integrate them with internal stimuli (interoceptive information from the body, somatic markers, the "felt experience").
>
> (Bromberg, 2011, p. xxiii)

Schore's (2003) formulations of the dynamics of dissociation help to clarify the processes involved. If we think of the affects of shame and humiliation as central to the trauma of having one's deepest fear of being exposed as being a fraud are about to be realized, then dissociation would appear to be the only way out of such a horrific eventuality. Schore suggests that the right hemisphere, which deals with all nonverbal communications, processes the negative affects. The shame responses reflect the activation of the conservation/withdrawal parasympathetic autonomic nervous system. This system leads to the dissociation of the events that stimulate the experience from the affects that they generate. In essence, the dissociation constitutes a defense against the psychic pain generated by these affects.

Dissociation: Angie

Angie, a 34-four-year-old woman with a severe executive function disorder, had been in therapy twice a week for two years when she came to this session.

As the therapist invited her in from the waiting room, he noticed that she was more disheveled than usual. Not only did her clothing seem ill-fitting, she came wearing slippers and her hair was not combed and her complexion gaunt. She looked like she had been crying.

She sat down and as usual put her feet under her, sitting cross-legged in the chair. She stared blankly into space. After a prolonged silence, the therapist being concerned about her state said, "You look like you've been through hell! What's happened?" After another long silence, she seemed to wake up from the trance and responded, "You're right!" After another long silence, which is not unusual for her, and more attempts on the therapist's part to make contact with her, she said, "I had a fire in my apartment last night!" "Where you hurt?" She responded, "No! But two of my cats died!" She had six cats around which her life centered. Feeding them and cleaning their litter boxes were the only activities that gave regularity to her life. She had been unemployed for a year, having lost her last job because she could not keep straight the irregular hours that were assigned to her.

It took several more weeks to piece together the fragments of her memory of the events surrounding that fire. The therapist knew, from descriptions she had given, that her apartment looked like that of a hoarder. She liked to read books and magazines, none of which she ever threw out. She seldom cleaned her place, always giving the pretext that she first wanted to finish the book she was reading before attending to the chores.

What they slowly reconstructed was that she was smoking in bed. She and the therapist speculated, although she had no clear recollection, that she must have fallen asleep. She was awakened by the fire alarm in her bedroom, by which time the flames had engulfed most of the bedding and some of the books surrounding her. Although she had no recollection of how she got there, all she could clearly recall was that next she was sitting in her car in the parking lot of the building with four of her cats. Tears were streaming down her cheeks as she wondered what happened to the other cats. The firefighters knocked on the car windows and offered to take her to the emergency room, but she refused.

She thinks she fell asleep in the car and was aroused early the next morning by her cats pawing at her, clamoring to be fed. She got back to her apartment, which was now in total shambles, retrieved some of the cat food, which she offered to cats, and sat in the middle of the floor unable to take in what happened. As she searched for the missing cats with no success, a neighbor knocked on her door and informed her that the firefighters had found them dead and removed them. She was overcome with guilt and shame at the catastrophe for which she was responsible.

The devastating consequence of that event was that it plunged her into a deep depression that medication could not relieve. She dismissed the therapist's suggestion that she be hospitalized; instead, she chose to struggle by keeping actively organized around her cats and cleaning up the mess that engulfed her apartment.

The psychodynamics of patients who use dissociation as a defense are different from those who use disavowal. For those who resort to dissociation, the experience of confronting the consequences of their deficit is so devastating as to lead to the fragmentation of their sense of self – that is, of the temporary or permanent loss of the capacity for self-cohesion. They split off the affects generated by the experience from their ability to process the experience cognitively. They could not make meaningful sense of what had happened to them. It is as though the only solution to which they could resort was to withdraw from their surround and figuratively hide from others in their context.

The outcome of these psychodynamics is that such patients do not have any established patterns of interaction with others or of addressing tasks that they confront. Their responses emanate from the random images or sensory stimuli that the present circumstances evoke. Their hyperarousal leads them to be chronically vigilant in anticipation of a recurrence of the trauma.

I should note that in both examples given above, the clinical issues the therapists address are the defenses brought to bear by the patients' efforts to deal with deficits in selfobject functions – that is, in the emotional consequences, the shaming and humiliating experiences resulting from their neuropsychological deficits. Left untouched are the deficits in the adjunctive functions that lay behind their responses. Those deficits, as we will see in Chapter 6, will require separate treatment.

In summary, the presence of a neuropsychological deficit may create the condition that leads to an unstable sense of self that is prone to fragmentation. Depending on the severity of the deficits, the patient's response to it, and the environment's ability to provide complementary functions, these may either mitigate the effects or enhance the constraints on the patient's capacity to accommodate successfully to the context. Often, the narcissistic injuries the patients suffer lead to rage responses that serve as attractors around which patterns of responses cluster. The justification for the rage is often rationalized as due to the frustrations related to an unresponsive environment. They feel that others are responsible for their failures. The fact that the neuropsychological self-deficit is transparent to them only reinforces this view of reality.

Self-understanding

Another preference or bias that engages a person's sense of self is the preference for self-understanding. The capacity to integrate the unique meanings that we construe from specific experiences is a system preference. Our capacity for self-understanding is an essential component of our individuality. Self-awareness and self-reflection bring with them insights that result in self-understanding. The affect states that predominate at the time the events took place inform those meanings. Affects then are not only critical to the organization of self-experience, but also serve to enhance the capacity for self-understanding.

From the perspective of the self as a complex adaptive system, we can regard the preference for self-understanding as a central organizer of experience. Galatzer-Levy and Cohler (1993) stated: "Not only do we commonly organize ongoing experiences as narratives, but also we often try to live a prescribed story, to approximate an ideal, or 'normal,' development. These efforts shape ongoing development and determine our evaluations of development" (p. 6).

The self-narrative that emerges from patients' attempts to integrate their experiences mediates self-understanding. Embedded within the self-narrative are themes that organize the "plot" of the narrative. Such are the experiences that patients with neuropsychological deficits encounter when confronted with failures, humiliations, or severe narcissistic injuries. The encoded patterns, which are rich in intense affect, lead patients to reinterpret their past, to reshape their view of their present lives, and to anticipate how their future will unfold. Patients enact the narrative themes as interactions that form part of a closed system that is not readily accessible to change. In other words, these themes become attractor basins around which habitual patterns of interaction will accrue.

Self-narratives as organizers of experience

Through the preference for self-understanding, patients organize the historical events of their experiences around affect-laden scripts or themes, which lead to the emergence of a *self-narrative*. Self-narrative refers to the broad set of meanings that individuals construe from their experience and through which patients have organized those experiences (Cozolino, 2006). The neuropsychological strengths and weaknesses that patients bring to the process in part determine the interpretations patients make of their experiences.

Self-narratives are generally *nonconscious* organizers of experience. They provide individuals with a sense of continuity that when given expression in social context is regarded as that person's history (see Brandell, 2000; Bruner, 1987, 1990; Cohler, 1982; Cohler & Freeman, 1993; Saari, 1991; Schafer, 1980, 1981, 1983, 1992; Spence, 1982; Stern, 1989). When shared, patients' self-narratives can provide a window into their subjective experiences (Klitzing, 2000). When given verbal expression, we may think of the self-narrative as an autobiographical story that represents the integration of the meanings patients assigned to their experiences as well as the meanings the community conferred on those experiences. For Fernyhough (2012), "[N]arrative is a key organizational force in autobiographical memory, allowing memories to represent the passage of time and the human push toward the reaching of personal goals. Memories are told like stories, to others and to oneself" (p. 239).

Tomkins (1979, 1987), in his *script theory*, details the way in which affect states, which initially represent analogues of experiences of interactions with the environment, become encoded into scripts. He proposed that the amplified and magnified experiences, as retained in non-declarative memory, take the form of scripts or thematic models that serve as interpreters of subsequent experiences. A script reflects the process through which a set of experiences, such as those of having a self-deficit, becomes organized around an attractor state. The script encodes the totality of the experience at the time of its formation, which includes the affects, the event, and the personal meaning that the event acquired. Some of these scripts serve as major organizers of how patients perceived events at the time of their formation. Scripts encode the events that are prototypical of a set of experiences.

As patients integrate and synthesize the meanings of their experiences, their self-understanding develops and their self-narratives acquire a structure and content (Cohler, 1993). As with all stories, the self-narrative has its own structure. It has characters who represent figures in the person's past, a *protagonist*, who is the central figure of the story, and a *plot* that ties the elements of the story together (Scholes & Kellogg, 1966). The person is generally the protagonist (i.e. the central character of the story). The content of the narrative is organized around the plot. Embedded in the plot is a *central theme or scripts* that tie together the elements of the patient's self-narrative. The plot generally encapsulates a statement that people make about repetitive experience, such as "This is the story of my life! I keep reliving the same scenario, unable to change the outcome!" It represents a unifying theme that ties most of the elements of a person's life together. A nodal experience in childhood or a traumatic event may become a central theme of a person's view of their life. At times, more than one theme is embedded in a self-narrative, which can result in conflicting view of the person's values and life goals. These themes are related to the integration of experience, the establishment and maintenance of a sense of continuity, or as Sander (2002) proposed, the sense of "coherence" – that is, the processes that are involved in the experience of wholeness and in sustaining a sense of integration as human beings.

Narrative coherence is an emergent property that results from the self-organizing processes active at the time the person is attempting to integrate a set of experiences. Having a coherent self-narrative enhances feelings of integration and self-understanding. Coherence reflects the stability and integrity of that set of meanings (Saari, 1986a, 1986b). However, coherence depends on the interpretations that people give to their experiences rather than something that is inherent in the phenomena themselves. As a result, a tension may exist between a narrative that is considered coherent by a patient and how others view the coherence of the narrative.

The self-narrative is comparable to the latent content of a dream that is descriptively unconscious – that is, often not necessarily available to the person without self-reflection and introspection. An autobiographical statement is comparable to its manifest content. The latter is no more than an edited rendition of a larger and deeper story that patients cannot retell through conscious statements. In an autobiographical statement, we become the narrators of a story in which we are the protagonists. We may present a self-serving account that justifies our actions and course of life or a confession that we hope will evoke forgiveness or absolution for our misdeeds (see Bruner, 1990). An autobiographical statement is often a highly edited version of one's life as presented publicly. It differs from an account of a self-narrative in that the latter focuses specifically on the unfolding of one's personal life with all the personal meanings that entered the formation of one's view of oneself (Farrar & Goodman, 1990).

Therapists have traditionally identified the explanations that patients give themselves for their problems as "fantasies," because these explanations do not to match the reality to which they refer. From this perspective, the therapeutic process involves having the patient reveal the explanations that are part of their self-narratives, which are then corrected so that they can match the probable reality at the time of their formation (Beebe & Lachmann, 2014).

One question this point of view raises is whether it is correct to call the patient's self-narratives *fantasies*. If we subscribe to the view that these expressions are fantasies, then we must distinguish the products of a patient's imagination from explanations patients reach about actual events. On the other hand, if we view the explanations as *beliefs* patients have reached to help them interpret their world, then we are left with the disparity between these beliefs as personal meanings and the meanings that others ascribe to the events as explanations for the same occurrences. In the latter case, we may make a distinction between a fantasy and an explanation proposed as a hypothesis (Gopnik, Meltzoff, & Kuhl, 1999). Patients' autobiographical accounts are the product of connections they have made between events as they experienced them.

I suggest that we may view self-narratives as beliefs to which patients arrive based on their experiences, rather than fantasies. This is not to negate that patients sometimes embellish their explanations with fantasies. We have seen this in patients' reports of their early histories. I would call these embellishments *secondary elaborations*. The addition of fantasies expands the nucleus of truth, which come in the form of a memory drawn from other sources. Fantasies replace some personal meanings. Patients may be vulnerable to such secondary elaborations when they have suffered a trauma or when they wish to please someone.

In this connection, Spence's (1982, 1987) contribution is interesting to consider because of the different interpretation of analysis he proposes. For him, the patient's recollections of childhood events are narrative creations whose accuracy can never be confirmed. The analytic process does not involve the reconstruction of childhood events but simply the construction of a coherent narrative that has sufficient explanatory power and aesthetic quality to satisfy the patient. He suggests that it is idle to speculate whether the constructed history parallels what actually occurred (Palombo, 1991).

In summary, individuals acquire self-understanding within a shared contextual experience. Both personal and shared experiences derive their meaning from lived episodes that are translated into scripts. Some of these scripts become themes included within the plot of the self-narrative. The themes lend a distinctiveness to the self-narrative and include the nucleus of a *world view*. This world view, which is organized around an attractor, is a major theme that plays an active role in shaping future experiences.

A counterpart to the patients' self-narrative is the narrative that therapists construct based on their interpretation of the patients' psychodynamics and life histories. Those narratives are embedded in the therapists' theoretical framework. As we will see in the chapters on the therapeutic dialogue, these narratives become powerful determinants of the types of interventions that therapists can make.

Neuropsychological deficits and narrative incoherence

There are several ways to think about the coherence of a self-narrative. One is from the patient's perspective, who has tried to make sense of events in her life by stitching segments as best she could to make meaning of what occurred. The other is from the outlook of the community to which the patient belongs. From the community's perspective, if a concordance exists between the personal meanings that the patient has assigned to events and the shared meanings the context gives to them, then a match exists. The patient's narrative is coherent to both herself and others in the community.

However, often what is lacking in both those narratives is the contribution of the neuropsychological deficits to patients' senses of self as well as the effects they have had on their lives. Neither the patients nor the community may take into account the impact of the impairment in the specific functional areas of the brain, of which informed practitioners are much aware.

Another manifestation of coherence occurs when the patients' understanding of what has happened clashes with that of the community's. While their narratives are coherent to themselves, they are incoherent from the community's outlook, as when an adolescent devalues the academic standards and expectations set by parents and seeks alternative lifestyles. The two sets of meanings are not concordant. Problems arise when patients act on their own understanding, which others perceive as out of step with theirs. Differences exist between the types of explanations patients provide themselves, as contrasted with the accounts that others in the community provide, as happens when patients act on beliefs or even paranoid misconceptions that the community finds inexplicable.

As we will see, in the clinical setting, therapists strive for coherence that will incorporate information about the neuropsychological deficit, information that the patient may not possess or may not have fully integrated. These patients may have explained to themselves what occurred through interpretations given to them by others or by creative connections that they have made between disparate events. For example, others may have called them lazy or stupid and criticized them for what others interpreted as a lack of motivation. Having internalized these criticisms, they embrace these views of themselves and incorporate them as themes into their self-narratives.

Most patients with neuropsychological deficits come to treatment with incoherent narratives. The incoherence may stem from their puzzlement at their lack of success or from their inability to come to grips with the limitations that their deficits impose on them. Sometimes, incoherence may occur either because the patient's integrative capacities are overtaxed, or because the neuropsychological deficits interfere with the integrative task. Patients may ask themselves: "Why am I having so much trouble? Why do relationships always end up disastrously?" At a different level, they are aware of and puzzled by their own neuropsychological strengths and weaknesses. They ask themselves: "Why can't I be as successful as my friends, I am smarter than they are. Why am I such a good problem solver, yet I can't keep a job?'

For patients with neuropsychological deficits whose narratives have elements of incoherence, the experience of having the sources of the disturbances understood reduces the incoherence. The therapist contributes information about the effects that the neuropsychological deficits produce on the patient's view of events. Once the patient can grasp the significance and impact of the deficits, a set of shared meanings is created that leads to a reduction in incoherence. The therapist may then help sort out and interpret the psychodynamic factors at play in the patient's problems. In a study on the life course of adults with dyslexia, McNulty (2000, 2003) examined the life stories of adults diagnosed with dyslexia as children:

> [The] findings indicated that self-esteem problems might emerge by early childhood as individuals contend with aspects of their learning disabilities that interfere with typical development. By school age, all participants noted self-esteem problems when they experienced struggles or failures in school, which could feel traumatic. Testing and diagnosis improved self-esteem when conducted in a relevant manner that led to adaptation. The central plots of the participants' lives were characterized by the interplay between the functional challenges of their learning disabilities and the related self-esteem issues.
> (p. 363)

A further complexity of incoherence arises because of developmental factors. Younger patients' capacity to understand causal relationships is less well developed than that of older patients. Consequently, they will often associate events that they accidentally or temporally link together, believing them as causally connected. The themes in their self-narrative may incorporate these relationships between events and generalizations made from them. Subjectively, the narrative is coherent, but from the perspective of others, it makes little sense. As the child grows older, these seemingly archaic explanations may become modified, elaborated, or embellished. Nevertheless, their nucleus may remain unchanged, leading to beliefs that guide the child's conduct in problematic areas. The age at which such themes crystalize determines, to a degree, whether personal or shared meanings will predominate. Ultimately, the therapeutic process may resolve these tensions within the self-narrative.

Two common themes that recur and that contribute to the coherence or incoherence of patients' self-narratives are *conventionalization* and *emplotment* (see J. Palombo, 2008, pp. 95–100). *Conventionalization* refers to the expectations that society presents members of its community, such as "pre-designed" narrative themes that its members should embrace. Those themes include the social norms and expectations of the social group. Individuals feel pressured to conventionalize their narrative by making their lives approximate the normative narrative (i.e. the canonical narrative) of the social/cultural milieu (Bruner, 1990). The challenge that patients with neurocognitive deficits face is that of conventionalizing their self-narratives by having their lives conform to that of the larger community's expectations. In order to maintain the selfobject ties to the members of the larger social group, patients must embrace the values that the group maintains. It means that they have to align or modify their lives and their self-narrative to bring them closer to the expectation of those whose opinions they value or suffer the consequences for their differences.

The concept of *emplotment* (J. Palombo, 2008, p. 95) is used in narrative theory to delineate the ways in which patients become characters in another person's narrative, or become engulfed into their own narrative. Children become emplotted in their caregivers' narratives and try to conform to their caregivers' expectations by taking on the themes of the narratives of those they wish to please or not to please. Some caregivers come to the task of parenting with ready-made narratives of their own, which they configured out of their own experiences that include the meaning the child has for them and the role the child is to play in their lives. In effect, the parents experience their infant as a character in their own plot. If the child appropriates these attitudes and behaviors and includes them as subplots within his narrative, the child thus becomes emplotted into the caregivers' narrative characterizations of him (cf. Winnicott, 1960, concept of the true and false self). As we will see in the case that follows, Jim not only became emplotted into his father's view of him, but also seemed to have integrated unambivalently that view into himself.

Case illustration: Jim

Jim was an obese young man, a high school freshman, who had a receptive language problem, an impairment in auditory memory and auditory processing. His ability to understand verbal communications was mildly impaired. While he could hear clearly and could process verbal communications that were simple, he had difficulty fully understanding other people's spoken words if they were not couched in simple sentences. Even with the assistance of a tutor, he struggled to get a C average in courses that involved listening to teachers' lectures. In subjects that involve reading texts and in math, he consistently got high grades.

Psychoeducational testing at age 10 revealed a Verbal IQ of 95, a Performance IQ of 106, and a Full Scale IQ of 100. The diagnostician indicated that testing "Reveals a language/learning disability in: (1) receptive, integrative and expressive language; (2) word retrieval; (3) auditory memory and processing; (4) auditory closure; and (5) auditory synthesis. Visual/motor perceptual integration is inconsistent. The above problems appear to be causing interferences, particularly in his ability to understand and integrate directions, in reading comprehension and math reasoning and computation. Disruptions in the above area of processing can negatively affect the learning process, as the acquisition of academic skills requires the integration of a complex set of receptive and expressive functions. In his long-term memory, what he has learned is not necessarily available for retrieval on demand."

Referral was made to a specialized audiologist for testing for a possible central auditory processing problem. The report of the audiologist stated, "Central testing confirmed the presence of moderate/severe auditory/language processing weakness at this time. Performance profile suggested moderate deficits in the ability to perceive and discriminate/decode auditory information (specifically speech) and to tolerate noiseless severe weakness inability to integrate and coordinate auditory/language information. Overall performance was similar to that obtained for a 6-year-old child."

The parents did consult a clinical social worker to help them resolve the conflict and to decide on whether Jim should be in therapy. The father, who also was opposed to having Jim in individual therapy, rejected a recommendation for family therapy outright. Instead, they opted for intensive tutoring by a speech and language specialist to help Jim academically. The mother kept in intermittent touch with the social worker and provided him with the following information.

Jim's perception of himself, in his high-achieving family, was that of someone who could never attain the success that his parents and siblings had attained. Consequently, he was chronically depressed and had lapsed into a passive stance in which he took no initiative in any activity. His preferred form of entertainment was playing video games, at which he became expert. In addition, he was unable to control his food intake as he resorted to eating as a way to comfort himself. This habit, combined with his sedentary lifestyle, led him to be more than 60 lbs overweight. His large-boned frame masked his obesity and made him look like an ideal football player.

Jim's father had a similar physique. He had come from a large family in which he had to fend for himself. He became highly successful by being aggressively competitive. While he intellectually understood his son's problems, he felt utterly frustrated by his son's passivity. He became enraged whenever he saw Jim watching TV and munching on snacks or playing video games. To him, Jim was a lazy slug who would never amount to much. He took the approach of "motivating" Jim by berating him, presenting him with the image of failure that he would become unless he did something with himself now. He constantly compared him with his high-achieving siblings, tried to restrict his food intake and TV watching, and pushed him to engage in sports. Jim inevitably responded by increasing his food intake and putting even less effort into homework than he usually did.

When Jim entered high school, his father decided that the solution to the problem was for Jim to try out for football. He felt that participation in football would not only involve him in a healthy athletic program, but also would encourage him to become more assertive. Jim hated the idea. Being afraid of bodily contact and not well-coordinated, he saw only failure and humiliation ahead of him. However, he felt caught between his own desire to remain regressed and his desire to please his father and gain his approval and affection. For his part, his father dangled the prospect of more fun times together should Jim comply, while he threatened to withdraw from Jim if he did not comply.

On the other hand, Jim's mother was enraged at her husband's treatment of the boy. She felt that the constant criticism and threats to withdraw were erosive of Jim's self-esteem and activated his negativism. Jim would stubbornly defy his father, get into loud arguments with him, and become so enraged that she feared that physical confrontations would follow. She actively defended Jim in front of his father, setting up a division among the parents that Jim would often try to exploit. Clearly, Jim had become emplotted into the family's dynamics as he felt pulled in one direction by his father's insistence that he joined the football team and in another direction by his mother's opposition because of her fears that he would suffer a sports injury.

His father's criticism, while motivated by a desire to have his son succeed, was extremely harsh and punitive. Jim's mother would often intervene, feeling that her husband was doing more harm than good to their child. Arguments broke out between the two parents about the best strategy to take to help Jim. His mother would have long talks with him, interpreting his father's behavior to have a detrimental effect on him, and clarifying his intentions in dealing with him so harshly. She realized that the boy needed these explanations to process his father's treatment of him. For his part, Jim appeared unable to deal with the complexity of the interactions around him. To him, the issues were clear-cut: His father was displeased with him, and his mother did not like that. The simple solution was for him to do what his father wanted him to do. The fact that he got recognition and acceptance for that meant that he had made the right decision. Eventually, the gains Jim felt he would make in pleasing his father overcame his resistance.

Football turned out to be a painful but bearable experience for Jim. Jim's size impressed the coach, who saw him as a promising linebacker who could contribute to the team's success. He took a great interest in Jim's training, praised him for the efforts he made, and rewarded him by publicly recognizing any success on the field. The rest of the team became equally invested in Jim's success since they needed him; they made him an integral part of the group and accepted him as one of their own. Jim's wish to become like the other athletes on the team led to efforts "to be like the others." He saw the salvation from his problems as lying in the "direction of conventionalizing his behavior so that he appeared to more 'normal.'" A scenario unfolded in which he began to daydream of being a star on the football team. It felt as though he wished to shape his identity into one that could conform to his father's expectations of him.

Psychodynamic profile

Initial conditions: During his growing years, prior to the diagnosis of his condition at age 10, Jim's passivity and failure to perform academically had puzzled his concerned parents. They alternated between encouraging him to be more active socially and to try harder in school and berating him for his lack of initiative. Once they understood the nature of his neuropsychological problems, a change in their attitudes occurred. However, serious differences arose between the parents as to how to deal with Jim. His mother insisted on an empathic approach that took account of the constraints under which he functioned, whereas his father was adamant that Jim not be permitted to use his learning disorder as an excuse to avoid taking on challenges.

Preferences: The nature of the neuropsychological deficit did not affect Jim's sense of self-cohesion markedly, although initially, he did respond with demoralization and discouragement prior to its diagnosis. He felt stable in the support he received from his mother, as she was vocal about what she considered as abuse by the father. Fortunately, for Jim, he was sufficiently receptive to the tutorial interventions he received that he made considerable gains. In fact, the academic gains bolstered his self-esteem enough for him to develop a close friendship with a classmate, which opened the possibility to have a wider circle of peers.

Processes that guided his psychodynamics: Of interest in this case is the fact that the learning disorder was not the primary organizer of Jim's problems. The tutorial help that he received provided sufficient support to help them succeed in school. The focal issue was the conflict between the parents. His emplotment into his father's narrative seems to have been a central theme of his self-narrative.

Since Jim was not seen in therapy, it is difficult to speculate as to the attractors that became organizers of his experiences. It is possible that the central issues for him would not be those of his learning disability, but rather that of the residues that the conflict between the parents produced. The capacity to develop an intimate relationship with a partner might later on replicate what he experienced in his family. To his credit, his receptivity to involving himself in football led to the emergence of a pattern of success that enhanced his sense of agency and his ability to achieve a higher level of maturation that he would have otherwise.

Therapeutic implications: This case provides an example of a child who in spite of his emplotment into the family's dynamics could find an avenue of success that helped restore a measure of self-esteem in an activity into which he had been pushed. While the initial impetus for his trying out at football was a desire to please his father, the responses he got from his coach and teammates transformed his involvement in the activity. The desire to be like others, to be accepted as part of the group, became a powerful force for his continued involvement in football, in spite of his initial fearfulness and his lack of aggressiveness.

Summary

Two preferences guide the self as a complex adaptive system: the preference for self-cohesion and for a coherent self-narrative. Self-cohesion is associated with positive affect states, such as feeling of pride, competence, and vitality. Patients with a neuropsychological deficit may feel cohesive because the context complements their deficits and because they have a coherent narrative. The understanding that they have a neuropsychological deficit that requires someone to complement them in order to function satisfactorily may enhance their self-cohesion. This is the case as when a patient who understands and accepts that she must rely on others to help her organize her work space because of her disorganization. A different patient with a similar neuropsychological deficit may feel cohesive because of the support she gets from her family and partner, even though she may not understand the nature of her neuropsychological deficit. She could not generate a coherent narrative to explain her difficulties. The positive affects associated with self-cohesion (Demos, 2007) dispose individuals to value conditions that produce such self-states over those that lead to destabilization or fragmentation.

We also value self-understanding for the benefits it confers on our ability to control our lives. We learn from experience and incorporate that learning into our histories. Our histories find expression in the self-narratives that we construct. These self-narratives are nonconscious, but at times, it is possible to articulate them into autobiographical statements. The preference of self-understanding finds expression in a self-narrative that provides a sense of agency (i.e. being a locus of activity, power, and control). It gives expression to intentionality, to have the capacity for volition, and to have a sense of coherence.

The transformations and reorganization that occur in a person's narrative over the lifespan represent the person's autobiography. Narratives are not created in a vacuum; they are always connected to a context in which they evolve. Consequently, the community within which a person organizes her narrative plays a constitutive role both in the structure and in the context of the narrative and of the meanings that it incorporates. To the extent that they are cohesive, patients can often give a coherent account of themselves through their self-narrative. To the extent that they are troubled and lack cohesion, they often fail to create a coherent narrative out of their life experiences. In a sense, their distress arises from the fact that they have been unable to make meaningful what has happened to them. The absence of coherence in their narrative may be in direct proportion to the level of their distress. Patients experience fragmentation states as a loss of inner organization and the loss of the meanings associated with their experiences; it reflects the absence of coherence in the patient's self-narrative.

Writing of older adults who confront their mortality, Cohler and Freeman (1993) stated:

> A sense of psychological well-being in later life is assumed to be associated with enhanced preservation of meaning, expressed as a purposive or coherent life story. Failure to maintain this coherent life story leads to feelings of lowered morale and a sense of personal depletion, as exemplified by the older patient who had lost her sense of personal significance.
>
> (p. 108)

Patients with neuropsychological deficits from an early age were exposed to situations in which they were expected to complete tasks that were beyond the abilities, but which were performed with ease by their peers. As a result, their shortcomings became evident to them as well as to others. The ridicule and criticism to which they were exposed from others only compounded their own assessment of their failures. As a result, feelings of embarrassment, shame, and humiliation pervaded their daily lives.

Depending on the intensity of the affects generated by those experiences, they suffered either a narcissistic injury or a serious trauma. The defenses of disavowal served to mitigate some of the effects of those narcissistic injuries, whereas the defense of dissociation accompanied the traumatic experiences. Consequently, their capacities for self-cohesion and their abilities to construct coherent narratives were compromised. They became vulnerable to fragmentation and were unable to comprehend the sources of their distress, since the neuropsychological deficits were transparent to them. Not only did these experiences affect the trajectory of their development, but as we will see, their precarious state also affected the quality of the relationships that they formed and their ability to accommodate to the context.

References

Beebe, B., & Lachmann, F. M. (2014). *The origins of attachment: Infant research and adult treatment*. New York: Routledge.
Bowlby, J. (1969). *Attachment and loss, volume I: Attachment*. New York: Basic Books.
Brandell, J. R. (2000). *Of mice and metaphors: Therapeutic story telling in children*. New York: Basic Books.

Bromberg, P. M. (2003). Something wicked this way comes: Trauma, dissociation, an conflict: The space where psychoanalysis, cognitive science, and neuroscience overlap. *Psychoanalytic Psychology, 20*, 558–574.

Bromberg, P. M. (2011). *The shadow of the tsunami and the growth of the relational mind*. New York: Routledge.

Bruner, J. S. (1987). Life as narrative. *Social Research, 54*(1), 11–32.

Bruner, J. S. (1990). *Acts of meaning*. Cambridge, MA: Harvard University Press.

Cohler, B. J. (1982). Personal narrative and life course. In P. Baltes & O. G. Brins (Eds.), *Lifespan development and behavior* (Vol. 4, pp. 205–241). New York: Psychology Press.

Cohler, B. J. (1993). Aging, morale, and meaning: The nexus of narrative. In T. R. Cole & W. A. Achenbaum (Eds.), *Voices and visions of aging: Toward a clinical gerontology* (pp. 107–133). New York: Springer.

Cohler, B. J., & Freeman, M. (1993). Psychoanalysis and the developmental narrative. In G. H. Polloch & S. L. Greenspan (Eds.), *The course of life* (Vol. 5, pp. 99–177). Madison, CT: International Universities Press.

Cozolino, L. (2006). *The neuroscience of human relationships: Attachment in the developing social brain*. New York: W. W. Norton.

Cozolino, L. (2014). *The neuroscience of human relationships: Attachment in the developing social brain* (2nd ed.). New York: W. W. Norton.

Damasio, A. R. (1994). *Descartes' error: Emotion, reason, and the human brain*. New York: G. P. Putnam's Sons.

Darwin, C. (1998). *The expression of emotion in man and animals*. New York: Oxford University Press.

Demos, E. V. (2007). The dynamics of development. In C. Piers, J. P. Muller, & J. Brent (Eds.), *Self organizing complexity in psychological systems* (pp. 135–163). New York: Jason Aronson.

DeYoung, P. A. (2015). *Understanding and treating chronic shame: A relational/neurobiological approach*. New York: Routledge.

Farrar, M. J., & Goodman, G. S. (1990). Developmental differences in the relation between scripts and episodic memory: Do they exist? In R. Fivush & J. A. Hudson (Eds.), *Knowing and remembering in young children* (pp. 30–64). NY: Cambridge University Press.

Fernyhough, C. (2012). *Pieces of light: How the new science of memory illuminates the stories we tell about our pasts*. New York: Harper.

Frie, R. (2009). Reconfiguring psychological agency: Postmodernims, recursivity, and the politics of change. In R. Frie & D. Orange (Eds.), *Beyond postmodernsims: New dimensions in clinical theory and practice* (pp. 162–181). New York: Routledge.

Frie, R., & Orange, D. M. (Eds.). (2009). *Beyond postmodernism: New dimensions in clinical theory and practice*. New York: Routledge.

Galatzer-Levy, R. M., & Cohler, B. J. (1993). *The essential other: A developmental psychology of the self*. New York: Basic Books.

Gopnik, A., Meltzoff, A. N., & Kuhl, P. K. (1999). *The scientist in the crib: Minds, brains, and how children learn*. New York: William Morrow & Co.

Hainer, M. L. (2016). The Ferenczi paradox: His importance in understanding dissociation and the dissociation of his importance in psychoanalysis. In E. F. Howell & S. Itzkowitz (Eds.), *The dissociative mind in psychoanalysis: Understanding and working with trauma* (pp. 57–69). New York: Routledge.

Howell, E. F., & Itzkowitz, S. (Eds.). (2016a). *The dissociative mind in psychoanalysis: Understanding and working with trauma*. New York: Routledge.

Howell, E. F., & Itzkowitz, S. (2016b). From trauma-analysis to psycho-analysis and back. In E. F. Howell & S. Itzkowitz (Eds.), *The dissociative mind in psychoanalysis: Understanding and working with trauma* (pp. 20–32). New York: Routledge.

Janet, P. (1907/2012). *The major symptoms of hysteria: Fifteen lectures given in the medical school of Harvard University.* Retrieved from www.forgottenbooks.org.

Klitzing, K. v. (2000). Gender-specific characteristics of 5-year-olds' play narratives and associations with behavior ratings. Journal of the American Academy of Child & Adolescent Psychiatry, 39(8), 1017–1023.

Kohut, H. (1977). *The restoration of the self.* New York: International Universities Press.

Kohut, H. (1984). *How does analysis cure?* Chicago: The University of Chicago Press.

Kohut, H., & Wolf, E. S. (1978). The disorders of the self and their treatment: An outline. *International Journal of Psychoanalysis, 59*, 413–425.

LeDoux, L. (1996). *The emotional brain: The mysterious underpinnings of emotional life.* New York: Simon & Schuster.

McNulty, M. A. (2000). The life stories of adults diagnosed with dyslexia as children: A dissertation submitted to the faculty of the Institute for Clinical Social Work in Partial Fulfillment of the Degree of Doctor of Philosophy. Qualitative Study, Institute for Clinical Social Work, Chicago, IL.

McNulty, M. A. (2003). Dyslexia and the life course. *Journal of Learning Disabilities, 36*(4), 363–381.

Morrison, A. P. (1994). The breadth and boundaries of a self-psychological immersion in shame: A one-and-a-half-person perspective. *Psychoanalytic Dialogues, 4*, 19–35.

Ogden, P. (2009). Emotion, mindfulness, and movement: Expanding the regulatory boundaries of the window of affect tolerance. In D. Fosha, D. J. Siegel, & M. F. Solomon (Eds.), *The healing power of emotion: Affective neuroscience, development, and clinical practice* (pp. 204–230). New York: W. W. Norton.

Palombo, J. (1990). The cohesive self, the nuclear self, and development in late adolescence. In S. C. Feinstein (Ed.), *Adolescent psychiatry* (Vol. 17, pp. 338–359). Chicago: University of Chicago Press.

Palombo, J. (1991). Bridging the chasm between developmental theory and clinical theory, part I: The chasm. In A. Goldberg (Ed.), *The annual of psychoanalysis* (Vol. 19, pp. 151–174). Hillsdale, NJ: The Analytic Press.

Palombo, J. (1994). Incoherent self-narratives and disorders of the self in children with learning disabilities. *Smith College Studies in Social Work, 64*(2), 129–152.

Palombo, J. (1996). The diagnosis and treatment of children with nonverbal learning disabilities. *Child & Adolescent Social Work Journal, 13*(4), 311–332.

Palombo, J. (2001a). *Learning disorders and disorders of the self in children and adolescents.* New York: W. W. Norton.

Palombo, J. (2001b). The therapeutic process with children with learning disorders. *Psychoanalytic Social Work, 8*(3/4), 143–168.

Palombo, J. (2008). Mindsharing: Transitional Objects and Selfobjects as Complementary Functions. Clinical Social Work Journal, 36, 143–154.

Palombo, J. (2008). Self psychology theory. In B. A. Thyer (Ed.), *Comprehensive handbook of social work and social welfare: Human behavior in the social environment* (Vol. 2, pp. 163–205). Hoboken, NJ: John Wiley & Sons.

Panksepp, J. (1998). *Affective neuroscience: The foundation of human and animal emotions.* New York: Oxford University Press.

Panksepp, J. (2001). The long-term psychobiological consequences of infant emotions: Prescriptions for the twenty-first century. *Infant Mental Health Journal, 22*(1/2), 132–173.
Saari, C. (1986a). *Clinical social work treatment: How does it work?* New York: Gardner Press.
Saari, C. (1986b). The use of metaphor in therapeutic communication with young adolescents. *Child & Adolescent Social Work Journal, 3*(1), 15–25.
Saari, C. (1991). *The creation of meaning in clinical social work.* New York: The Guilford Press.
Sander, L. W. (2002). Thinking differently: Principles of process in living systems and the specificy of being known. *Psychoanalytic Dialogues, 12,* 11–42.
Sander, L. W. (2008). Awareness of inner experience: A systems perspective on self-regulatory process in early development. In G. Amadei & I. Bianchi (Eds.), *Living systems, evolving consicousness, and the emerging person: A selection of papers from the life and work of Louis Sander* (pp. 205–214). New York: The Analytic Press.
Schafer, R. (1980). Narration in the psychoanalytic dialogue. In W. J. T. Mitchell (Ed.), *On narrative* (pp. 25–50). Chicago: The University of Chicago Press.
Schafer, R. (1981). *Narrative actions in psychoanalysis.* Worcester, MA: Clark University Press.
Schafer, R. (1983). *The analytic attitude.* New York: Basic Books.
Scholes, R., & Kellogg, R. (1966). *The nature of narrative.* London: Oxford University Press.
Schore, A. N. (1994). *Affect regulation and the origin of the self: The neurobiology of emotional development.* Hillsdale, NJ: Lawrence Earlbaum.
Schore, A. N. (2003). *Affect dysregulation and disorders of the self.* New York: W. W. Norton.
Solms, M., & Turnbull, O. (2002). *The brain and the inner world: An introduction to the neuroscience of subjective experience.* New York: Other Press.
Spence, D. P. (1982). *Narrative truth and historical truth.* New York: W. W. Norton.
Spence, D. P. (1987). *The Freudian metaphor: Toward a paradigm change in psychoanalysis.* New York: W. W. Norton.
Stern, D. N. (1985). *The interpersonal world of the infant.* New York: Basic Books.
Stern, D. N. (1989). Developmental prerequisites for the sense of narrated self. In A. M. Cooper, O. F. Kernberg, & E. S. Person (Eds.), *Psychoanalysis: Toward the second century* (pp. 168–178). New Haven, CT: Yale University Press.
Stolorow, R. D., Brandchaft, B., & Atwood, G. E. (1987). *Psychoanalytic treatment: An intersubjective approach.* Hillsdale, NJ: The Analytic Press.
Tomkins, S. S. (1962). *Affects, imagery, consciousness, volume I: The positive affects.* New York: Springer.
Tomkins, S. S. (1963). *Affect, imagery, consciousness, volume II: The negative affects.* New York: Springer.
Tomkins, S. S. (1979). Script theory: Differential magnification of affects. In H. E. Howe & R. A. Dienstbier (Eds.), *Nebraska symposium on motivation* (Vol. 36, pp. 201–236). Lincoln, NE: University of Nebraska Press.
Tomkins, S. S. (1987). Script theory. In J. Aronogg, A. I. Rabin, & R. A. Zucker (Eds.), *The emergence of personality* (pp. 147–216). New York: Springer.
Tomkins, S. S. (1991). *Affect, imagery, consciousness, volume III: The negative affects: Anger and fear.* New York: Springer.

Tomkins, S. S. (1992). *Affect, imagery, consciousness, volume IV: Cognition: Duplication and transformation of information.* New York: Springer.

van der Hart, O. (2016). Pierre Janet, Sigmund Freud, and dissociation of personality: The first codification of a psychodynamic depth psychology. In E. F. Howell & S. Itzkowitz (Eds.), *The dissociative mind in psychoanalysis: Understanding and working with trauma* (pp. 44–56). New York: Routledge.

Van Der Kolk, B. A. (2014). *The body keeps the score: Brain, mind, and body in the healing of trauma.* New York: Viking.

Winnicott, D. W. (1960). Ego distortion in terms of true and false self. *The maturational processes and the facilitating environment* (pp. 140–152). New York: International Universities Press.

Chapter 5

Self-deficits
The interpersonal domain (L-III)

The interpersonal (social) domain (L-III) is the third domain that we consider. In this domain, the objects of study are the person's modes of interactions with others. Within this level of analysis, the attributes of patients' interactions with others are their interconnectedness and their capacity to dialogue with others. The questions we confront in a discussion of the interpersonal domain are: What impact does the presence of neuropsychological deficits have on the patterns of interactions that patients have with others and on the type of attachments that they form to others? How do the feelings they have about themselves affect their capacity to communicate with others? Answering these questions leads to an exploration of the broad topic of the modes of interactions we have with others.

Our modes of interaction

The interpersonal domain addresses our interconnectedness with others, which includes the broad range of processes and functions that deal with our "object relatedness" – that is, the mental functions that permit us to retain in memory a schema of ourselves, of others, and of the patterns of our interactions with them. In addition, it includes the channel through which we maintain those modes of interactions – that is, the language system that permits us to communicate with others – which I call the *capacity for dialogue*. I believe that Aron (1996) proposes the concept of "mutuality" to encompass many of the processes that I include in the domain.

The two aspects of this domain, our interconnectedness and capacity to dialogue, are deeply entwined. Whether it is through our investment in others or our attachment to others, how we relate has a communicative dimension. The feelings, thoughts, and behaviors through which we display our involvement with others have meanings associated with them that others interpret as representing our intentions. A further overlap lies in the fact that both sets of processes, interconnectedness, and communication often occur through nonverbal as well as verbal modalities. We will see that not only do many of our patterns of interaction occur verbally and explicitly but that a significant component of our communication with others also occurs nonverbally and implicitly. Each of these facets of the interpersonal domain has implications for individuals with neuropsychological deficits and for our modes of intervention with those patients.

In what follows, I discuss our interconnectedness and our capacity to dialogue separately, although they are deeply entwined. The distinctions at which we arrive will permit us to clarify some of the confusion that exists in discussions of the relational patterns that we establish with others and the relationship between the ways in which we communicate with others.

Our interconnectedness: relational patterns

Psychoanalytic theories have always considered the development of an adequate capacity for object relatedness as central to mental health. Conversely, deficits in that capacity were indicators of psychopathology. Freud proposed that the processes through which relationships to others (object relatedness) occurred resulted from the libidinal investment of others. Fairbairn (1963) maintained that "[t]he ego, and therefore libido, is fundamentally object-seeking" (p. 224). Object relations theorists describe these processes as caused by the internalization of relational patterns experienced in childhood (Kernberg, 2001). Bowlby offered the concept of "Internal Working Models" to refer to the psychological processes through which children form schemas of themselves, of others, and of the relationships between themselves and others (J. Palombo, Bendicsen, & Koch, 2009). Stern (1985, 1989a) proposed the concept of RIGs (Representations of Interactions Generalized). Self psychologists, on the other hand, explain relationships to others as related to the empathic responses of caregivers who provided selfobject functions to their children. Relational theory has shifted "away from inner processes toward relational processes" (Beebe & Lachmann, 2003, p. 379). Finally, the Boston Change Process Study Group (2010) found that the procedural mode of implicit relational knowing (IRK), when placed within the context of a moment-to-moment, mutual regulation model of co-constructed exchanges, provides an explanation for the replication of relational patterns in relationships with others (Lyons-Ruth, 1998).

Each of these theories explains the process that from a dynamic systems perspective I designate as our *interconnectedness* (Piers, 2000). Jacobs (2013) summarizes the central themes of this view in her statement that "every behavior, every experience is dynamically interconnected with foundational themes, with adaptive adjustments, with self-protective patterns, with longings, and with imaginative and creative capacities. Nothing we say or do stands alone" (p. 515).

In this section, I pick up two different views of the processes involved in our interconnectedness. The first view deals with the laying down of relational patterns in memory, and the second comes from attachment theory and the regulatory functions that are critical to development. A large literature exists on the social and emotional disorders associated with specific neuropsychological deficits (see J. Palombo, 2000, 2006). However, few studies exist that examine the relationship between the presence of a neuropsychological deficit and the type of attachment that patients form. I summarize the few studies that exist because of my conviction that such studies can open up areas of investigation that will greatly enhance our understanding of the psychodynamics of individuals with these disorders.

The encoding and retrieval of relational patterns

A set of patterns of interactions is laid down during development that act as organizers of experience and become predictive of how we expect others to respond to us. These patterns are the product of each person's unique givens, the unique meanings that individuals confer on their experiences with others, and their experiences within the social context in which they mature (Beebe & Lachmann, 1998; Frie, 2011).

A discussion of our interconnectedness is incomplete without a profound understanding of the function of memory in the retention of relational patterns acquired early in life (Pally, 1997). The question we must address is: How do we retain in memory the patterns of our relationships to others? To answer this question, we must explore the contributions that our memory system makes to the process, in particular the declarative and non-declarative memory systems (Schacter, 1996; Schacter & Scarry, 2000; Squire & Kandel, 1999; Squire & Knowlton, 1993).

Our memory system

There are two long-term memory subsystems: the declarative, which is generally verbal and conscious, and the non-declarative, which is generally nonverbal and nonconscious (Squire & Kandel, 1999; Squire & Knowlton, 1993). Both declarative and non-declarative memory systems serve as organizers of experience. Through its function, declarative memory brings together the conscious elements of a person's experience and the associated affects that lead to the formation of autobiographical memory, whereas the non-declarative memory system serves to store the relational patterns that the person forms nonconsciously (Fuster, 1995; Kohler, 2014).

Declarative memory is well-suited for connecting pieces of information together; it allows us to build models of the external world. It is fast but not always reliable (i.e. forgetting and retrieval failures can occur); it is flexible in the sense that it is accessible to multiple response systems (Zola & Squire, 2003). Declarative memory has two components: semantic and episodic memory.

Semantic memory is a network of associations that stores concepts that underlie our basic knowledge of the world, such as word meanings, categories, facts, and other information that we have acquired over the years. Semantic memory is the repository from which we draw upon with the assistance of the central executive among other functions to communicate, formulate ideas, and undertake projects.

Episodic memory involves the storage of information in the form of stories or scenarios. Whether we deal with historical events, events about which we have read, or autobiographical occurrences, the data are bound together by the interpretations that we have given them (Howe & Courage, 1997). In other words, the information that we store in episodic memory always involves the subjective interpretation that we made of the events to which we were exposed, an example being the types of scripts discussed in Chapter 4. During conscious recall, we retrieve aspects of what was originally stored and bring the fragments together to serve the purpose of the moment. The recall is not a videotape of the original experience but a reconstruction. Episodic memory is particularly vulnerable to a variety of inaccuracies that Schacter (1999) described in this paper, "The Seven Sins of Memory."

Memories of past experiences are not fossilized artifacts that are recovered unchanged. They are recollections that were modified by their interrelationships with other experiences in the person's life. The system of recollection and the context in which the recollection occurs determines some of the meanings past events will have. Depending on the motives that operate at the time of recollection, the meaning of what is recalled will serve a function for the person. The context largely contributes to the meanings extracted from occurrences to which the person is exposed. Some of the themes function as motives to a person and become central to the understanding of the person.

Autobiographical memories are stored in episodic memory. Consequently, when retrieved, they too are mental constructions, created in the moment. The very process of recalling them changes them. These memories can also be changed by subsequent events. As Fernyhough (2012) stated, "To remember the past, you tell a story about it" (p. 98). He goes on to say that memories are told like stories to others and to oneself.

Non-declarative memory includes procedural memory and priming; it also includes associative learning, which deals with positive and negative reinforcement which we will not address in this work. In Chapter 9, I will discuss the process of priming, which is the process through which the fragment of an event or an association will bring to mind the entire event. An example of priming is what occurs in enactments that are activated by a random event that opens the floodgates of memories of a past traumatic experience.

Habitual activities, in which we engage sometimes on a daily or hourly basis, are encoded in procedural memory. Procedural memory is also a kind of bodily memory; it is memory of habitual motor skills. An important feature of procedural memory is that it functions implicitly, that is, nonconsciously. The process through which procedural memories are formed may begin with a conscious activity that is stored in episodic memory. For example, learning to drive a car initially entails consciously learning the steps involved. After a period of habituation, the entire process becomes automatic and is stored in procedural memory; its retrieval occurs nonconsciously. In a similar manner, patterns of relationships that are initially experienced consciously, but when encoded in procedural memory become nonconscious habitual modes of relating to others.

Encoding of relational patterns

As we have seen with the encoding of narrative themes or scripts, a similar process is involved in the encoding of relational patterns. An event or set of events that has recurred multiple times is stored as a pattern of interaction either in declarative or non-declarative memory (cf. Stern's RIGs, 1985). One of the major features of non-declarative memory is that it encodes all information nonverbally. In the next chapter on mindsharing, I discuss one aspect of the domain of nonverbal information, which is large and complex.

In the psychoanalytic literature, the terms *implicit memory* and *procedural memory* are often used interchangeably, in particular in the use of the concept of "implicit relational knowing" (Lyons-Ruth, 1998). Technically, procedural memory is only one of the processes involved in non-declarative memory. Since the psychoanalytic literature does not make a clear distinction between procedural memory and non-declarative memory, for the sake of simplicity, in what follows I will refer to procedural memory and its features to include both types of memory, even though that is technically incorrect.

Most relational patterns are encoded nonconsciously in procedural memory (Ogden, 2009). However, some patterns are first experienced consciously at some point during development. At times, a single incident may lay down a script that shapes all future encounters. At other times, the recurrence of a set of responses may also lead to the formation of a pattern of expectations that for the person become predictive of how others will respond. Since these patterns are initially stored in episodic memory, upon recall of particular experiences, their meanings are subject to elaboration, modification, or embellishment.

However, given the nature of episodic memory, there can be no certainty as to the match between what is recalled and what occurred. This phenomenon is central to patients who have suffered from a trauma that resulted in a post-traumatic stress disorder, since during such traumatic experiences the capacity to process cognitively the events to which the person was exposed is impaired. The residue of the experience is primarily of the intense somatic and affective stimuli that have been aroused. What are laid down in episodic memory are fragments of the events and the overwhelming bodily sensations and emotions (Van Der Kolk, 2014). In brief, from the standpoint of the procedural memory system, when experiences are encoded in memory as habitual patterns of response, they begin to function as "mental structures" or as attractors onto which patterns of responses have been interwoven. These become organizers of future experiences (cf. Stern, 1989b).

The relevance of understanding the relationship among memory function, relational patterns, and neuropsychological deficits are now laid bare. First, the understanding provides insights into the effects such deficits have on early relational patterns and their encoding in memory. Second, it provides a basis for understanding the formation of autobiographical memories and their contribution to self-understanding that patients with such deficits recollect. Finally, it allows us to interpret the extent to which the deficits contributed to any trauma the patients may have suffered.

Retrieval of relational patterns

Critical to our understanding of the manner in which we relate to others is not only the way in which we form and store patterns of interaction, but also how we retrieve them and the circumstances that evoke their enactments. As we have seen, habitual patterns are laid down nonconsciously in procedural memory. Among these are the day-to-day modes of interaction that occur from birth on. These patterns are not necessarily processed consciously, but often pass unnoticed into the person's repertoire of interactions with others. Retrieval under everyday circumstances consists of the nonconscious habitual modes of relating, which Lyons-Ruth (1998) called "implicit relational knowing."

When we speak of the enactment of a past relationship, we are therefore often referring to the nonconscious replication of a pattern previously encoded in procedural memory that emerges in the clinical setting. In the transference-countertransference configuration, the therapist not only evokes a past pattern of interaction, but also participates by personifying the character in the patient's history that shaped the encoded pattern.

Attachment and regulatory functions

Whereas Bowlby proposed that attachment was the product of an innate drive, a residual of our evolutionary heritage to seek proximity to our caregivers to be protected from predators, Schore (2001) has documented the contributions of the regulatory function associated with attachment as evidence of our interconnectedness. He has described in detail the neural processes involved in self-regulation (see also Cozolino, 2014; Shane, Shane, & Gales, 1997; Siegel, 1999). Schore hypothesizes that attachment is a regulatory theory. Its primary function is that of regulating the child's affect states. Regulation is a central organizing principle of human development. He proposed a psychoneurobiological view of the origins of the self, stating that psychological functions are the product of the brain structures that undergird them. The social environment affects brain development, and the regulation of emotions is a critical part of this process.

Attachment in patients with neuropsychological deficits

Except for a few studies, we unfortunately lack systematic research on the relationship between the incidences of specific neuropsychological deficits, whether mild or severe, and the type of attachments to their caregivers these children form. Of the few studies that I was able to access, none were conducted in the US. They were conducted in countries as disparate as Israel, Australia, the UK, and the Netherlands. It is not surprising that the criteria for what constituted a learning disability differed or were unspecified, and the variations in the instruments used to measure attachment also differed and were often not comparable. Nevertheless, I summarize some of the results of these studies for what we may learn from them.

In a series of studies, Al-Yagon (2007, 2012) and Al-Yagon and Mikulincer (2004a, 2004b) investigated the mediating role played by attachment factors on the socio-emotional and academic adjustment of Israeli children with learning disabilities. They used the diagnostic criteria for learning disabilities set by law in Israel, which must include

> (a) achievement test scores at least two years below grade level and (b) average verbal intelligence with a marked deficit in academic achievement. Exclusion criteria were (a) absence of extreme behavioral or attentional difficulties that would impede completion of the study measures, (b) absence of frank neurological problems, (c) absence of sensory impairments, and (d) absence of problems presumed to be due to environmental, economic, or cultural factors.
>
> (Bauminger & Kimhi-Kind, 2008, p. 319)

All studies were of children who satisfied those criteria, but the investigators did not specify the type of learning disorder of the children. Consequently, the participants in those studies included a broad range of children with differing learning disorders.

In one study, Al-Yagon and Mikulincer (2004b) found that in children with learning disabilities, a significant association exists between the learning disorder and attachment-based factors. The investigators reported lower attachment security and more attachment avoidance and anxiety in close relationships. In another study, they (Al-Yagon & Mikulincer, 2004a) found that attachment style significantly correlated with socio-emotional adjustment but not with academic functioning. Interestingly, a substantial group of the children demonstrated resilience to their condition, as indicated by a high sense of coherence and low sense of loneliness; however, that resilience did not affect the type of attachment they formed.

In a study on the moderating role of maternal personal resources and its effects on the socio-emotional and behavioral adjustment of children with learning disabilities, Al-Yagon (2007) concluded with this significant statement, which affirms the positions taken in this work:

> Overall, the findings suggest that these children are more vulnerable to differences in maternal personal resources, which raises important questions regarding the contributions of the children's specific disabilities such as neurological factors, the children's perceptions and interpretations, which in turn may affect their vulnerability to a variety of maternal personal resources. Furthermore, the current findings may support the notion of multiple or "cumulative" risk models indicating that the group of children with LD, *well-adjusted functioning was better predicted by combinations of protective and vulnerable factors at different levels, such as the individual and maternal levels, than by individual factors alone.*
> (p. 214, italics added)

Finally, Al-Yagon (2012) in a study "explored children's [with LD] secure attachment with both parents versus one parent, as well as the unique role of children's patterns of close relationships with father and mother" (p. 170). The findings revealed that a

> secure attachment to both parents served as a protective factor, whereas the insecure attachment to both parents served as a risk factor.

> Secure attachment to only one parent did not serve as a protective factor for any of the child's adjustment measures, except the case of secure attachment to the father, which does serve as protection against loneliness.
>
> (p. 179)

Bauminger and Kimhi-Kind (2008) examined the contribution of attachment security and emotion regulation in middle-school boys with learning disabilities. Results revealed that children with LD who were securely attached to mothers fared better than their peers, whereas those with insecure attachments had more limited capacity to compensate for their insecurity. Clarke and Ungerer et al. (Clarke, Ungerer, Chahoud, Johnson, & Stiefel, 2002) investigated the relationship between attachment insecurity and ADHD. They found an association between ADHD and an insecure attachment.

Other studies (Clegg & Lansdall-Welfare, 1995; Klomek et al., 2013; Naber et al., 2007; Smith & McCarthy, 1996), using different methodologies with populations of different ages, investigated the relationship between a variety of neuropsychological deficits and the type of attachment the affected individuals manifested. In spite of the wide differences in the definitions of the deficits, all the studies supported the hypothesis of the coexistence of such deficits and some type of insecure attachment.

Although these studies find evidence for an association between the presence of a learning disorder and an insecure type of attachment, multiple factors confound and compromise the validity of the association. Consequently, the establishment of the relationship between the type of attachment that individuals form and the presence of a neuropsychological deficit remains a work in progress. This makes the application of the non-linear dynamic perspective to such studies all the more critical in establishing whether such a relationship exists. Furthermore, attachment theory ascribes heavy emphasis to the mother's sensitivity as contributing to the type of attachment the child makes to her; it does not account for the feelings the child might have about her as affecting the relationship. A child who is beset by shame, uncertainty, or insecurity because he has a serious learning disorder would respond differently to his caregiver's overtures than a child without such deficits.

Case illustration: ADHD: Alice

Attention-deficit/hyperactivity disorder (ADHD) is a heterogeneous disorder whose symptoms manifest with considerable variation. It is the most common condition for which patients are referred to mental health centers (Barkley, 1998). The question we face is that of understanding the relationship between this particular neuropsychological deficit and the patterns of interaction that individuals with this condition develop.

In his paper, Levin (2002), a psychoanalyst, discusses the neurobiology of ADD; he provided a "Neuropsychoanalytic Sketch." His focus is on "(1) how the patient with ADD might experience himself and his world, and (2) how others, including the analyst, might experience the ADD patient" (p. 337). He suggests that patients with this type of condition crave stimulation in an effort to avoid the experience of boredom. Their boredom avoidance "could reflect either disrupted object relations, a lack of self-cohesion, or an internal narcissistic or borderline state with various ego (self) deformations" (p. 347).

Alice was a 14-year-old with severe ADHD. She was impulsive, lacked any ability to manage frustration, and jumped from one topic to the next during conversations, maintaining a dizzying pace of verbalization. She often alienated her peers by her intrusive insensitivity, which they regarded as rude.

Alice presented in her initial contacts as a likeable, energetic, unreflective teenager, who entered the process unhesitatingly but with no concept of what the process involved. Until recently, Alice's mother had devoted herself to managing Alice's life. She had taken her for therapy when she was an infant regarding problems with attachment. She actively participated in the therapeutic process, often modifying her style of relating to Alice in order to facilitate Alice's development. She comforted Alice and helped to modulate her deregulated outbursts; she planned and orchestrated small group activities so that Alice might benefit from these experiences of socialization.

After doing this for eight years and getting little in return, Alice's mother felt burned out and decided to go to work, turning over most of Alice's caregiving task to the father. Alice felt abandoned and bereft of the one person who helped her mediate her environment. She interpreted her mother's going to work as a desertion, and even though her father took charge as best he could, in no way could he replace the psychological functions that her mother provided. The experience of her mother's detachment was magnified by Alice's own inability to modulate her affect states. Rather than coping in some constructive way with this turn of events, Alice went on a campaign to make her mother's life miserable. Her interpretation of the events was that her mother was responsible for her inability to modulate her feelings. She held her mother responsible for her problems because she felt her mother had constantly interfered with her activities. From Alice's perspective, she blamed her mother because she had no friends and had problems in school. Eventually, the father sought therapy for Alice in hopes of ameliorating the situation. However, her mother refused to be involved.

For two years, in this twice-a-week therapy, the therapist struggled to stabilize the situation. Working with her father, the school tried to help Alice modulate her responses. Unfortunately, Alice could not get over the injury suffered by her mother's abandonment. She was determined to "ruin my mother's life!" She became unmanageable at home and at school. Both parents were opposed to the use of medication to manage Alice's ADHD. Finally, both the father and the therapist concluded that the best solution was a placement in a therapeutic school. In that setting, after an initial period of resistance and upheaval, she settled down and graduated from high school with good enough grade to allow her to go to a small nurturing college.

Psychodynamic profile

The initial conditions that took precedence over other factors in Alice's development were the deficits in the capacity for self-regulation associated with her ADHD. Her mother attempted to complement those deficits through her caregiving; her efforts were sufficient for Alice to maintain a sense of self-cohesion only by devoting herself exclusively to the caregiving task. If she faltered, Alice would fragment.

As long as the attachment to her mother was sufficiently stable, Alice could maintain a sense of self-cohesion and could function adequately. Once that bond was broken, she had no anchor to stabilize her and help her regulate herself.

As a child, although Alice could not be introspective enough to note her impulsivity, the positive relationship with her mother provided her with a sense of security and stability. As long as her mother was an ally, she could discount what others said about her. However, once she felt that her mother had withdrawn from her, that stability was compromised. What at first appeared as a secure attachment to her mother led to a rupture that precipitated what we might consider as a reactive attachment disorder. However, whether motived by the disrupted attachment or her impulsivity, her volatility often brought reprimands from teachers and parents. Her responses to these negative comments were to feel injured and to defend herself that her actions had been misunderstood. She would alternately become enraged and throw a tantrum or pout for hours until someone came to rescue her.

As for her self-understanding, in spite of the cognitive explanations given to her, Alice had no idea what having ADHD meant or that it contributed to the conflicts with her mother. Her subjective experience was one of puzzlement as to why others around her responded so negatively to her. She felt no hesitation to act on her impulses and had no awareness of the effects of her actions on others. This was exemplified by her behavior upon being dropped off early to her session. She would begin to press repeatedly the buzzer in the therapist's waiting room announcing her presence, disrupting the therapist's session. She would continue doing that until it was time for her to be seen. All reminders to have her refrain from doing so were met with incredulity, as though that was the first time that she was being told not to do that.

A set of patterns of responses formed around the attractors that organized her thoughts, feelings, and behaviors. She would act impulsively, often outrageously in the perception of others, who would respond with escalating reprimands and an outpouring of negatively toned prolonged lectures. She would seem to listen and be sheepishly attentive, while her mind was evidently elsewhere. In the next moment, she would move on to an episode that repeated the pattern.

Given the neurological nature of her drivenness, verbal interventions were of little use. Whereas she cognitively was fully capable of understanding the explanations given to her, she could not benefit from those explanations. There seemed to be no avenue to bring the consequences of her behaviors to her awareness.

From the point of view of the therapeutic dyad, it was important to stabilize the major elements in her context before she could become self-reflective. This meant first attempting to restore the bond with her mother, a bond that had appeared to reflect a secure attachment but had now deteriorated to a disorganized type of attachment. The restoration of that bond would have helped Alice reinstate some – but not all – of the lost capacity for self-regulation and might diminish her impulsivity. Second, it meant getting others in her context, teachers and peers, to take a less critical and more benign attitude toward her. They needed to understand that Alice could not learn from verbal lectures, pointing out consequences, or even punishments. Such interventions were counterproductive and only served to make her feel bad. The challenge for her caregivers and her therapist was to find an environment that would permit her to respond positively.

Unfortunately, these challenges could not be met as long as she remained in the environment that was a constant reminder of her distress. The decision to place her in a therapeutic school seemed to be the only viable alternative.

The capacity to dialogue

As we turn to the second component of the interpersonal domain, the domain of social communication, we enter a world where communicative competence is essential not only for successful social discourse but also for the establishment of satisfactory relationships with others. The domain of communication is central to all interactions among components of a system. Social communication deals with the medium (i.e. verbal and nonverbal language) through which relationships are conducted, whereas social interactions dealt with the patterns through which people interacted with each other (i.e. feel attached to or disconnected from others).

The complexity of the domain of social communication is disclosed by the issues that we are required to address to avoid unnecessary confusion. I will separate these issues into two broad categories: those related to the medium through which we communicate (i.e. our language systems) that permits us to dialogue with others and those that deal with the distinction between verbal and nonverbal modes of communication.

The medium through which we dialogue

From an introspective perspective, meanings are attained through shared experiences with others and through the particular imprint that a person's innate givens lend to what is experienced (Lasser & Bathory, 1997). Meanings also have an organizing function for psychological events. They become encoded in a sign or language system that is unique to the social and cultural context in which the child is raised. They include the affective and cognitive dimensions of experience (see Palombo, 2006, Chapter 5, for a more detailed discussion). Without understanding the affective dimension, it would be impossible to understand fully how we acquire and process the meaning we attach to our experiences (Demos, 1988; Kaye, 1982). We may think of the developmental process through which the child acquires communicative competence as the capacity to dialogue. In this sense, the dialogue plays a fundamental role in the structuralization of self-experience and of relationships. The dialogue extends to all aspects of those human activities that are interpretable as having meanings (for an interesting discussion of Ferenczi's contribution to semiotic theory, see Harris & Aron, 1997).

All social interactions occur within a context that imbues those interactions with meaning. We all live in contexts that interpenetrate all of our experiences (Frie & Coburn, 2011). The community of others with whom individuals are connected and with whom they communicate represents the context that they inhabit. Within these contexts, caregivers convey to children the sense of the world as formed by their own acculturation. The social, cultural, and historical milieu pervades the caregivers' view of the world. The child is exposed to that particular view of the world as disclosed by the caregivers. Context gives meaning to behavior.

Context then serves to interconnect the components of the experience with the entirety of the setting within which it occurs. It dictates the functions and meanings of any individual component. Taken out of the whole, the component loses some aspects of its essential meaning. In meaning making, the idea of a "whole" prevails over the parts and leads to the notion of coherence. Coherence is a product of the relationships of parts to whole. It is the product of their interconnectedness and of the meanings that are construed out of the whole.

In what follows, I distinguish between the verbal, nonverbal, and preverbal dimensions of the dialogue. In Chapter 6, I discuss the process of mindsharing as a critical aspect of our interactions and the nonverbal dialogue that we conduct with others.

Contrasts between verbal, nonverbal, and preverbal communication

Experiences are encoded through a sign system that includes verbal and nonverbal components. Verbal language is one medium through which communication occurs. Other mediums are nonverbal forms of expression, such as gesture, musical sounds, affective expressions, and nonverbal patterns through which we interact with others (see J. Palombo, 2006). Through language, we convey our feelings and thoughts to others; they in turn attempt to grasp not just what we say, but also what we intend to convey. Affective communication and affect processing are integral to all social relationships. In addition, research into the neurobiology of social cognition is beginning to enhance our understanding of the mental processes that undergird sociality (Adolphs, 2001, 2003a, 2003b; Cozolino, 2014).

A distinction must be made between nonverbal and the preverbal modes of communication. Developmentally, all interchanges between caregiver and infant occur both preverbally and nonverbally until the age at which the infant acquires verbal language (Beebe, 1982). As children acquire verbal language, these nonverbal modes are integrated smoothly into their communicative styles. All preverbal communication is nonverbal, but it is not true that all nonverbal communication is preverbal (see J. Palombo, 2000, 2006; J. Palombo & Berenberg, 1997, 1999).

Preverbal experiences are encoded nonverbally. They are stored in nondeclarative (implicit or procedural) memory. However, even after the acquisition of verbal language, these nonverbal signs continue to exist within a nonverbal language system; they need not be translated into verbal signs for them to retain their meaning or to find expression in relational patterns or enactments.

During the preverbal period, the process of communication between infant and caregiver occurs nonverbally, a process that Schore (2001) describes as right-brain to right-brain communication. He refers to the caregiver's regulatory activities that occur through visual, vocal, and tactile modalities that the infant experiences as soothing and as having a positive valence. These interactions enhance the orbital frontal region and attenuate the amygdala's responses and its activation of the hypothalamic-pituitary-adrenal axis that regulate the autonomic nervous system. These experiences are then "remembered" (i.e. encoded and stored) in what attachment theory describes as Internal Working Models.

What we infer from this is that there are distinct differences between verbal and nonverbal modes of expression. Each is part of a separate developmental track, and both are inextricably intertwined with each other. The failure to trace the distinctive contribution that nonverbal expressions make to the development of the sense self can result in an incomplete understanding of the factors that share in the formation of the personality and the interactions in the clinical setting. As we will see, some patients who have a neuropsychological impairment that prevents them from understanding the codes used in the nonverbal language system can develop disorders of the self, as exemplified in the case illustration that follows.

Case illustration: Clark

Clark was a patient with a nonverbal learning disability, whose sense of self-cohesion was chronically threatened by his feelings about himself and his inability to cope with the demands that he faced. His case illustrates the complex interaction between our modes of social communication and the relational patterns that patients with nonverbal learning disabilities encounter. The neuropsychological deficits in this condition impair the patient's capacity to process social information, in addition to affecting the person's capacity to function in social contexts. The result is that from an early age the deficit interfered with the attachment process and with the development of satisfactory relational patterns. His capacity for self-regulation was impaired, and often a pattern of avoidance of social interactions emerged as a form of social phobia. It is important to note that in patients with nonverbal learning disabilities, they are highly skilled in verbal modes of communication but impaired in their abilities to communicate nonverbally, in either the expressive or the receptive modalities.

Patients with a nonverbal learning disability are unable to decode social cues involved in "reading" other people's body language, facial expression, and vocal intonations; they are inept in social situations. Affective communication is also problematic as they respond to affect-laden situations with sadness, anxiety, or withdrawal and appear to have problems modulating certain affects. For the patients with a nonverbal learning disability (NLD), all social interactions are fraught with anxiety. They tend to feel inadequate and have low self-esteem. Their considerable anxiety leads them to express irritation, display frustration, unhappiness, or sadness and appear worried, fidgety, and uncomfortable. Patients with NLD not only respond to stresses with a loss of cohesion but also may anticipate such a loss when confronting novel situations. A pattern of avoidance and isolation becomes a major defensive style, leading to a possible loss of the capacity for self-cohesion or for the successful accommodation to the context (see J. Palombo, 2006).

Clark, a 41-year-old man, is currently separated from his wife of eight years. They have a 4-year-old daughter. Clark called requesting a diagnostic evaluation to rule out the possibility that he has Asperger's disorder. He had been seeing a clinical social worker for psychotherapy for two years, who diagnosed him with dysthymia. In addition, he and his wife were seeing another therapist for their marital difficulties. A friend, who is a psychologist, suggested that he obtain a second opinion to determine whether he has Asperger's disorder.

Clark presented as anxious and uncomfortable. He spoke rapidly, in a loud uninflected voice. He also had a loud forced laugh, which came at inappropriate times. He made what seemed like good eye contact; however, his eye contact was not natural. When talking about issues, he spoke in an animated fashion that was not always appropriate to the content he was discussing. He pointed out that people tell him that his vocal intonation does not match the emotional content of his communications and that his eye contact bothers people because they feel that he stares at them. Finally, he mentioned that when people speak to him, he hears their words, but they appear to be jumbled at times. Only if he replays the words and sounds to himself can he decode them.

At the end of the first session, Clark asked me to remind him to talk about his obsessive-compulsive disorder (OCD) in the next session. When he returned, we picked up where we left off. He reported that he has had OCD symptoms for many years. When asked to describe them, he gave the following examples. He has to "even things up." If he turns over a book, he has to turn it back to its original position. If he moves a chair one way, he has to retrace his steps and move it back to its original place. The closet doors in his bedroom have to match up exactly. He has to check the locks on the doors many times. If he does something that requires a number of steps, he has to retrace the same steps exactly several times. When asked how much of his time these obsessions take up, he was clear that they require a small fraction of his time, and they never interfere with his ability to function. No one ever noticed any of them.

With regard to his history, he described his relationship with his father as distant. His mother was more involved with him, but he gave few details of that relationship. When asked to talk about his early school experiences, his first response was that he has few memories of that period in his life.

However, as he spoke he was able to reveal some significant events. For example, he remembered an incident in preschool where he was playing with boys and came across a girl's dress; he asked to put it on. When he was told that it was not appropriate, he could not understand why that was so. During that time, he also remembered "feeling strange." He felt that the activities at school were pointless and boring.

At a later point in the session, he told me that as far back as he could remember, he used to rock. He was vague in his recollections, although he thought that he would sit on the floor and rock for hours. This occurred during the day but not at night. He eventually stopped doing that in his teen years. He also described that he used to "crave pain." He was unclear as to what that was about except that he remembers sticking things like pencils in his eye.

He went to a public school for first and second grade, where he recalled that "I always got into a lot of trouble." He remembers that he was not allowed to go to recess because he picked fights with the other kids. He thinks he didn't know how to interact with the other children. One particular incident he remembers was that of being asked to draw a picture of his family. He drew four bodies and drew his father with a large penis. He remembers thinking to himself that if he has a small penis his father must have a much larger one. He was puzzled at the response he got to that picture. He believes that in those early years he took things extremely literally and concretely. He could not perform academically because "I didn't get it."

He stated that he had few friends in high school, had no interest in girls, and did not date. He enjoyed his freshman year in college and majored in sociology because he was interested in trying to figure out the rules by which society operates. Then he got interested in human development and social policy.

After college, he decided to go to law school. Law school was a "lousy experience." He didn't like law but in spite of that passed the bar exam. At that time, he looked at himself as an alien in society. He was fascinated by his observations of others much as an anthropologist who studies society observes its natives. As an experiment, he took an anthropology course in which he did very well and which he found to be fascinating.

What followed was a series of jobs working for law firms. The longest lasted two and half years, where he worked as a criminal defense attorney. In each case, he parted company with the people in the firm amicably. He decided that he was better off working for himself and established his own practice. However, he has had trouble developing a clientele and is considering going back to work for a law firm.

Up to this point, Clark had made no mention of his wife or child. He seemed totally focused on work. I therefore asked about other relationships prior to his meeting his wife. Aside from a woman with whom he had an eight-month relationship, he had a two-year relationship with another woman but did not consider that a serious relationship. He dated for a while until he met his wife at a church group. They dated for two years and then were married. They have been married for seven years, but the relationship has been a rocky one practically from the start. His wife complains about his excessive negativity and his mood swings. In trying to clarify these descriptions, it appears as though Clark does not really have mood swings but that he has exaggerated reactions that are either highly positive or highly negative. As he described them, when things go well, he jumps up and down with joy. When things do not go well, "Everything is shit!" He feels that he could stand her personality quirks, which he finds to be difficult. They have had many arguments about this. He considers her to be extremely stubborn and unwilling to try anything that is radically different. She is now asking for a divorce, although this is not what he wishes. He decided on divorcing when his therapist pointed out that their 3-year-old child was beginning to act out because of the stresses in the marriage. He is moving out of the apartment that weekend.

Discussion

There are several considerations in arriving at an understanding of Clark's psychodynamics. The primary concern is that of the extent to which his impaired capacity for social communication interfered with his ability to form relationships with others. He reported that during college and in law school, he struggled to uncover the rules by which people governed their conduct. Lacking the inborn capacity, which most people have to understand other people's intentions and motives, his responses to other people missed the mark. In his dealings with others, he applied rules of conduct he had developed, which did not take into account the context of his interactions.

Historically, children with this disorder begin to have social difficulties as early as preschool. They misunderstand social signals, often interpreting friendly ones as assaultive. This begins a vicious cycle of inappropriate aggression, which is condemned by adults and results in the child's frustration and feelings of being misunderstood. These interchanges not only contribute to the child's instability, but also bring forth defenses that lead to withdrawal and entrenchment into feeling victimized. The result is that the chronic frustration becomes intolerable, leading to meltdowns. This leaves untouched the conviction that the responses were appropriate. The person's self-system becomes prone to instability and closed to modification.

Clark's difficulties could be traced back to his early years. Absent the necessary affirmative responses, the negative responses to Clark's behavior set the stage for the erosion of his self-confidence and self-esteem. Furthermore, his view of adults was compromised because he could no longer experience them as protective of him or as models to emulate and idealize. Finally, the reinforcement of the sense of his being different from others excluded him from the community of peers. Not only was he an outsider, but he became the object of bullying and derision. All of these factors contributed to the erosion of his self-cohesion and heightened his vulnerability to fragmentation. To compensate for his deficits, Clark attempted to develop rules of conduct to guide him in his relationships with others and to interpret their responses. The fact that the application of such rules to specific contexts required the kind of social judgment that he lacked led to a miscarriage of his intentions and only obfuscated the process of relating to others. Furthermore, as is evident from the material he presented, he had no coherent self-narrative to explain to himself what was happening and why it was happening.

At the interpersonal level, a complex configuration of factors contributes to what became attractors for Clark. First was the neuropsychological deficit itself, which set off a cascade of negative responses both from his parents and from others. Often his behavior was mischaracterized as being "oppositional/defiant," which only accentuated his alienation from others. Second were the feelings generated by these interactions, which formed the nucleus of patterns of expectations that guided his responses to other people.

Finally, it was my impression that Clark suffered from a moderately severe form of a nonverbal learning disability that has had a marked impact on his development, his relationships, and career path. Since it did not appear that his marriage was salvageable, I recommended psychotherapy with a clinician experienced in NLD. In addition, I suggested that he join a specialized socialization group, where he could gain insight into the ways in which his inability to process other people's nonverbal cues affected his responses and where he might learn the elements of beginning to decode such communications.

Summary

In the interpersonal domain, I discussed two functions that define us as social beings: our interconnectedness to others and our capacity to dialogue with others. With regard to our interconnectedness, we are social beings who are interdependent and are sustained by other people's understanding and empathy for us. What we do or how we act can have consequences that extend far beyond the reaches of our imagination. We search for involvements that will give meaning to our experiences. Our greatest anxiety is the fear of isolation and disconnection from those who are significant to us. The failure to find meaning in our lives leads to despondency and despair. Furthermore, the context provides functions that complement each person's immature or deficient capacity to function independently. While people retain their individuality, they are not entirely separable from others. At the interpersonal level, the central concern is the individual's interpretation of and the responses to the social context and the person's experiences of those occurrences.

We may conceive of the processes through which we develop the capacity to establish and maintain a connection to others as occurring through the encoding in our memory systems of the relational patterns that we experience during our formative years. The facts stored as events in declarative memory are organized into episodes that form the core of autobiographical memory, which are then retained in non-declarative memories as a set of biases or beliefs that are not conscious (cf. Eichenbaum & Bodkin, 2000). However, as Squire and Knowlton (1993) noted, not all implicit relational knowing is unconscious, as some people can describe their destructive patterns of relating but feel helpless to change them. Some patients may be able to describe the origins of these patterns and recall the events that helped to shape them. These two phenomena have important implications for the therapeutic interventions that make it possible for a change to occur. A major component of the therapeutic process in this regard is the reorganization and reconsolidation that occurs through the reworking of non-declarative memory of the self-narrative. Insight into the origins of the patterns may also bring about a change.

In addition, we may think of the capacity for relatedness as part of an innate need to find a secure base that would protect infants from predators, as proposed by Bowlby's attachment theory. Through the interaction with caregivers, the attachment leads to the ontogenesis of brain functions that enhance the capacity for self-regulation; however, there are insufficient data to establish a connection between the presence of a specific type of attachment and a neuropsychological deficit. According to Al-Yagon (2007), whereas the presence of a learning disorder may play a mediating role between the socio-emotional and academic adjustment of some elementary school children and their lower attachment security, the specific contribution of the neuropsychological deficit to that type of attachment could not be established.

The second component of the interpersonal domain is the domain of social communication, which I call the capacity to dialogue with others. Social and communicative competencies are closely entwined. Our openness to sharing of ourselves with others and their sharing of themselves with us occurs through the verbal and nonverbal interchanges that we have. The importance of the context in which these interchanges occurs is highlighted by the fact that the context determines the meanings of what we convey and the interpretations that others make of what we communicate.

In recent years, we have seen a greater appreciation of the contributions of nonverbal communication both in interpersonal relationships and in clinical contexts (see Palombo, 2006). The failure to distinguish between preverbal and nonverbal modes of expression has led to the mistaken view that some disorders, such as narcissistic and borderline personality disorders, in which patients cannot give verbal expression to some of the origins of their problems, must have had their origins during the preverbal period. That is, if a patient cannot express verbally what they feel or have experienced, then it must be because those feelings or experiences had their origins in early infancy prior to the capacity for verbal communication. The issue revolves around the fact that whereas all preverbal modes of expression are nonverbal, not all modes of nonverbal expression are preverbal. It is possible to have suffered from a trauma after the development of verbal language and yet not to be able to give a verbal account of what happened.

References

Adolphs, R. (2001). The neurobiology of social cognition. *Current Opinion in Neurobiology, 11*(2), 231–239.

Adolphs, R. (2003a). Cognitive neuroscience of human social behavior. *Nature Reviews: Neuroscience, 4*(3), 165–178.

Adolphs, R. (2003b). Investigating the cognitive neuroscience of social behavior. *Neuropsychologia, 41*, 119–126.

Al-Yagon, M. (2007). Social emotional and behavioral adjustment among school-age children with learning disabilities: The moderating role of maternal personal resources. *The Journal of Special Education, 40*(4), 205–217.

Al-Yagon, M. (2012). Subtypes of attachment security in school-age children with learning disabilities. *Learning Disabilities Quarterly, 35*(3), 170–183.

Al-Yagon, M., & Mikulincer, M. (2004a). Patterns of close relationships and social emotional and academic adjustment among school-age children with learning disabilities. *Learning Disabilities Research and Practice, 19*(1), 12–19.

Al-Yagon, M., & Mikulincer, M. (2004b). Socioemotional and academic adjustment among children with learning disorders: The mediational role of attachment-based factors. *The Journal of Special Education, 38*(2), 111–123.

Aron, L. (1996). *A meeting of minds: Mutuality in psychoanalysis*. New York: Routledge.

Barkley, R. A. (1998). *Attention-deficit hyperactivity disorder: A handbook for diagnosis and treatment* (2nd ed.). New York: Guilford Press.

Bauminger, N., & Kimhi-Kind, I. (2008). Social information processing, security of attachment, and emotion regulation in children with learning disabilities. *Journal of Learning Disabilities, 41*(4), 315–332.

Beebe, B. (1982). Micro-timing in mother-infant communication. In M. Key (Ed.), *Nonverbal communication today: Current research* (pp. 168–195). New York: Mouton.

Beebe, B., & Lachmann, F. M. (1998). Co-constructing inner and relational processes: Self- and mutual regulation in infant research and adult treatment. *Psychoanalytic Psychology, 15*(4), 480–516.

Beebe, B., & Lachmann, F. M. (2003). The relational turn in psychoanalysis: A dyadic systems view from infant research. *Contemporary Psychoanalysis, 39*(3), 379–409.

Boston Change Process Study Group. (2010). *Change in psychotherapy: A unifying paradigm*. New York: W. W. Norton.

Clarke, L., Ungerer, J., Chahoud, K., Johnson, S., & Stiefel, I. (2002). Attention deficit hyperactivity disorder is associated with attachment insecurity. *Clinical Child Psychology and Psychiatry, 7*(2), 179–198.

Clegg, J. A., & Lansdall-Welfare, R. (1995). Attachment and learning disability: A theoretical review informing three clinical interventions. *Journal of Intellectual Disability Research, 39*(4), 295–305.

Cozolino, L. (2014). *The neuroscience of human relationships: Attachment in the developing social brain* (2nd ed.). New York: W. W. Norton.

Demos, E. V. (1988). Affect and the development of the self: A new frontier. In A. Goldberg (Ed.), *Frontiers in self psychology* (Vol. 3, pp. 27–54). Hillsdale, NJ: The Analytic Press.

Eichenbaum, H., & Bodkin, J. A. (2000). Belief and knowledge as distinct forms of memory. In D. L. S. Schacter (Ed.), *Memory, brain, and belief* (pp. 176–207). Cambridge, MA: Harvard University Press.

Fairbairn, W. R. D. (1963). Synopsis of an object-relations theory of personality. *International Journal of Psychoanalysis, 44*, 224–225.

Fernyhough, C. (2012). *Pieces of light: How the new science of memory illuminates the stories we tell about our pasts.* New York: Harper.

Frie, R. (2011). Culture and context: From individualism to situated experience. In R. Frie & W. J. Coburn (Eds.), *Persons in context: The challenge of individuality in theory and practice* (pp. 3–20). New York: Routledge.

Frie, R., & Coburn, W. J. (2011). Introduction: Experiencing context. In R. Frie & W. J. Coburn (Eds.), *Persons in context: The challenge of individuality in theory and practice* (pp. xv–xxx). New York: Routledge.

Fuster, J. M. (1995). *Memory in the cerebral cortex: An empirical approach to neural networks in the human and nonhuman primate.* Cambridge, MA: The MIT Press.

Harris, A., & Aron, L. (1997). Ferenczi's semiotic theory: Previews of postmodernism. *Psychoanalytic Inquiry, 17,* 522–534.

Howe, M. L., & Courage, M. L. (1997). The emergence and early development of autobiographical memory. *Psychological Review, 104*(3), 499–523.

Jacobs, L. M. (2013). Appreciating and arguing with some wonderful teachers: Review of Danielian and Gianotti's "listening with purpose: Entry points into shame and narcissistic vulnerability." *International Journal of Psychoanalytic Self Psychology, 8,* 514–523.

Kaye, K. (1982). *The mental and social life of babies.* Chicago: The University of Chicago Press.

Kernberg, O. F. (2001). Recent developments in the technical approaches of English-language psychoanalytic schools. *Psychoanalytic Quarterly, 70,* 519–547.

Klomek, A. B., Kopelman-Rubin, D., Al-Yagon, M., Mufson, L., Apter, A., Erlich, I., & Mikulincer, M. (2013). Changes in attachment representations during an open trial of a psychological intervention for adolescents with learning disorders. *Adolescent Psychiatry, 3*(4), 335–341.

Kohler, L. (2014). On the development of the autobiographical self and autobiographical memory: Implicit and explicit aspects. *International Journal of Psychoanalytic Self Psychology, 9*(1), 18–34.

Lasser, C. J., & Bathory, D. S. (1997). Reciprocal causality and childhood trauma: An application of chaos theory. In F. Masterpasqua & P. A. Perna (Eds.), *The psychological meaning of chaos: Translating theory into practice* (pp. 147–173). Washington, DC: American Psychological Association.

Levin, F. M. (2002). Attention deficit disorder: A neuropsychoanalytic sketch. *Psychoanalytic Inquiry, 22,* 336–354.

Lyons-Ruth, K. (1998). Implicit relational knowing: Its role in development and psychoanalytic treatment. *Infant Mental Health Journal, 19*(3), 282–289.

Naber, F. B. A., Swinkels, S. H. N., Buitelaar, J. K., Bakermans-Kranenburg, M. J., Van Ijzendoor, M. H., Deitz, C., & van Engeland, H. (2007). Attachment in toddlers with autism and other developmental disorders. *Journal of Autism and Developmental Disorders, 37,* 1123–1138.

Ogden, P. (2009). Emotion, mindfulness, and movement: Expanding the regulatory boundaries of the window of affect tolerance. In D. Fosha, D. J. Siegel, & M. F. Solomon (Eds.), *The healing power of emotion: Affective neuroscience, development, and clinical practice* (pp. 204–230). New York: W. W. Norton.

Pally, R. (1997). Memory: Brain systems that link past, present and future. *International Journal of Psychoanalysis, 78,* 1223–1234.

Palombo, J. (2000). A disorder of the self in an adult with a nonverbal learning disability. In A. Goldberg (Ed.), *Progress in self psychology* (Vol. 16, pp. 311–335). Hillsdale, NJ: The Analytic Press.

Palombo, J. (2006). *Nonverbal learning disabilities: A clinical perspective.* New York: W. W. Norton.

Palombo, J., Bendicsen, H., & Koch, B. (2009). *Guide to psychoanalytic developmental theories.* New York: Springer.

Palombo, J., & Berenberg, A. H. (1997). Psychotherapy for children with nonverbal learning disabilities. In B. S. Mark & J. A. Incorvaia (Eds.), *The handbook of infant, child and adolescent psychotherapy: New direction in integrative treatment* (Vol. 2, pp. 25–68). Northvale, NJ: Jason Aronson.

Palombo, J., & Berenberg, A. H. (1999). Working with parents of children with nonverbal learning disabilities: A conceptual and intervention model. In J. A. Incorvia, B. S. Mark-Goldstein, & D. Tessmer (Eds.), *Understanding, diagnosisng, and treating AD/HD in children and adolescents: An integrative approach* (pp. 389–441). Northvale, NJ: Jason Aronson.

Piers, C. (2000). Character as self-organizing complexity. *Psychoanalysis and Contemporary Thought, 23*(1), 3–34.

Schacter, D. L. (1996). *Searching for memory: The brain, the mind, and the past.* New York: Basic Books.

Schacter, D. L. (1999). The seven sins of memory: Insights from psychology and cognitive neuroscience. *American Psychologist, 54*(3), 182–203.

Schacter, D. L., & Scarry, E. (Eds.). (2000). *Memory, brain, and belief.* Cambridge, MA: Harvard University Press.

Schore, A. N. (2001). Minds in the making: Attachment, the self-organizing brain, and developmentally-oriented psychoanalytic psychotherapy. *British Journal of Psychotherapy, 17*(3), 299–328.

Shane, M., Shane, E., & Gales, M. (1997). *Intimate attachments: Toward a new self psychology.* New York: Guilford Press.

Siegel, D. J. (1999). *The developing mind: Toward a neurobiology of interpersonal experience.* New York: Guilford Press.

Smith, P., & McCarthy, G. (1996). The development of a semi-structured interview to investigage the attachment-related experiences of adults with learning disabilities. *British Journal of Learning Disabilities, 24*(4), 154–160.

Squire, L. R., & Kandel, E. R. (1999). *Memory: From mind to molecules.* New York: Scientific American Library.

Squire, L. R., & Knowlton, B. J. (1993). The organization of memory. Paper presented at the The Mind, the Brain, and Complex Adaptive Systems, George Mason University, Fairfax, VA.

Stern, D. N. (1985). *The interpersonal world of the infant.* New York: Basic Books.

Stern, D. N. (1989a). Developmental prerequisites for the sense of narrated self. In A. M. Cooper, O. F. Kernberg, & E. S. Person (Eds.), *Psychoanalysis: Toward the second century* (pp. 168–178). New Haven, CT: Yale University Press.

Stern, D. N. (1989b). The representation of relational patterns: Developmental considerations. In R. N. Emde & A. Sameroff (Eds.), *Relationship disturbances in early childhood: A developmental approach* (pp. 52–69). New York: Basic Books.

Van Der Kolk, B. A. (2014). *The body keeps the score: Brain, mind, and body in the healing of trauma.* New York: Viking.

Zola, S., & Squire, L. R. (2003). Genetics of childhood disorders: XLIX. Learning and memory, part 2: Multiple memory systems. *Journal of the American Academy of Child & Adolescent Psychiatry, 42*(4), 504–506.

Chapter 6

The nonverbal dialogue
Mindsharing

Our interconnectedness and our dialogue with others find expression in verbal and nonverbal modes of communication. However, a significant segment of those interactions occurs at the nonverbal/implicit level. It is for this reason that increasingly in recent years, greater attention has been given to this domain of human relationships than had previously been given to it (Jacobs, 1994; Knoblauch, 1997; Lyons-Ruth, 1998; Pally, 2001). Whereas in the literature the focus of the discussion has been on the nonverbal dialogue, in this work, I add to that communicative dimension the psychological functions, such as selfobject and adjunctive functions, that we provide one another. I propose the concept of mindsharing to encompass both the nonverbal dialogue and the psychological functions that we implicitly provide each other. The Boston Change Process Study Group (2010) stated:

> Clinically, the most interesting aspect of the intersubjective environment between patient and analyst is the mutual knowing of what is in the other's mind, as it concerns the current nature and state of their relationship. It may include states of activation, affect, feeling, arousal, desire, belief, motive, or content of thought, in any combination. These states can be transient or enduring, as mutual context. A prevailing intersubjective environment is shared. The sharing can further be mutually validated and ratified. However, the shared knowing about the relationship may remain implicit.
>
> (p. 7)

From a systems perspective, the concept of mindsharing, as a nonverbal mode of communication, brings together the various domains of knowledge of the self as a complex adaptive system: the neuropsychological, the introspective, and the interpersonal, as well as its self-deficits. Within the neuropsychological domain, the concept helps us to identify other people's self-deficits, as well as their sequelae.

From a subjective perspective, through our capacity for empathy, the concept allows us to understand our patients' needs for the selfobject and adjunctive functions that will enhance their ability to maintain self-cohesion and help them to attain self-understanding.

At the interpersonal level, the concept highlights the manner in which our interdependence provides a milieu through which these processes may come to fruition. Through our capacity for empathy, mindsharing is one of the mediums by which communication with others occurs. It is part of the nonverbal, nonconscious dialogue that we conduct with patients. Its activities often occur within the implicit relational domain. Mindsharing, therefore, includes the capacity to remain interconnected with others while being in a dialogue with them. It forms part of the interpersonal domain of lived experiences.

What is mind?

Before addressing the concept of mindsharing in greater detail, it is necessity to take a brief detour to discuss the nettlesome issue of "what is mind?" (cf. Frith, 2007; Morowitz & Singer, 1993). The question of mind as an emergent property of brain function has received a great deal of attention, although it remains an area of considerable controversy (Goldberg, 2015). If we agree that to be a self is equivalent to having a mind, then we must distinguish what it means to be a self, as a set of mental functions, from what it means to be an embodied self, as a set of mental functions that brain structure undergirds.

As we have seen, being a self includes the attributes of historical continuity, agency, and consciousness. The sense of agency entails a capacity for purposive behavior and thought. Activity is a defining characteristic of the self, as the person. Thought is a form of activity. It is also a form of dialogue with oneself (cf. Searle, 2005). To be a self is to possess intelligence and to have a mind as the activity through which we create and acquire meanings. Mind is a reflection of people's capacity to render into linguistic signs, whether verbally or nonverbally, the experiences to which they are exposed. To speak of "mind" is another way of talking about the activities of the *sense of self*. The content of the sense of self may be described as the mind (LeDoux, 1996).

However, mind is not divisible from the matter in which it is embodied. To speak of the brain is not to negate that mind exists, nor is it to equate the two. Psychological functions (i.e. the abilities to think, feel, and behave) reflect the workings of underlying neural processes and the functional organization that gives rise to these mental events. Nevertheless, the self is not located in any place in the brain. The organism is not something in which the self resides.

To talk of mind, therefore, is not necessarily to talk of anything as separate from the neurological events that constitute mind. As Damasio (1994) stated, "[T]he body contributes more than life support and modulatory effects to the brain. It contributes a content that is part and parcel of the normal mind" (p. 226). Neuroscience, through such tools as MRIs, can point to brain activities that co-occur with specific thoughts, behaviors, or affect states. However, equating these neurological events with the meaning-making activities with which we are concerned is reductionistic. From a philosophical perspective, this view is consistent with the philosophical principles of scientific realism in that it accepts the position that some call the "dual aspect" theory of the mind/body problem (Solms & Turnbull, 2002). Mind and body are two sides of the same coin, each viewed from a different perspective.

Shared minds

Clinicians are familiar with the phenomenon in which one person provides psychological functions to another that enhance their capacity to function or that are essential to their psychological survival. In the psychoanalytic literature, we find a set of concepts that bear a family resemblance to each other that conceptualizes this phenomenon. Examples of such concepts are *transitional objects* (Winnicott, 1953), *auxiliary ego functions* (Spitz, 1965), *selfobject functions* (Kohut, 1966, 1977), *mental state resonance* (Siegel, 1999), *complementary and adjunctive functions* (J. Palombo, 2011), *intersubjective sharing* (Stern, 2004), *interactive regulation* (Beebe, Rustin, Sorter, & Knoblauch, 2005), *shared brains* (Schore, 2012), *mentalization* (Allen, Fonagy, & Bateman, 2008), and *dyadic consciousness* (Tronick, 1998). Mitchell (2002) summarizes these views in his statement:

> These are the common assumptions: that minds interpenetrate each other and are shaped in relation to each other; that the patterned

processes inside minds reflect the patterned processes between minds; that ways of being with oneself are inseparable from ways of being with others; and that subjectivity develops always in the context of intersubjectivity. But each system has its own focus, its own language, its own center of gravity.

(p. 66)

In their discussion of intersubjectivity, Beebe and Lachman (2002) referred to the exchange of *interactive regulatory functions* between caregivers and infants. They note that the "[m]ind begins as *shared* mind" (see Beebe, Knoblauch, Rustin, & Sorter, 2005, p. 49, italics in original). They state, "Meltzoff, Trevarthen, and Stern all endorse the position that mind begins as shared mind" (Beebe, Rustin et al., 2005, p. 57). Tronick (2007) described the processes through which a dyadic expansion of consciousness results from the mutual regulatory interchanges between caregivers and their infants. He proposed that

> The dyadic consciousness hypothesis states that each individual is a self-organizing system that creates its own states of consciousness – states of brain organization – *which can be expanded into more coherent and complex states in collaboration with another self organizing system.* When the collaboration of two brains is successful, each fulfills the system's principle of increasing its coherence and complexity.
>
> (p. 408, italics added)

Kohut's (1984) concept of selfobject functions most closely describes what we may call the sharing of minds. Infants require psychological functions they do not possess to maintain a sense of self-cohesion. The caregivers' mirroring, alter ego, or idealizing functions perform those tasks. Infants are most often unaware of their needs for those functions unless they are deprived of them. When that occurs, the distress becomes evident, and if no response is forthcoming for prolonged periods, the experience may shatter their sense of self. Restoring the function repairs the patient's self-cohesion and restores a functional sense of self.

Furthermore, as we have seen, Schore (2003), in his discussion of attachment as a regulatory process, refers to the brain-to-brain communication that occurs between infants and caregivers as enhancing the development of the infant's capacity for self-regulation. In his description of the face-to-face dialogue of caregivers and their infants, he stated:

> Dynamically fluctuation moment-to-moment state-sharing represents an organized dialog occurring within milliseconds, and acts as an interactive matrix in which both partners match states and then simultaneously adjust their social attention, stimulation, and accelerating arousal in response to the partner's signals. In this mutually synchronized attunement of emotionally driven facial expression, prosodic vocalization, and kinetic behaviors, the dyad co-constructs a mutual regulatory system of arousal.
>
> (p. 96)

From an evolutionary viewpoint, the recognition process is the process by which an organism can find a match between its functional capacities and the conditions in the environment that enable the person to accommodate successfully to the context that it inhabits. It is through mindsharing that the recognition process becomes actualized in the psychological domain. The process moves beyond the simple identification of the other's need for psychological functions; it permits others to provide the missing function. The enhanced adaptability that results allows the person to maintain a stable sense of self-cohesion and to accommodate more successfully to the context. Furthermore, as we will see, mindsharing is a central component of the processes involved in the therapeutic interactions between therapists and patients.

Implied in this view of shared minds is that we have evolved as human beings as part of a matrix of social and cultural activities that required our participation in other people's lives. Not only are we embedded in this matrix by our interconnectedness to others but we are also actively engaged in the web of the minds of others with whom we are intimately associated. We are part of a hierarchy of human systems that ranges from the closest and most intimate to the broader and the most extended. As Jonas Salk (1983), who discovered the polio vaccine, stated:

> We are in touch with the minds of others, their thoughts, their imaginations, their fears and reassurances. We are disturbed or comforted, menaced or uplifted. It is for this reason that we need to be concerned

with others, with how their minds work, and with the effects this has on the way they behave. All this is to say that in the world today, we are more openly and instantly exposed to each other even over vast distances of space and through reaches of time.

(p. 95)

I review the contributions of these authors because each of their concepts refers to or attempts to describe a psychological function that another person performs for the subject and that the subject requires to maintain a sense of well-being, a homeostatic inner balance, or a cohesive sense of self. Lyons-Ruth (1999) uses the term "scaffolding"[1] to describe situations in which the partner lends her strength and varieties of functions. The common denominator in these functions is that a person shares part of another person's psychic organization. I suggest that we might subsume many of these phenomena under the more comprehensive construct of mindsharing (J. Palombo, 2008).

Mindsharing

I define mindsharing as follows:

> Mindsharing is a form of interconnectedness in which one person can understand the mental state of another and/or can provide psychological functions that complement another's psychological functions. The interchanges between such dyads are often reciprocal, with the subject being the recipient of others' understanding and complementing functions.

I distinguish between two senses of the term *mindsharing*. In one sense of the term, we may speak of mindsharing as the set of phenomena in which one person can understand what is on another person's mind. An example of this sense of the term is the capacity for empathy, in which one person might comprehend what another person thinks or feels. This capacity includes the mental ability for Theory of Mind by which we can grasp another person's intentions, desires, or beliefs (Baron-Cohen, 1997; Baron-Cohen & Swettenham, 1997). The second sense of mindsharing is the one that Stern (1983) calls "self-other complementing." I call these experiences performing *complementary functions* (J. Palombo, 2001).

From a dynamic systems perspective, each person is the recipient as well as the provider of such functions.

Mindsharing and empathy

Mindsharing includes the ability to share mental states with another through verbal and nonverbal communication. This process extends over the capacity to be attuned or to empathize with the inner state of another person nonverbally (Pally, 2001). We are in continuous dialogue with others. Much as we share in other people's emotional experiences through empathy, we enter another's world through language.

Kohut (1959, 1981) defined empathy as the capacity to introspect vicariously about another's mental state. It involves entering the other person's experience so as to resonate with that person's affect state and come to a cognitive understanding of the meaning that person has construed of her experiences. Demos (1984) extended the use of the concept to include the role that affects play in the exchanges between infants and mothers as well as between adults.

From a dynamic systems perspective, empathy is a type of mindsharing that represents a form of "mental state sharing and tuning" (Stern, 1983, p. 50). The human capacity for empathy differentiates us from our evolutionary and biological ancestors. We alone of all biological organisms can feel and perceive ourselves in others. Empathy is the act through which we apprehend the contents of another person's mind, a process that leads to an understanding of how the other feels, thinks, perceives reality, and gives meaning to his perceptions. By empathically reflecting on another person's experience, we can understand that person's perception of the events that impinged upon that person and the manner in which these affect her. Frith (2007) stated:

> By making models of the minds of others (the same way that it makes models of the physical world), my brain enables me to enter a shared mental world. By sharing in the world with others, I can also learn from their experiences and adopt the models of others that are better than my own. From this process, truth and progress can emerge, but so can deception and mass delusions. . . . We are embedded in the mental world of others just as they are embedded the physical world. What we're currently doing and thinking is molded by whoever we

are interacting with. But this is not how we experience ourselves. We experience ourselves as agents for the minds of our own. This is the final illusion created by our brains.

(pp. 183–184)

Recent research in brain function has uncovered a set of neurons, called mirror-neurons, that are activated whenever a subject observes another perform a goal-directed behavior (Rizzolatti & Craighero, 2004; Rizzolatti & Sinigaglia, 2006). Rizzolatti and Arbib (1998) proposed that these neurons have the capacity to represent actions and ultimately "represent the link between sender and receiver" that allows the receiver to "understand" the action and use this "understanding" to formulate an appropriate response to the performed action. They suggest that these may be the gestural underpinnings of the beginnings of communication. In humans, when observing a grasping activity, there was a significant activation of the superior temporal sulcus as well as the inferior parietal and inferior frontal gyrus. According to Iacoboni (2008), "the mirror neuron system is indispensable to that *sharing of experience which is at the root of our capacity to act as individuals but also as members of a society*" (p. xii, italics added).

From a neurobiological perspective, some investigators have explored the brain mechanisms that appear to be involved in understanding others. Decety and his colleagues (Decety & Jackson, 2006; Decety & Lamm, 2006; Jackson, Brunet, Meltzoff, & Decety, 2006), studying the mechanism associated with the capacity for empathy, found support for a model of empathy that highlights the role of specific brain regions, notably the insula, the anterior cingulate cortex, and the right temporo-parietal region (see also Terman, 2006). Finally, Cozolino (2006) contends that "[i]n one sense, a child 'borrows' the prefrontal cortex of the parent while modeling the development of its own nascent brain on what is borrowed" (p. 86).

In summary, the concept of mindsharing provides a bridge between concepts of neuropsychology and self psychology, thus integrating the two perspectives. By encompassing our modes of understanding others, the construct makes it possible to outline a line of development that enriches our understanding. Mindsharing can enhance our understanding of what occurs when deficits exist and provide a larger repertoire of interventions than were possible previously.

Mindsharing and complementary functions

The second sense of mindsharing is the one that Stern (1983) calls "self-other complementing" (p. 50). I refer to these experiences as performing psychological "complementary functions," a concept under which are subsumed selfobject functions and adjunctive functions (Palombo, 2008). It is significant that most mindsharing functions occur nonverbally. They take the form of activities that seem not to require verbal expression as part of the interchanges that occur between people, such as empathizing with another person, comforting another by holding or hugging them, or following their gaze when they look at something (Palombo, 2001).

Complementary functions are psychological functions, which we provide others or others provide us, that supply missing functions associated with person's self-deficits. For individuals with self-deficits, their "search for complementary functions" is a system attribute. It represents the recognition process or the search for contexts or persons that provide the missing function. This process most often occurs nonconsciously, although it may become conscious and intentional. It is triggered by the response we have to other people's emotional or cognitive needs, even though these are often not expressed explicitly. In addition, the recipients of the function may have little awareness of the specific nature of the function that others provide; their only experience is that they feel more cohesive and are able to accommodate more successfully to the demands made of them than they could previously.

Joan Riviere (1952), coming from a Kleinian object relations perspective, aptly describes this phenomenon:

> We tend to think of any one individual in isolation; it is a convenient fiction. . . . There is no such thing as a single human being, pure and simple, unmixed with other human beings. Each personality is a world in himself, a company of many. That self, that life of one's own . . . is a composite structure which has been and is being formed and built up since the day of our birth out of countless never ending influences and exchanges between ourselves and others. They begin with heredity and are succeeded by every emotional experience undergone as the days of life pass; and every one of these emotional experiences is bound up in feeling with one or more other persons in our lives, with "loved and hated objects". . . *These other persons are in fact therefore parts of ourselves, not indeed the whole of them but such parts or*

aspects of them as we had our relation with, and as have thus become parts of us. And we ourselves similarly have and have had effects and influences, intended or not, on all others who have an emotional relation to us, have loved or hated us. We are members one of another.

(pp. 166–167, italics added)

When viewed from the perspective of the three levels of analysis of self-experience, we may identify three types of complementary functions that we mutually provide each other: first, the neuropsychological, associated with adjunctive functions, which are part of the psychological supports the person needs to survive and which include the cognitive functions of attention, executive functions, memory, expressive, receptive, and language processing; second, the introspective, associated with selfobject functions, which include the provision of approval, admiration (mirroring), regulation of affective states (idealizing), and the creation of a sense of belonging to a community of like-minded others (twinship/alter ego); third, the interpersonal, associated with regulatory functions and connectedness with others, as well as those of social and emotional communication.

Mindsharing and neuropsychological deficits

Earlier, I listed some of the neuropsychological functions that may be impaired and identified through neuropsychological assessment. Here, I turn to a description of the ways in which others may complement some of these missing adjunctive functions. *Adjunctive functions* consist of the cognitive, moral, and spiritual nourishment necessary for us to function as contributing members of the community. Since our concern is the patients with neuropsychological deficits, I focus exclusively on the psychological functions associated with functional areas of the brain involved in cognition, in the processing of social information, the patterns of social interactions, and the capacity for emotional communication, with self and others. The critical place of some of the functions in this large repertoire of functions in determining whether a person can retain a sense of self-cohesion has been given little attention in the psychoanalytic literature. Much as the evidence for selfobject functions is found when they are absent; so it is with these functions. We take them for granted until they are unavailable or fail to operate. In everyday life, others finish our sentences, they fill in words when we cannot recall them, they remind us of tasks that we need to perform, and they help us to calm down when we feel overwrought. In a seamless way, dyads operate in concert with one another so that the effects of those relatively minor self-deficits become invisible to its members.

When others perform adjunctive functions, to which Spitz (1965) refers as performing *auxiliary ego functions*, they may help by structuring or organizing a person's life in several ways. They may translate events or other people's actions so that those may become meaningful to the person, they may guide the subject by instructing her in the rules of conduct that socializes behaviors, or they may act as moral beacons for subjects to follow. Some of these activities are cognitive functions that occur along the developmental spectrum, encompassing the entire lifespan. They range from the developmental needs of immature children to adults' requirements for complementarity to function effectively. They denote the interdependence we have on each other for more than emotional sustenance, but also for supports in many areas of functioning.

For example, in the cognitive areas, I can think of no more vivid or poignant illustration of the performance of adjunctive functions by a partner than the situation in which a person is slowly sinking into senility and losing cognitive abilities. Caregivers who are charged with the care of patients with impaired cognitive functions, such as those with emerging signs of senility or Alzheimer's disease, find themselves having to make up for the short-term memory impairments of their charges. Caregivers must remind them of the names of relatives or of self-care activities they must perform. With the decreases in their processing speed and a slowing in the capacity to understand and integrate materials, caregivers must patiently pace them through the steps necessary to undertake day-to-day tasks and make up for their diminished ability to sequence activities correctly, such as when to take pills and when not to take them or testing blood sugar levels before eating breakfast. They must help with severe word retrieval problems, as the patient struggles to express thoughts and feelings. They must deal with attentional problems, resistance to novelty, perseveration, and heightened affective reactivity, including reactions to their own neuropsychological limitations. In all these efforts, the caregivers must attune themselves to the needs of their charges and through mindsharing provide for self-deficits as these emerge.

Children with neuropsychological deficits tend to elicit adjunctive functions from caregivers that serve to complement their immature or deficient psyches. What is different about these children is that the adjunctive functions they require are not those that are usually identified as part of the parenting process. Sometimes, it is impossible to identify specific delays or deficits early in infancy. Caregivers' capacities for mindsharing will, at times, determine their abilities to complement a child's self-deficits. Alternatively, the limitations in a child's capacities may act as a barrier to the caregivers' efforts at providing for the self-deficits.

Parents are often in the dark about what the child requires. Some caregivers respond intuitively. Through their empathic capacities, they can fill in the child's neuropsychological deficits. In fact, these parents, if they have had other children, recognize the differences in the child and feel they must respond as they do or cause the child serious distress. When parents either cannot or do not complement the child's deficits, the child suffers. The reason for the child's distress is seldom evident early on. Parents often feel much puzzlement and guilt as they assume that they are the cause of the problem.

In those cases, when active, the process of mindsharing may provide a protective factor that makes it possible for the person to compensate for some self-deficits. Furthermore, it may prevent neuropsychological deficits from becoming attractors around which unsuccessful accommodations will cluster. Since the person's self-cohesion or self-organization depends on those providers, failures in mindsharing could disrupt those capacities. The stability of the person's sense of self depends on the availability of the providers of the adjunctive functions that fill in the self-deficits. Mindsharing is a necessary but not a sufficient condition for self-cohesion. Unsuccessful accommodations may result when the capacity for mindsharing is absent or, if present, is unstable. The absence of this capacity would indicate the presence of a deficit in the sense of self.

For some patients with neuropsychological deficits, their neuropsychological strengths and weaknesses and the impact of their self-deficits may constrain their capacities to benefit from the resources that may be available to them. Caregivers may be ready and willing to provide for the person's needs; however, the person's deficits can interfere with their abilities to use what they provide, much as they cannot soothe a colicky baby in spite of the caregiver's best efforts. Similarly, the presence of ADHD limits the caregiver's capacity to soothe the child because her physiological system is too highly aroused to respond or benefit from the caregiver's interventions. On the other hand, the caregiver's sensitivity to the child's psychological state may result in a secure type of attachment, in spite of the constraints on the caregiver's attempts to relieve the child's distress. Children with neuropsychological deficits who suffer from disorders of the self but have strong positive relationships with their caregivers sometimes display this seemingly paradoxical phenomenon. What this means is that at times the neuropsychological deficits may be the primary contributor to the system's dysfunction, whereas at other times the dysfunction may be due to the effects of other factors, such as the environment's response the patient or to the trauma caused by the deficit itself. (For a discussion of the ontogeny of mindsharing, see Palombo, 2008.)

Mindsharing and selfobject deficits

Kohut's concept of *selfobject*, one of his most seminal concepts, describes a particular aspect of the relationship between self and others. To the extent that the others are emphatically responsive to the person's psychological needs is the extent to which the person will experience others as selfobjects. It is in the nature of selfobject experiences that as long as an empathic connectedness exists through which requisite functions are performed, the person will experience a sense of wholeness and intactness. The person may have no awareness that others are performing any functions, much less any awareness of the source or location of the performing agent. Only when the functions are absent does the person experience discomfort and an awareness that something is amiss. Eventually, the person may acquire some of these selfobject functions and develop the capacity to maintain internal harmony, although people can never totally dispense with the need for selfobjects.

Providers of selfobject and adjunctive function must negotiate the complex task of recognition that will result in the fitting together between the person's self-deficits and the required psychological functions. This suggests that often a unique dyad can function effectively as others cannot replicate what the dyad provides. This is often the case when a couple has functioned effectively only to discover that when a breakup occurs one or both are so bereft that they cannot regain the sense of self-cohesion they formerly possessed.

Emotions permeate the selfobject functions that people provide others. Selfobject functions always carry a positive emotional valence. Three common selfobject functions are those of *idealizing, mirroring*, and *twinship* (*alter ego*).

Idealizing selfobject functions

Caregivers of children function as psychological protectors and as providers of emotional support. Caregivers are responsible for seeing to it that children feel safe from external dangers. For children to experience such feelings of safety, they must have faith that the caregivers are sufficiently powerful. In addition, caregivers must direct their efforts at modulating and regulating the child's affective states so that they do not become overstimulated or overwhelmed. The provision of these selfobject functions can result in the internalization of self-control, self-discipline, and self-regulation.

Mirroring selfobject functions

For self-esteem to develop, children must experience their caregivers as cherishing and affirming their uniqueness and specialness, as treating them as the center of the caregivers' universe. When parents mirror their children's worth by expressing and displaying their delight and joy, the children experience a sense of worth, positive self-regard, dignity, and self-respect.

Twinship (alter ego) selfobject functions

The experience of a common bond with others that ties all human beings together and that leads to feelings of kinship with others is critical to the healthy development of all children, but particularly to children with neuropsychological deficits. These experiences lead to the development of alter-ego selfobject functions. Once internalized, these functions permit the children to feel intact and healthy. The functions provide a sense of well-being and wholesomeness without which they can feel dehumanized. Togashi (2014) summarizes Kohut's views:

> For Kohut, self-experience always emerges within the context of the other's responsivity. In other words, selfhood involves both authentic being and experiences of relatedness. The idea is most clearly described in his definition of the twinship experience as being "a human being" among other human beings. . . . In my view, the twinship experience is organized by two people who are "mutually finding himself and not-himself in each other". . . . This is an experience

organized between emotionally connected people who recognize the differences and similarities vis-à-vis one another.

(p. 270)

Selfobject functions are psychological functions with which people are not born. They represent enduring functions that accrue to the self through the maturational process. These functions are essential for a person to sustain the sense of self-cohesion and integration. Kohut drew an analogy between the need for selfobject functions and the human need for an environment that includes oxygen to survive. Without oxygen, people would suffocate. The awareness of the need for the function is most urgently felt when we deprive a person of the function. It is then that the means to sustain a sense of well-being ceases to exist. At other times, when the function is available, it is taken for granted.

Developmentally, selfobject functions follow a maturational path from concrete manifestation to abstract and symbolic forms of expression. We may trace a developmental line in the performance of selfobject function by others. A child in pain may need to be physically held and comforted, whereas a grieving adult may find solace in words of sympathy and understanding. What this means is that there is a relationship between our capacity to perform the functions for ourselves and our need to have others perform those functions for us. The less we are able to do for ourselves, the more others have to fill our selfobject deficits. Furthermore, the greater the deficit, the more concrete the form of expression that others must institute to fill in the deficit. The more mature the person, the greater their level of self-organization and the less concrete their need for the expression of selfobject functions.

It is important to note that at times we may consciously choose to forego having our emotional needs met when faced with exceptional circumstances. Such are the circumstances when we are required to sacrifice ourselves to care for someone who is ill, to devote ourselves to serving our community, or even to endanger ourselves because of a belief or adherence to a set of ideals, which we value over our lives. The rewards for such altruism lies in the satisfaction we gain in giving expression of a core of our sense of self, without which our sense of self-cohesion would be endangered or life would not be worth living (see Kohut, 1985).

It is often difficult to make a clear-cut distinction between selfobject and adjunctive functions when people are involved in the performance of these functions. In addition to selfobject functions, patients with self-deficits often draw adjunctive functions from others that complement their immature or deficient psyches. These processes are most evident in patients with neuropsychological deficits, where through their neuropsychological deficits they call out to us for complementary responses. Whether they are open to receiving what we have to offer will depend on the level of their distress or whether their defenses will stand in the way of their availability to use what is offered (i.e. whether as a system their sense of self is open or closed). What will become evident is that the processes involved in these interchanges will replicate themselves in the clinical setting and will inform the type of relationship established between a patient and a therapist.

In the case of adjunctive functions, we use others as an extension to serve a specific purpose, usually that of performing tasks that we are unable to perform, and the person that performs the function may be exchanged with others who can provide the same function. However, in the case of selfobject functions, the situation is different. The person performing the functions is not interchangeable; since the functions performed are in the psychological area, the person performing the function assumes a special value that makes that relationship distinctive and not interchangeable.

Mindsharing and deficits in interconnectedness

As we have seen, evidence from the studies on attachment lends support to the proposition that our interconnectedness to others is a critical aspect of our need for others. The quality of those connections will often be a contributing factor as to whether individuals will accommodate successfully to the environment they inhabit or whether they will fail to attain the goals they desire to achieve. However, we must remind ourselves that our interconnectedness is but one element of the complex adaptive system of which we are constituted, the others being our neuropsychological strengths and weaknesses and our subjective responses to the events to which we are exposed. The endowment that each person brings to the relationships with others will contribute to the type of relationship the person will develop; this includes the diversity of each person's memory system. The meaning of the connections we make with others will differ with each individual. Finally, the context that each person inhabits will frame how that person relates to others.

Affect regulation, a component of our interconnectedness and of our interactive regulation, is a central organizing principle in human development and a central motivator of behavior (Schore, 2003). Mindsharing is the process through which the emotional interchanges between infant and caregiver as well as the processing and regulation of emotional information by the infant take place. The socio-emotional information that the members of the dyad exchange facilitates attachment, regulates bodily states, regulates affective states, and assists in dealing with stress (cf. Bendicsen, 2013).

For patients with neuropsychological deficits, mindsharing is critical to the change processes that occur within the therapeutic process. Communications may represent *inputs that may become change agents*; they may constitute functions, such as selfobject functions, or adjunctive functions that complement an individual's self-deficits. Internal communication among the components or communication with the external environment may provide feedback that leads to modification of the system. Such interchanges may threaten their stability, or they may enhance their preferences for self-cohesion and self-understanding. When their stability is endangered, they may approach the edge of chaos and fear lapsing into a state of fragmentation. Alternatively, this instability may offer an opportunity for self-reorganization and growth. Patients can then evolve because of these interchanges with the environment. In dynamic systems theory, the integration of information makes the system more complex; it increases its coherence and leads to more organized states and therefore greater self-organization. The hoped for outcome of therapeutic intervention would be that the interventions, whether verbal or nonverbal, would lead to a greater sense of self-cohesion and greater differentiation and individuation.

Case illustration: Sally

The following case of an adult illustrates the unstable sense of self-cohesion that was associated with the effects of having an executive function disorder and the absence of others who could complement her adjunctive deficits.

Sally was a 34-year-old woman referred by a therapist who was seeing her and her husband for marital counseling. The therapist was requesting a consultation because the treatment was stalemated and she felt that Sally was contributing to that stalemate because of an inability to change her behavior.

Sally described herself as always being behind in her work. She worked many hours, was constantly tardy, and had a messy desk. This pattern dated back to high school. She remembered her father having to chase after her to drop off assignments she had forgotten to take with her. Being on time is a huge problem. Each of the three times we met, Sally was late for her appointment, although she noted that the extent of her lateness decreased with each session. She feels considerable embarrassment at having to explain her lateness and to give excuses for her irresponsibility. In her current position, they expect her to be at work at 8:30 a.m., but she has never been able to get there on time. This is a source of tension between her and her supervisor, who is critical of her tardiness. She has worked on this, trying to develop strategies to deal with the problem. However, these would only work for brief periods. She would then revert to her old patterns.

She is also late bringing her daughter to preschool as well as in picking her up. As an example, she related an incident that occurred following one of her sessions. She left the session with plenty of time to pick up her daughter. However, on the way to the day care center, she passed a Toys R Us store and remembered that she had some items to return. She looked at her watch and decided that if she did not dally, she could make it. When she went into the store, hurried around, and remembered that she needed to buy a birthday gift for the party to which her daughter was invited. By the time, she got to the checkout counter, there were five people ahead of her. She became furious at herself as she realized that again she would be late picking up her daughter. She sped through traffic, hoping not to get a ticket as she had a few months back. Ultimately, she arrived at the day care center about 20 minutes late. The staff at the day care center was furious at her, and her child had been crying because mom was nowhere to be found. She sees this as a pattern in her life.

At work, her attention to detail made her lose sight of the bigger picture. As a result, she got into areas beyond those that concerned her. She did not set boundaries on her work assignments and consequently got distracted and behind in her work. She related that in a previous position, in order to be assured that she completed her work, she asked a secretary to sit by her side to keep her focused on what she was supposed to do. Without that assistance, she would wander from one thing to the next, ending up being late in completing the work.

In part, according to Sally, the problem seemed to stem from the fact that she took on much more than she could complete within the allotted time. As a result, she got behind in her work and appeared disorganized. She lost track of time and had trouble stopping what she was doing to move on to the next task. She also procrastinated. In part, she felt that when confronted with a new task, she became overwhelmed and put it off. However, once she started, she could generally find ways of attacking the problem and completing it. She did misjudge how much work she could accomplish in a given period. This had the effect of her not being able to limit what they asked her to do. Since she had difficulty saying no and wanted to please her bosses, she ended up having to work far too many hours to complete her tasks. Often, she felt so exhausted by these demands that she stopped functioning. She collapsed and had to take a sick day off. She then stayed in bed all day trying to recover.

Sally also stated that, at home, the pattern was just as bad. She and her husband constantly argued because chores were not done and he felt that he carried the major burden of running the household. During these arguments, she felt panicked that he might leave her and dissolved in uncontrollable tears. In fact, that was the reason they sought marital counseling.

In speaking of her childhood, Sally reported that the relationship between her parents was highly discordant. They fought openly in front of her. During her high school years, she remembers witnessing her father hitting her mother. On the other hand, her mother would respond by going after her father with a knife. Her father was more nurturing than her mother was. He was a wonderful cook who would prepare the meals for the family. He started as a sales clerk and was promoted to plant manager. Her mother worked as a nurse. She worked "crazy hours." When Sally was 19 years old, her mother had a breakdown and was diagnosed with a bipolar disorder. She was hospitalized. It appears that her mother never recovered.

Sally started junior college while still living at home. There was much chaos in her life until her husband, Tom, came into her life. She decided to marry, just to get away from home. She finished college, easily found work, and by the age of 24 had advanced in her position at work to senior manager of the company, earning a salary commensurate with her title. Her boss, who was 55 years old, was demanding and manipulative. He started making sexual overtures, which led her to leave the company. She went to work for another company. There again, her boss sexually harassed her.

She filed a sexual harassment suit against the man and left that position for her current employment a year ago.

Approximately three years ago, she and her husband began marital counseling. After seeing her briefly, her therapist referred her to a psychiatrist who prescribed Prozac for her depressive mood, which helped reduce the fluctuations in her feeling states but did not bring any changes in her capacity to be more organized.

Psychodynamic profile

From a neuropsychological perspective, Sally presented with all the features of an executive function disorder and ADHD. Her difficulties centered on her disorganization, her poor time management, and her impulsivity. Besides these was the inability to sustain attention and focus on tasks for long periods. Her neuropsychological deficits left their unique imprint on her personality.

Her neuropsychological deficits were major contributors to her inability to make a successful accommodation to the demands made of her. These deficits represented sequestered components, which in tandem with the relational patterns that she acquired during her early years became self-organized attractors that governed her relations with others. In spite of her best efforts, she was incapable of modifying her conduct to minimize their effects on her life.

From a subjective perspective, she paid a heavy price for the constraints set by her neuropsychological endowment. She periodically lost the ability to sustain a sense of self-cohesion, either becoming dysfunctional or dissolving into uncontrollable tears. The guilt, self-criticism, and demoralization she felt in being unable to control her symptoms contributed to her distress. She was chronically under stress, her self-esteem suffered, and she blamed herself for her neuropsychological deficits seeing them as flaws in her personality. Her demoralization manifested as depression. Her early childhood experiences, in a household in which her parents were in constant conflict, further complicated these responses. At an emotional level, Sally was temperamentally kind, gentle, and eager to please. She disliked confrontations and angry outbursts. As a child, she tried to placate her parents to stop their fighting. Now, she found it difficult to say "no" when pressured to do something that she believes is not in her best interest. At work, these habitual patterns of interaction have not served her well.

Preferences

Her struggles affected her capacity to remain cohesive and process the reasons for her actions. Her husband was critical of her and saw her as incompetent in dealing with day-to-day household chores. He felt she was negligent in the care of their daughter and inattentive to her needs. A complicating factor resulted from her reactions to other people's responses to some of her cognitive problems. Since these problems had clear consequences in her relationships to others, she found herself criticized and that she was not performing up to expectations. This not only made her feel guilty but also played into her desire to be liked and led to her desire to regain the lost approval. While she was able to use other resources to compensate for deficits, the demands that others made on her and that she had to make of herself would periodically exhaust her and lead to fragmentation. Finally, her reactions to her own cognitive problems compound her difficulties. She was aware of her difficulties and saw herself as failing to live up to her own expectations. The confusion this produced led her to question her motives, to be self-critical, and feel that she was not in control of her life.

Processes that guided her psychodynamics

As a neuropsychological deficit, and executive function disorder had a pervasive effect on her life. It invaded most areas of day-to-day functioning as well as her ability to process and anticipate future events. At times, it also affected her ability to think sequentially and to maintain the focus on a task. This deficit became an attractor basin that organized her experiences. For Sally, this meant that the dysfunctional patterns replicated themselves in multiple areas of her life, her relationship to her husband, to her employers, and to her daughter's caregivers. In addition, the extensive use of disavowal resulted in her seeming unawareness of the consequences of her actions. Outwardly, her actions and expectation of her performance appeared to others as grandiose and unrealistic. However, when confronted by those consequences, she felt humiliated and became enraged at herself for what she believed was her stupidity.

Therapeutic implications

In cases such as Sally's, interventions are called for at multiple levels. Among these is individual therapy for her to address the erosion of her self-esteem, her shame, and her puzzlement at the course her life has taken.

At the marital level, couples' therapy is needed to help both she and her husband understand that Sally's problem was not due to irresponsibility or neglect, but simply due to her neuropsychological makeup. Remediation by a specialist who would help her develop techniques for time management, organization, and planning is also required. Neuropsychological testing, if possible, would be important to confirm the clinical impressions and possibly to uncover areas of strength that she might be able to use to compensate for the deficit.

Summary

We may describe the activities to which we refer as mental processes as reflecting the presence of "mind." At some point, as complex adaptive systems, we become conscious and self-reflective, seeking to understand ourselves. We not only respond to the internal and external stimuli that we receive, but we also use the learning that occurs from these inputs to modify ourselves and to readjust our responses to others. We re-process recursively what we have learned historically to anticipate how we will respond. In the process, the capacity for self-observation leads us to monitor our responses to our inner states and our responses to others. This monitoring permits us to judge the success of failure of our ability as a system to attain the goals we intend to achieve.

As social beings who are complex adaptive systems, we are in constant interaction with others. Several psychological processes are active at a conscious and nonconscious level. Among these processes is the emergent property of mindsharing. Mindsharing encompasses the processes involved in the empathy through which we understand other people's mental states and they in turn understand ours. These processes include sharing mental states that are often identified as intersubjective experiences. Moreover, they are part of the processes through which we provide others with psychological functions that they lack and reciprocally that they provide us. The concepts of mindsharing and of self-deficit are foundational constructs of the neuropsychodynamic perspective.

The concept of mindsharing proposes that we are in unremitting communication with others at the affective and cognitive levels. In these exchanges, we bring patterns of interactions that were structured by our self-deficits and the attractor states to which they gave rise. These patterns became encoded in our non-declarative memory systems and nonconsciously structured the nature of the relationships we form with others. Depending on the fit created by those patterns, the relationships may lead to successful or unsuccessful accommodations.

As a system of communication among human beings, mindsharing plays a significant role in our capacity to maintain our interconnectedness with each other. It permits us to monitor the self-state of those with whom we are attached and as a means for complementing others and being complemented by others; it serves the function of helping maintain our sense of self-cohesion. Since it functions primarily as a nonverbal form of communication, it has a parallel function to that described by Lyons-Ruth (1998) in her concept of implicit relational knowing. We know each other in the sense that we understand that others have feelings, beliefs, and intentions through our capacity for empathy, but also through the responses we make to their needs for complementarity.

I distinguished three types of complementary functions that the context provides through mindsharing and that we mutually provide each other. One type is that of the adjunctive functions that others provide to patients' cognitive and physical capacities, the second type is the selfobject function, and the third type is associated with our interconnectedness to others, which as social beings is essential to our survival.

Note

1   It is important to distinguish the concept of complementary functions as I use it from two concepts used in the cognitive and educational literature: the concepts of "scaffolding" and of the "zone of proximal development." Scaffolding was introduced in the cognitive literature by Wood, Bruner, and Ross (1976) to describe the assistance given by tutors to students attempting to learn a task that was initially beyond their capabilities. It does not take into account the emotional dimensions or the nonconscious provision of the function. Vygotsky (1978) introduced the concept of the zone of proximal development to describe a similar process but which was not necessarily limited to cognitive challenges.

References

Allen, J. G., Fonagy, P., & Bateman, A. W. (2008). *Mentalization in clinical practice.* Washington, DC: American Psychiatric Publishing.

Baron-Cohen, S. (1997). *Mindblindness: An essay on autism and theory of mind.* Cambridge, MA: The MIT Press.

Baron-Cohen, S., & Swettenham, J. (1997). Theory of mind in autism: Its relationship to executive function and central coherence. In D. J. Cohen & F. R. Volkmar (Eds.), *Handbook of autism and pervasive developmental disorders* (pp. 880–893). New York: John Wiley & Sons.

Beebe, B., Knoblauch, S., Rustin, J., & Sorter, D. (2005). Forms of intersubjectivity in infancy research and adult treatment: A systems view. In B. Beebe, S. Knoblauch, J. Rustin, & D. Sorter (Eds.), *Forms of intersubjectivity in infant research and adult treatment* (pp. 1–28). New York: Other Press.

Beebe, B., & Lachmann, F. M. (2002). *Infant research and adult treatment: Co-constructing interactions*. Mahwah, NJ: The Analytic Press.

Beebe, B., Rustin, J., Sorter, D., & Knoblauch, S. (2005). An expanded view of forms of intersubjectivity in infancy and their application to psychoanalysis. In B. Beebe, S. Knoblauch, J. Rustin, & D. Sorter (Eds.), *Forms of intersubjectivity in infant research and adult treatment* (pp. 55–88). New York: Other Press.

Bendicsen, H. (2013). *The transformational self: Attachment and the end of the adolescent phase*. London: Karnac.

Boston Change Process Study Group. (2010). *Change in psychotherapy: A unifying paradigm*. New York: W. W. Norton.

Cozolino, L. (2006). *The neuroscience of human relationships: Attachment in the developing social brain*. New York: W. W. Norton.

Damasio, A. R. (1994). *Descartes' error: Emotion, reason, and the human brain*. New York: G. P. Putnam's Sons.

Decety, J., & Jackson, P. L. (2006). A social-neuroscience perspective on empathy. *Current Directions in Psychological Science*, *15*(2), 54–58.

Decety, J., & Lamm, C. (2006). Human empathy through the lens of social neuroscience. *The ScientificWorld Journal*, *6*, 1146–1163.

Demos, E. V. (1984). Empathy and affect: Reflections on infant experience. In M. B. J. Lichtenberg & D. Silver (Eds.), *Empathy II* (pp. 9–34). Hillsdale, NJ: The Analytic Press.

Frith, C. (2007). *Making of the mind: How the brain creates our mental world*. Oxford: Blackwell Publishing.

Goldberg, A. (2015). *The brain, the mind and the self: A psychoanalytic road map*. New York: Routledge.

Iacoboni, M. (2008). *Mirroring people: The new science of how we connect with others*. New York: Farrar, Straus, Giroux.

Jackson, P. L., Brunet, E., Meltzoff, A. N., & Decety, J. (2006). Empathy examined for the neural mechanisms involved in imagining how I feel versus how you feel pain. *Neuropsychologia*, *44*, 752–761.

Jacobs, T. J. (1994). Nonverbal communications: Some reflections on their role in the psychoanalytic process and psychoanalytic education. *Journal of the American Psychoanalytic Association*, *42*(3), 741–762.

Knoblauch, S. H. (1997). Beyond the word in psychoanalysis: The unspoken dialogue. *Psychoanalytic Dialogues*, *7*(4), 491–516.

Kohut, H. (1959). Introspection, empathy and psychoanalysis. *Journal of the American Psychoanalytic Association*, *7*, 459–483.

Kohut, H. (1966). Forms and transformations of narcissism. *Journal of the American Psychoanalytic Association*, *14*(2), 243–272.

Kohut, H. (1977). *The restoration of the self*. New York: International Universities Press.

Kohut, H. (1981). On Empathy. In P. H. Ornstein (Ed.), *The search for the self: Selected writings of Heinz Kohut: 1978–1981* (Vol. 4, pp. 525–536). Madison, CT: International Universities Press.

Kohut, H. (1984). *How does analysis cure?* Chicago: The University of Chicago Press.

Kohut, H. (1985). *Self psychology and the humanities: Reflections on a new psychoanalytic approach*. New York: W. W. Norton.

LeDoux, L. (1996). *The emotional brain: The mysterious underpinnings of emotional life*. New York: Simon & Schuster.

Lyons-Ruth, K. (1998). Implicit relational knowing: Its role in development and psychoanalytic treatment. *Infant Mental Health Journal, 19*(3), 282–289.

Lyons-Ruth, K. (1999). The two-person unconscious: Intersubjective dialogue, enactive relationsal representation, and the emergence of new forms of relational organization. *Psychoanalytic Inquiry, 19*(4), 576–617.

Mitchell, S. A. (2002). The texture of fields: Commentary on the contributions of Louis Sander. *Psychoanalytic Dialogues, 12*, 65–71.

Morowitz, H. J., & Singer, J. L. (1993). The mind, the brain, and complex adaptive systems. Paper presented at the The Mind, the Brain, and Complex Adaptive Systems, George Mason University, Fairfax, VA.

Pally, R. (2001). A primary role for nonverbal communication in psychoanalysis. *Psychoanalytic Inquiry, 21*(1), 71–93.

Palombo, J. (2001). *Learning disorders and disorders of the self in children and adolescents*. New York: W. W. Norton.

Palombo, J. (2008). Mindsharing: Transitional objects and selfobjects as complementary functions. *Clinical Social Work Journal, 36*, 143–154.

Palombo, J. (2011). Executive function conditions and self-deficits. In N. H. Heller & A. Gitterman (Eds.), *Mental health and social problems: A social work perspective* (pp. 282–312). New York: Routledge.

Riviere, J. (1952). The unconscious phantay of an inner world reflected in examples from English literature. *The International Journal of Psychoanalysis, 33*, 160–172.

Rizzolatti, G., & Arbib, M. A. (1998). Language within our grasp. *Trends in Cognitive Sciences, 21*(5), 188–194.

Rizzolatti, G., & Craighero, L. (2004). The mirror-neuron system. *Annual Review of Neuroscience, 27*, 169–192.

Rizzolatti, G., & Sinigaglia, C. (2006). *Mirror in the brain: How our minds share actions and emotions* (F. Anderson, Trans.). New York: Oxford University Press.

Salk, J. (1983). *Anatomy of reality: Merging of intuition in recent*. New York: Columbia University Press.

Schore, A. N. (2003). *Affect dysregulation and disorders of the self*. New York: W. W. Norton.

Schore, A. N. (2012). *The science of the art of psychotherapy*. New York: W. W. Norton.

Searle, J. R. (2005). The self as a problem in philosophy and neurobiology. In T. E. Feinberg & J. P. Keenan (Eds.), *The lost self: Pathologies of the brain and identity* (pp. 7–19). New York: Oxford University Press.

Siegel, D. J. (1999). *The developing mind: Toward a neurobiology of interpersonal experience*. New York: Guilford Press.

Solms, M., & Turnbull, O. (2002). *The brain and the inner world: An introduction to the neuroscience of subjective experience*. New York: Other Press.

Spitz, R. A. (1965). *The first year of life: A psychoanalytic study of normal and deviant development of object relations*. New York: International Universities Press.

Stern, D. N. (1983). The early development of schemas of self, other, and "self with other." In J. D. Lichtenberg & S. Kaplan (Eds.), *Reflections on self psychology* (pp. 49–84). Hillsdale, NJ: The Analytic Press.

Stern, D. N. (2004). *The present moment in psychotherapy and everyday life*. New York: W. W. Norton.

Terman, D. M. (2006). Empathy and neuroscience. Paper presented at the Self Psychology Conference, Chicago, IL.

Togashi, K. (2014). A sense of "being human" and twinship experience. *International Journal of Psychoanalytic Self Psychology*, *9*(4), 265–281.

Tronick, E. Z. (1998). Dyadically expanded states of consciousness and the process of therapeutic change. *Infant Mental Health Journal*, *19*(3), 290–299.

Tronick, E. Z. (2007). *The neurobehavioral and social-emotional development of infants and children*. New York: W. W. Norton.

Vygotsky, L. S. (1978). *Mind in society: The development of higher psychological processes*. Cambridge, MS: Harvard University Press.

Winnicott, D. W. (1953). Transitional objects and transitional phenomena: A study of the first not-me possession. *International Journal of Psychoanalysis*, *34*, 89–97.

Wood, D., Bruner, J. S., & Ross, G. (1976). The role of tutoring in problem solving. *Journal of Child Psychology & Psychiatry*, *17*, 89–100.

Chapter 7

The therapeutic dialogue
An overview

At this point, it is timely to take stock of where we are conceptually. The focus in this work has been on the patients' experiences of having neuropsychological deficits that are innate in their origins. In considering these patients' self-experience, I called attention to the affect states that were instrumental in the formation of those experiences: specifically, the feelings of shame associated with their awareness that something about themselves is amiss, often not knowing the specific source or cause of the discomfort and the reasons for the subsequent disruptions in their capacity to accommodate successfully to their context.

In terms of their day-to-day functioning, patients met those challenges in different ways. Some avoided tasks that required the functions associated with the self-deficits or compensated for them and consequently could accommodate successfully to the demands made of them. For others, the impairments made it difficult for them to accommodate to the demands made of them. Most, however, seemed to seek unconsciously relationships with others who could provide them with the missing function, thus hoping to have their sense of self complemented by others. When successful, these attempts led to a restoration of self-cohesion and the capacity to accommodate successfully to the context they inhabited. When they failed, patients confronted problems at multiple levels of functioning. However, I emphasized that not all individuals who are born with such self-deficits follow this path. Some negotiate successfully the obstacles that these self-deficits present and are able to lead successful and productive lives.

To organize the data of these patients' experiences, it became essential to introduce a metatheory that would illuminate the complexity involved in assigning a share of the contribution each of the three domains involved makes to the person's developmental trajectory and the person's capacity to accommodate successfully to the context he or she inhabits. I suggested a levels-of-analysis perspective that clustered each set of experiences around the neuropsychological, the introspective, and the interpersonal domains. The evolutionary viewpoint into which this metatheory is embedded required that we consider that all human activity occurs within a context that defines its meaning but also that results from interactions and communication with others. Nonlinear dynamic systems theory was most suited to fulfill the requirements of the task of bringing together the interaction among the three domains of experience (Palombo, 2013a, 2013b).

I proposed that the neuropsychological deficits represented impairments in specific functional areas of the brain, which present challenges to patients who possess them. These self-deficits formed part of the initial conditions that often determined the patients' developmental trajectory. At the subjective level, the intense feelings generated by the self-deficits had an impact on the patient's sense of self-cohesion and on her self-understanding. At the interpersonal level, the self-deficits interfered with the formation of adequate relational patterns and the ability to communicate with others in social contexts.

I also proposed that the capacity for mindsharing is the process through which we are able to empathize with other people's experiences and they with ours. As part of mindsharing, three broad types of complementary functions that are essential for the development of a stable sense of self-cohesion are *selfobject functions, adjunctive functions* (Palombo, 2008), and *functions related to our interconnectedness to others* (see Aron's, 1996, concept of mutuality). Mindsharing also gives rise to our propensity, through the recognition process, to respond to others by feeling urged to complement their missing functions as they do for us. As we have seen, complementary functions are psychological functions that others provide to enhance or help patients maintain a sense of self-cohesion.

While the sharing of information between patients and therapist is essential for the establishment of a mutuality of understanding, for therapists, a statement of patients' psychodynamics provides a road map of the path through which the attractors organized their conscious, nonconscious, and unconscious mental states into interlinked enduring patterns of feelings, thoughts, and behaviors. These patterns are embedded in the social and emotional context that the patients inhabit. The three sources of data from which we obtain an insight into patients' psychodynamics are the data from neuropsychological assessments; their subjective feelings, thoughts, and behaviors; and reports from others in their social context, such as professionals or family members.

From patients' perspectives, the defenses they use, such as dissociation or disavowal, engendered by the pain and anxieties associated with their feelings, led to the formation of attractors that organized their experiences into distinctive psychodynamics. In other words, the shame they felt or the humiliations they suffered, which activated those defenses, formed a set of dynamics that became attractor states that served as organizers of future experiences. These experiences were encoded in procedural memory. The patterns replicated themselves at multiple levels of feelings, thoughts, and actions. While for some patients the self-righting processes can help them heal the effects of their self-deficits, others require the assistance that therapy provides to achieve that end.

Treatment becomes a joint endeavor in which both patients and therapists are active participants. However, therapists confront the challenge of addressing questions such as: What processes bring about changes in patients' psychological makeup that may lead them to develop a greater capacity for successful accommodation than was possible before their involvement in therapy? How do the therapist's activities produce these changes, and how much do they further the patient's own sense of agency? How much does the proactive participation of the patient in the process, in acquiring new skills and in effecting changes in their own lives, contribute to the outcome? As Jonas Salk (1983) so aptly stated:

> Although the power of the mind to heal itself and to restore itself is great, training and experience are needed to master this power. Just as the mind needs nourishing food and the nourishing diet biologically and metabiologically, so it can be malnourished and even poisoned. When this occurs, its capacity to self-regulate and to self-heal is impaired and maybe destroyed, resulting in various kinds of pathological manifestations. The capacity to self-regulate, to self-heal, and to self-renew may be one of the most important functions of the mind not only for itself but also in relation to others. *There must be a capacity for some minds to nourish to heal others, and some minds provide this function, protecting both self and society.*
>
> (p. 98, italics added)

The collaborative efforts may lead to an understanding of the patients' selves as a complex adaptive system, of the contributions that self-deficits make to their unsuccessful accommodations, and of their efforts at seeking others to complement their self-deficits.

In this chapter, I will now present a brief overview of the therapeutic process, which I will discuss in more detail in the three chapters that follow. However, before proceeding with that overview, three issues deserve our attention because of their importance to a system's view of the therapeutic process. These issues are the functionality of the therapeutic dyad, the problem of the mutative factors that are change agents in the therapeutic process, and the construct of the therapeutic dialogue as occurring during moments that encapsulate the issue most pertinent for the dyad to address.

The functionality of the therapeutic dyad

From the moment of their first encounter, the therapist and patient form a new dyad (i.e. a new complex adaptive system). This system lays out a set of initial conditions to which each member contributes her own individual perspective. Among the patients' initial conditions are the type and severity of their neuropsychological deficit, the stability or instability of their sense of self as reflected in the capacity for self-cohesion, and their capacity to benefit from interventions that are change agents.

A set of attractors has organized patients' experiences and established recurrent patterns of expectations. Patients instituted a set of defenses to deal with their feelings of humiliation, which maintain the stability of those recurrent patterns. Whereas their overt symptoms often do not correlate with the underlying psychodynamics, those symptoms represent their best efforts at dealing with their anxieties.

For their part, as members of the system, therapists contribute to the initial conditions. Therapists' theoretical orientation, their competence and experience, their personality structure, cultural interests, and position within the professional and broader community are factors that enter into the interaction with the patients. Each dyad is unique in the sense that no two pairs of therapist and patient are alike. Some are better "matched" and function effectively, whereas others are mismatched and do not function as optimally. This view places emphasis on the fact that both members of the dyad contribute to the adequate functioning of the system.

The optimal functioning of the therapeutic dyad depends on the "recognition" process, which is the process through which therapists are successful in identifying their patients' selfobject and adjunctive needs, while patients participate by feeling safe to expose those needs. That is, whether a "fittedness" can exist between the two members of the dyad through mindsharing. If the recognition process is unsuccessful, aspects of the therapists' personality or theoretical orientation may undermine the patients' sense of agency, diminish their capacity for fittedness, inhibit the integration of new information, derail the dialogue, and restrict mindsharing.

The functionality of the therapeutic dyad, therefore, is always a dimension of the individuality of each of its members. Each dyad is unique; consequently, that distinctiveness will determine the content of the dialogue. As therapists, we have often wondered whether a patient would address the same issues with a different therapist than those with which we dealt. In my view, the answer to that question is that, in all probably, they would not. Whether they would have benefitted more from seeing someone else is an unanswerable question. It is true, however, that some patients terminate their therapy satisfactorily but years later see a different therapist only to find that some core issues had remained untouched by the previous therapy. Similarly, many speculate what it would have been like to have been born to different parents or in a different culture. These counterfactual fantasies lend credence to the notion that the initial conditions in which we find ourselves always constrain the path that lies ahead and determine the trajectory of our lives no matter what we may wish for ourselves.

Mutative factors in the therapeutic process

The psychoanalytic literature records a long history on the issue of how the therapeutic process brings about changes in patients (Fosshage, 2013; cf. Boston Change Process Study Group, 2010). Ever since Strachey's (1934) landmark paper, "The Nature of Therapeutic Action of Psycho-Analysis," contributors to the literature on the therapeutic effects of psychoanalysis have struggled with the question of how a therapist's interventions lead to changes in a patient's psychic organization. The term *mutative factor* has been use to describe the change agents that modify patients' psychodynamics.

Today, the field seems divided into those who believe that change comes about because of the *relationship* established between therapist and patient as well as the nonverbal affective interchanges that occur within that relationship (Bromberg, 2003, 2011, 2013; Fosshage, 2013; cf. Stern, 2004) and those who maintain that it comes about through *understanding and interpreting* the patient's psychodynamics (Goldberg, 2015; Kohut, 1984).[1] The problem with the first view is that it diminishes the place of understanding as a change agent, which for patients with neuropsychological deficits would leave them feeling that the sources of their difficulties were mysterious. The second view perpetuates the idea of linear causality of how change occurs (i.e. an interpretation provided by the therapist becomes a link in the causal chain that produces change). This view underplays the collaborative nature of the process.

I propose that we need to take what is of value from both positions, incorporating them into the reconceptualization of the therapeutic process. Furthermore, we must supplement both positions with a third, which is the proactive engagement of patients in their quest for change. As active collaborators in the therapeutic process, patients, by exercising their sense of agency, become empowered to undertake changes in their lives.

However, from a dynamic systems perspective, an important caveat is that psychological changes derive from complex sources. Understanding, interpretations, and relationships are among many other factors to which people usually respond. One way to define the effect that we have on patients is that we act as catalysts that activate our patients' motives to bring about changes in themselves. What we say or do are not the only sources of the changes that patients make; patients use what we offer in conjunction with other factors to make changes in how they feel, think, or act.

As therapists, we have to balance what we believe to be our influence on our patients and their own activities in their determination to bring about changes in their lives. I suggest that one way to achieve such a balance, which is consistent with a systems approach, is to shift away from a heliocentric view of the therapist as the center of the patient's world (Fosshage, 2013). We should approach our role as agents of change with some humility.

In line with this approach, I suggest that an essential constituent of any complex adaptive system is the communication that occurs between its components. When applied to the therapeutic context, we may talk about this system of communication between therapists and patients as the *therapeutic dialogue*. This dialogue occurs through multiple channels: verbal, nonverbal, and affective. At the verbal level, the members of the dyad often process cognitively the content of that dialogue at a conscious level. While the exchanges take place verbally and are processed consciously, these are always accompanied by affect states that color the interactions. At the nonverbal level, the content is disclosed nonconsciously through vocal intonations, facial expressions, gestures, body language, and other forms of paralinguistic expressions. The channel through which we conduct the dialogue varies with the patient's age, verbal ability, personality style, and other factors. For younger patients, it may consist of activities such as fantasy play or drawings (Levy, 2008); for adults, it may consist of verbal exchanges, dreams, or even silence.

Within the narrow confines of the therapeutic dialogue that occurs in the clinical setting, I turn to a discussion of three sets of processes that constitute change agents: the relationship, the search for complementarity, and the patient's proactive engagement in the process. In Chapter 10, "The Therapeutic Dialogue: Disjunctive Moments," I discuss the possibility that the rupture and repair sequence may also turn into a change agent.

The relationship as a change agent

The question we ask in connection with the relationship between patient and therapist as a change agent is: What is it about the therapeutic encounter that permits patients' relational patterns to change? As we have seen, relational patterns and attachment styles are encoded in procedural memory, which are nonconscious. The patterns may have been acquired in early childhood or may have evolved and been amended at later points during the person's development. In any case, they may be reproduced in other relationships. From a dynamic system's point of view, the self-similarity that we encounter in the transference and patients' relational patterns is a function of that encoding.

The relationship between therapists and patients then becomes a space for patients to have a different set of experiences from those they have had in their past. Through the relationship, the therapeutic process *engages patients in an experience* in which they can relive an old pattern of interaction and create a new pattern in which feelings are deeply engaged and made more meaningful (Shane, Shane, & Gales, 1997). One way to conceptualize this process is to think of the system's openness as a condition for its readiness to change. A closed system is incapable of learning from experience; its ability to utilize the feedback that the recognition process provides is limited, and therefore its adaptability is impaired.

This aspect of the dialogue becomes a silent change agent that permits patients to use their experiences to reorganize their view of themselves around different themes and scripts than those they previously held. This reorganization may occur nonconsciously, resulting in emergent patterns of greater self-cohesion and complexity. The nonverbal dimensions of the interchanges contribute to the change process and complement the verbal dimension of that process (Amore, 2012; Levy, 2008, 2011).

The search for complementarity

Illustrative of the change agents that are activated during complementary moments, I have selected two sets of processes that were discussed earlier: the preference for self-cohesion and that of self-understanding. Since the attainment of both these sets of experiences in patients involves a collaborative effort with therapists, I focus in both instances on the dimension of the transference and countertransference as the vehicle through which a resolution of the issues brought forth occurs (see Aron, 1996, on mutuality).

The restoration of self-cohesion

For patients, the attainment of restoration of self-cohesion involves the working through of the emotional turmoil that the self-deficits have caused. This includes dealing with the shame or humiliation they experienced, their rage at the unjustified criticisms directed at them, their flight or withdrawal from situations that would have potentially revealed their perceived "incompetence." The problematic place of interpretations made by therapists requires serious examination. Traditionally, interpretations were considered to provide patients with insight into the unconscious or nonconscious aspect of their mental functioning and to identify their defenses and help them understand the functions those serve in dealing with the psychic pain and anxieties the feeling engendered. Perhaps a better way to conceptualize the process is that the dialogue is a joint voyage of discovery through which both therapists and patients undertake the exploration of the territory that constitutes the patients' mental organization. Through the healing that occurs during that process, patients may regain the lost sense of self-cohesion.

The co-created narrative

Central to the development of the patient's self-reflective capacities and self-understanding is the co-creation of a coherent narrative. From a dynamic systems perspective, such an understanding must include the nature and place of the neuropsychological deficits in the formation of the patient's personality. Without the validation of these self-deficits as contributors to the patient's difficulties, a critical component would be missing. Explanations given by the therapist may facilitate the process of self-understanding by permitting patients to clearly identify the types and sources of their self-deficits, whether of selfobject, adjunctive functions, or those related to the interconnectedness to others, and allowing them to begin to think about the effects these have had on their lives. The insights that these explanations provide give patients a comprehensive picture of what occurred and are vital to the healing process.

The formulation of a patient's psychodynamics by a therapist may be similar to the construction of a narrative that incorporates themes from the three levels of analysis. In a manner of speaking, we can say that those formulations constitute the therapist's narrative. I propose that from a narrative perspective, we view what it means to make an interpretation as a comment that facilitates the co-construction of a narrative that furthers the shared understanding that therapists and patients have of issues activated in the transference/countertransference interchanges.

The narratives that therapists use to formulate the patients' dynamics differ from those that patients have put together. Therapists find different or deeper meanings to the events than patients thought existed. Informed therapists have explanations for the patients' distress and experiences that the patients lacked. The therapeutic dialogue permits patients to reorganize their self-narratives by integrating the new information gained through the process. As Bromberg (2011) noted:

> Psychoanalysis must provide an experience that is *perceived* different from the patient's narrative memory. . . . The patient's old narrative frame is expanded by providing an interpersonal experience that for all its familiarity is perceptibly different. Enactment is the primary

perceptual medium that allows this kind of change to take place. Expanded, *consensually validated narratives containing events and experiences of self/other configurations formerly excluded begin to be constructed because these events and experiences* . . . are not simply a new way of understanding the past but entail a new symbolization of perceptual reality.

(p. 162, italics added)

The outcome hoped for is that along with the modification of the patient's self-narrative, the dyad arrives at the co-construction of a more coherent narrative, which integrates the patient's narrative with that of the therapist. Such an outcome would also enhance the patients' capacity for self-cohesion, helping them understand their strengths and weaknesses and what happened to them historically.

The patients' proactive activities as change agents

A stated earlier, from a dynamic systems perspective, psychological changes derive from complex sources. Interpretations and relationships are only one among many other factors to which people usually respond. An additional factor that contributes to a successful outcome of the therapeutic process is patients' capacity for self-initiation and their ability proactively to bring about changes in their lives. As previously discussed, for Sander (Amadei and Bianchi, 2008), the sense of agency appears as an emergent property. Agency is the product of the child's experience of the caregiver's recognition of its needs, which heightens the child's awareness of its capacity to affect the world that it inhabits. It is to that sense of agency that I refer in this discussion of patients' proactive initiation of alterations in their daily lives that they undertake on their own behalf. When patients take an active stance in relation to finding solutions to their difficulties, they feel empowered to overcome the adversities that they face. Their capacity for self-reflection may enhance their understanding and serve as a catalyst to change.

An integral part of this approach is that patients receive remediation for their self-deficits, much as patients who have suffered a major injury must go through a rehabilitative process to recover lost functions. Therefore, there is a *rehabilitative component* to the restoration of the self in patients with self-deficits. It involves the remediation of the self-deficits through the acquisition of new skills or other forms of intervention. I suggest that much as patients with traumatic brain injuries require physical rehabilitation to regain some of their former levels of functioning, so do patients with neuropsychological deficits (L. Miller, 1991, 1992). In the case of the latter, therapists direct their interventions to the realm of their adjunctive deficits rather than to the physical realm.

Since most therapists are not equipped to provide the types of instruction that these patients often require, a referral to appropriate specialists, such as occupational therapists, speech and language therapists, educational therapists, or other specialists ought to be made. For example, speech and language therapists may remediate a phonological processing deficit through specialized programs; occupational therapists can help individuals with sensory motor deficits; group therapy can assist individuals with social skills deficits; psychiatrists may prescribe medication for individuals with ADHD. As Van Der Kolk (2014) suggested for patients with PTSD, modalities such as dance, music, theater, and athletic activities can have beneficial effects in healing the dissociative defenses that the trauma produced.

Other interventions consist of helping patients acquire practical ways of dealing with their adjunctive self-deficits. Examples are the outright avoidance of tasks that depend on those skills for their successful completion, compensatory activities that permit the patients to accomplish tasks by using alternative means, or remediation that permits strengthening areas of weakness. The challenge that therapists confront is the extent and form their interventions must take in helping patients to deal with these adjunctive deficits. Some of these interventions require therapists to give their patients specific forms of instruction based on their knowledge of those types of neuropsychological deficits. Some are educational or didactic directives that inform patients of their limitations or of available resources. The outcome hoped for is that, by feeling empowered, the interventions will diminish the patients' feelings of shame, will enhance their self-esteem, and will permit them to accommodate more successfully to their context than they could previously.

The question of timing, however, is dependent on the patients' readiness to accept such offers. At times, this kind of supplemental support may have to be postponed until the patient is sufficiently settled emotionally to begin to learn. There are times when some preparatory work is necessary before patients can accept the fact that they would benefit from such help and are ready for a referral. In such instances, therapists must be prepared to demonstrate to their patients the usefulness of undertaking such work. This entails having sufficient knowledge of the types of interventions the patients require so that the therapists may illustrate the gains made by working with such specialists. I discuss the specific complication that this modification in technique produces in Chapter 9 on complementary moments.

Some patients find ways of compensating for their self-deficits in creative and unpredictable ways. Without interpretation or prompting, some will discover a talent or skill that begins to provide ways of compensating for their deficits. In those cases, the outcome may be just as successful. Eventually, success obtained through compensatory activities may lead to renewed efforts in the performance of challenging tasks. The old aversive reactions to those situations may give way to efforts at mastery.

The therapeutic dialogue as moments

As stated earlier, from its inception, the encounter between the therapist and the patient constitutes a new complex adaptive system. Applying an evolutionary viewpoint, we can conceive of this system as subject to all of the principles that guide the processes within it. These processes include the capacity for self-organization, development, and evolution (Miller & Sammons, 1999). The therapeutic process does not proceed in a linear fashion; it unfolds in a meandering and unpredictable manner. Through mindsharing and the creation of a holding environment, patients engage in the process expecting therapists to address their expectation for complementary responses. From a dynamic perspective, the process begins with a set of initial conditions that the diversity of the components of the system (i.e. the patient's neuropsychological strengths and weaknesses) in part define. To these initial conditions, we must add those that exist in the therapist, which while structurally mirroring the mental functions of the patient, in many respects are different from the patient's.

Conceptualizing the therapeutic dialogue as paralleling the developmental dialogue is in some respects accurate, but in other respects, it does not account for the multiplicity of factors that contribute to the maturational process. From a developmental perspective, there are similarities between some of the patterns that contribute to the initial presentation and those that emerge in the enactments of old patterns in the transference. However, much has happened to the patient during the intervening years since their childhood experiences structured their psychological makeup. Our assessment of the initial conditions in the present differs from those that existed earlier. Whether we think of a 9-year-old or a 49-year-old, as a complex adaptive system, the variables that contributed to the dynamics have deflected the developmental path in many ways. The current formulation must take into account the added factors.

The task then is to integrate the available data with what we know about development and psychopathology into a meaningful therapeutic dialogue. The efforts at integration are directed at enriching the explanatory powers of the therapists' understanding of their patients' problems and enhancing the possibility of a successful outcome to treatment.

A useful way to conceptualize the flow of the dialogue is to think of the process as producing changes in patients that reflect the system's self-organizing properties. The outcome that one hopes for is for the patients' sense of self to attain greater openness, greater stability, greater self-understanding, greater capacity for flexible relatedness, and a resumption of the maturational process. To these, Sander (2002) adds the outcome for increased coherence of organization of consciousness and changes in awareness of the patient's sense of self as agent. Through the exchanges with the therapist, patients can transform rigidly closed systems of self-organized attractors into more open, more complex systems that enhance their sense of agency and their ability to become more differentiated from others, which would permit them to achieve a greater level of complexity. Keep in mind that the changes are not confined to the patient alone, as the increased complexity of the system is important (i.e. the dyad produces changes in each member), which of course means that therapists are also the beneficiaries of those changes.

In contrast to the linear view of the therapeutic process as unfolding sequentially with a beginning, a middle, and a termination phase, and consistent with the dialogical nature of the process, I conceptualize *the treatment process of patients with neuropsychological deficits as a series of moments*. We may deconstruct the therapeutic dialogue as a series of moments during which nodal occurrences are in the foreground of the interaction (cf. Pine, 1985).

Moments in therapy are organizing events that capture the essence of the issues with which the patient is struggling at a given time during the process. Moments are activated when specific types of exchanges in the process between the therapist and patient are in the foreground of the interaction. By foreground, I mean periods during which the ebb and flow of the process is focused on a set of patterns that emerges in the transference. These moments are short units of time during which something important is happening (contrast with the concept of moments as used by the Boston Change Process Study Group, 2010). They produce emergent properties characteristic of a complex, dynamic system and represent nonlinear leaps in the process. Such moments activate mindsharing responses by the therapist – that is, they evoke empathy or the desire to complement the patient's deficits.

These moments do not necessarily occur sequentially but arise episodically; they become organizing events that capture the essence of the issues with which the therapist and patient are struggling. As such, they present opportunities for the therapist to intervene through supportive statements, interpretations, or other interventions. I conceptualize three types of moments: *concordant moments*, *complementary moments*, and *disjunctive moments* (cf. Racker, 1968, 1972)

Concordant moments

Concordant moments involve the therapist's immersion in the patient's experience through empathy and the creation and maintenance of a holding environment. The processes of *recognition* and *fitting in* are applicable to these moments as each member of the dyad attempts to explore the dimensions of the relationship. The patient brings to the setting what Anna Ornstein (1984) called the "curative fantasy," while the therapist brings what Spitz (1959) described as the "diatrophic attitude." Once a concordance is established between these two sets of experiences, the process moves on to the initial conditions that will begin to determine the direction of the flow of the dialogue. Such moments provide the bedrock on which the ongoing therapeutic work will take place.

The therapeutic dimension of concordant moments lies *in patients' experience of the relationship with the therapist*. I believe that we may subsume such moments under the types of experiences to which Lyons-Ruth (1998) refers as "implicit relational knowing." The therapist becomes attuned and resonates with what the patient brings to the session. By attending to what therapists see and hear, they listen to the feelings and associations that are evoked. The therapist's empathy provides an experience that is affirming and reinforcing to a patient that may lead to a spontaneous resumption of growth through the integration of experiences that may have remained dissociated from the rest of the person's life. The wounds of the past may be healed, compensated for, or simply set aside. The person can then go on to resume a life that is both full and productive. The essential component in this experience is the comfort derived by patients from having been able to share what was private and what they may never have exposed to anyone. The dominant change agent during such moments is the relationship. It is in this sense that we may say that the relationship, without the necessity for an interpretation of the patient's dysfunctional patterns, becomes a change agent.

An additional set of interactions in which patient and therapist engage during these moments is the empowerment of the *patient to take charge proactively* of the recovery process. Once that occurs, a therapeutic alliance carries the prospect of moving the process forward. As stated earlier, this rehabilitative process includes the development of skills to compensate for the self-deficits and the enhancement of the ability to advocate for accommodations. Patients may become free to act as centers of initiative or self-initiating agents. They will have moved up the hierarchy of self-organized complexity that will allow them to accommodate more successfully to the demands that they face. Such moments lead to more complex modes of integration, greater differentiation, and individuation, and therefore an enhanced sense of agency, than existed prior to the onset of therapy.

Complementary moments

Complementary moments are episodes that occur when the transference/countertransference dimension occupies the foreground of the dialogue. Two facets of this dimension emerge for explorations and for understanding through interpretations: the system's preference for self-cohesion, and the efforts directed at the co-constructions of a coherent self-narrative.

During complementary moments, the therapeutic dialogue also engages the patient's capacity for self-reflection. It explores the possibility that these exchanges will lead to the capacity for a reorganization of patterns of expectations. Patients thirst for stability and continuity within their context. Their capacity for self-reflection may enhance their understanding and serve as a catalyst to change. If the process produces changes in the patient's psychic organization, then the hoped-for outcome is greater openness, great stability, greater self-understanding, and greater capacity for flexible relatedness than previously existed. These processes lead to the emergence of a self as a complex adaptive system that is more hierarchically structured, more complex, and more capable of successfully accommodating to the demands placed on it. Although, as stated earlier, the process unfolds in a meandering and unpredictable manner in which a set of ruptures and repairs produce an initial disorganization in patients that will permit a reorganization of their patterns of expectations.

An important caveat is that not all patients who seek therapy are interested in becoming more self-reflective or in attaining a deep self-understanding of their condition. Some only seek symptom relief and are satisfied with the results obtained from the relationship with the therapist. For those patients, the therapeutic dialogue centers on concordant moments and on the repair of whatever disjunctions may occur. The co-construction of a coherent self-narrative appears to be unnecessary.

Disjunctive moments

Disjunctive moments involve the disruption of mindsharing; an interruption occurs in the dialogue. This is the process that Beebe and Lachmann (2002, 2014) and Schore (2003) called the "disruption and repair sequence." The disruption may be due to factors related to the therapist or the patient. When such a disjunction occurs, the treatment is in crisis, and it is then essential that the therapist heal the rupture and reestablish the concordance between herself and the patient. In such moments, the therapeutic process engages both patient and therapist at the deepest levels of their senses of self. Countertransference reactions that stem from the therapist's own problems are subsumed under disjunctions; however, the concept is meant to include a much broader set of contributors to the disruptions that occur between patient and therapist. A possible outcome of the rupture and repair sequence is that a new configuration in the relationship between patients and therapists emerges that permits the patients to accommodate more successfully to their context.

Termination

The readiness to terminate comes as a logical conclusion to the dialogue. From the patient's perspective is the hope that the process has transformed his rigid and closed psychodynamics into a system that is more complex and more open than previously existed. The therapeutic process has helped the movement from simple to complex, from lesser to greater differentiation, and will lead to the emergence of new patterns of relating and enhance the patient's differentiation from others and affirm his individuality.

The patient then feels ready to go on with life in a joyous optimistic mood. The future is ahead, and the road to further self-discovery, self-fulfillment, and achievement is open. One can then speak of a termination that the patient experiences as a triumph, rather than as the mournful loss of her symptoms. The relationship has served to open the channel to the future rather than merely set aside the past (J. Palombo, 1982).

We may identify several indicators that presage the readiness of the termination of therapy. Among these is a new level of stability and self-cohesion that reflects a more complex degree of self-organization. Patients experience themselves as less prone to the repetition of old patterns and are more aware of the sources of these patterns, which help them to differentiate themselves for others and from their past. They experience a heightened sense of uniqueness even as they realize that their reliance on others and their interconnectedness to others is an essential aspect of their humanity. However, the self-deficits may still be present, but the patients' accommodations permit them to be more successful in the achievement of their goals than it was possible for them in the past.

If the therapy has been meaningful to the patient, then for the therapist a small bit of history has been lived out and shared. The therapist has gained in having succeeded in helping someone. Patients gain both in knowledge and in wisdom that come from having participated and shared in a meaningful relationship.

Summary

Most patients with neuropsychological deficits come to therapy seeking relief from anxieties or discomforts they feel are due to the threats to their self-cohesion or to their inability to solve life problems they face. Their anxiety reflects their destabilized sense of self. For these patients, their self-deficits in interaction with the context and their subjective interpretation of what they experience result in an unstable sense of self. However, those self-deficits are embedded within the patient's larger psychodynamics. The psychodynamics include the unsuccessful accommodations they made in trying to prevail over the adversities that they face. They also include the overlay of defenses that they instituted to deal with the psychic pain they endured. Added to those are the attachment style and the relational patterns that were encoded in procedural memory.

From the moment of their first encounter, the therapist and patient constitute a new complex adaptive system. As Stanley Palombo (2007) stated, "The patient and the analyst are components of a therapeutic ecosystems" (p. 1). As we have seen, a set of principles guides the processes within every system. These include their initial conditions, their preferences or biases, and their capacity for self-organization and for the development of emergent properties. The neuropsychodynamic perspective of individual psychotherapy applies this systems perspective to the therapeutic process and enlarges upon the manner in which these principles organize the process.

In conceptualizing the restoration and healing the self, we confront a challenge that involves the modifications in the way we thought about the therapeutic process in treating patients with a neuropsychological deficit. To heal is to restore the system's capacity to accommodate successfully to the circumstances in which patients find themselves (see Jaenicke, 2013). Therefore, one way to conceptualize the flow of the therapeutic dialogue is to think of the process as producing changes in the patients' psychic organization that reflects the system's self-organizing properties.

I proposed three types of activities that define the mutative factors of the therapeutic process. These are the relationship between the therapist and patient, the search for complementarity, and the patient's proactive activities. Each of these constitutes what I call *change agents* that are essential constituents of the therapeutic process. In brief, the relationship offers patients an opportunity to experience something new and different from what they anticipate from others. These new experiences may serve to reorganize their expectations and undo the attractors around which former unsuccessful accommodations were shaped. No interpretations of these patterns need occur to achieve a positive outcome.

The second type of interchange addresses the patient's subjective experience of self-deficits. Through the transference and countertransference exchanges, the patient's sense of self-cohesion is restored. This includes, through the co-creation of a narrative, the enhancement of the patient's self-understanding of the nature of the neuropsychological dysfunctions and the impact these have had on her life. Part of that impact includes the shame and humiliation they experienced when confronted by situations that require their performance of tasks for which they did not have the requisite skills. Furthermore, defenses such as disavowal and dissociation helped to mitigate the psychic pain that accompanied those experiences but brought with them their own set of problems.

The third type of activity consisted in empowering patients to engage actively in the process of bringing about changes in their lives. These activities included advocating for the provision of accommodations that would diminish the impact of their self-deficits, learning new skills that might compensate for their self-deficits, and avoiding placing themselves in situations in which they would inevitably confront failures.

I conceptualize the treatment process of patients as a collaborative effort that occurs as a series of moments. Moments in therapy are organizing events that capture the essence of the issues with which the patient is struggling at a given time during the process. These moments do not necessarily arrive sequentially but occur episodically. Moments are activated when specific types of exchanges in the process between the therapist and patient are in the foreground of the interaction. By foreground, I mean periods during which the ebb and flow of the process focuses on a set of patterns that emerge in the transference. Such moments activate mindsharing responses by the therapist – that is, they evoke empathy or the desire to complement the patient's deficits. I conceptualize three types of moments: concordant moments, complementary moments, and disjunctive moments.

Finally, attempting to develop a model technique, which is applicable to most cases, is not advisable and is contrary to the nonlinear dynamic systems view that I advocate in this work. Such a technique would stultify the creative nature of the process and of the engagement in the dialogue. The fluidity of the ebb and flow of the engagement is fundamental to this approach. This means that few rules are inviolable and few techniques are beyond challenge under certain circumstances. For beginners, for whom direction is necessary, reading about such an approach may seem to say that anything the therapist does is acceptable. This would be a deep misunderstanding of the intent of this approach. The ease with which the outcome is achieved comes through much practice and discipline. What seems simplest and easiest for the experienced and talented therapist comes about as a result of long struggles at self-understanding and at understanding others.

Note

1 I leave out of consideration as change agent processes such as "mentalization" (Fonagy & Bateman, 2006; Fonagy & Target, 1998) and "mindfulness" (Siegel, 2007, 2012, 2013), which require separate treatment.

References

Amore, M. (2012). Clinical scenarios of "remembering": Somatic states as a process of emerging memory. *Psychoanalytic Dialogues, 22*, 238–252.

Aron, L. (1996). *A meeting of minds: Mutuality in psychoanalysis*. New York: Routledge.

Beebe, B., & Lachmann, F. M. (2002). *Infant research and adult treatment: Co-constructing interactions*. Mahwah, NJ: The Analytic Press.

Beebe, B., & Lachmann, F. M. (2014). *The origins of attachment: Infant research and adult treatment*. New York: Routledge.

Boston Change Process Study Group. (2010). *Change in psychotherapy: A unifying paradigm*. New York: W. W. Norton.

Bromberg, P. M. (2003). Something wicked this way comes: Trauma, dissociation, an conflict: The space where psychoanalysis, cognitive science, and neuroscience overlap. *Psychoanalytic Psychology, 20*, 558–574.

Bromberg, P. M. (2011). *The shadow of the tsunami and the growth of the relational mind*. New York: Routledge.

Bromberg, P. M. (2013). An interview with Phililp M. Bromberg, Ph.D. *Contemporary Psychoanalysis, 49*(3), 323–354.

Fonagy, P., & Bateman, A. W. (2006). Mechanisms of change in mentalization-based treatment of BPD. *Journal of Clinical Psychology, 62*(4), 411–430.

Fonagy, P., & Target, M. (1998). Mentalization and the changing aims of child psychoanalysis. *Psychoanalytic Dialogues, 8*(1), 97–114.

Fosshage, J. L. (2013). Forming and transforming self-experience. *International Journal of Psychoanalytic Self Psychology, 8*, 437–451.

Goldberg, A. (2015). *The brain, the mind and the self: A psychoanalytic road map*. New York: Routledge.

Jaenicke, C. (2013). When the bell tolls: A systems view of cure. *International Journal of Psychoanalytic Self Psychology, 8*, 245–264.

Kohut, H. (1984). *How does analysis cure?* Chicago: The University of Chicago Press.

Levy, A. J. (2008). The therapeutic action of play in the psychodynamic treatment of children: A critical analysis. *Clinical Social Work Journal, 36*, 281–291.

Levy, A. J. (2011). Neurobiology and the therapeutic action of psychoanalytic play therapy with children. *Clinical Social Work Journal, 39,* 50–60.

Lyons-Ruth, K. (1998). Implicit relational knowing: Its role in development and psychoanalytic treatment. *Infant Mental Health Journal, 19*(3), 282–289.

Miller, L. (1991). Psychotherapy of the brain-injured patient: Principles and practices. *The Journal of Cognitive Rehabilitation, 9*(2), 24–30.

Miller, L. (1992). Cognitive rehabilitation, cognitive therapy, and cognitive style: Toward an integrative model of personality and psychotherapy. *The Journal of Cognitive Rehabilitation, 1*(2), 18–29.

Miller, N. B., & Sammons, C. C. (1999). *Everybody's different: Understanding and changing our reactions to disabilities.* Baltimore, MD: Paul H. Brookes Publishing Co.

Ornstein, A. (1984). Psychoanalytic psychotherapy: A contemporary perspetive. In P. E. Stepansky & A. Goldberg (Eds.), *Kohut's legacy: Contributions to self psychology* (pp. 171–181). Hillsdale, NJ: The Analytic Press.

Palombo, J. (2008). Mindsharing: Transitional Objects and Selfobjects as Complementary Functions. Clinical Social Work Journal, 36, 143–154.

Palombo, J. (1982). The psychology of the self and the termination of treatment. *Clinical Social Work Journal, 10*(1), 15–27.

Palombo, J. (2013a). The self as a complex adaptive system, part I: Complexity, metapsychology, and developmental theories. *Psychoanalytic Social Work, 20*(1), 1–25.

Palombo, J. (2013b). The self as a complex adaptive system, part II: Levels of analysis and the position of the observer. *Psychoanalytic Social Work, 20*(2), 115–133.

Palombo, S. R. (2007). Complexity theory as the parent science of psychoanalysis. In C. Piers, J. P. Muller, & J. Brent (Eds.), *Self-organizing complexity is psychological systems* (pp. 1–14). New York: Jason Aronson.

Pine, F. (1985). *Developmental theory and clinical practice.* New Haven, CT: Yale University Press.

Racker, H. (1968). *Transference and countertransference.* New York: International Universities Press.

Racker, H. (1972). The meaning and uses of countertransference. *Psychoanalytic Quarterly, 41,* 487–506.

Salk, J. (1983). *Anatomy of reality: Merging of intuition in recent.* New York: Columbia University Press.

Sander, L. W. (2002). Thinking differently: Principles of process in living systems and the specificy of being known. *Psychoanalytic Dialogues, 12,* 11–42.

Amadei, G., & Bianchi, I. (Eds.). (2008). *Living systems, evolving consicousness, and the emerging person: A selection of papers from the life and work of Louis Sander.* New York: The Analytic Press.

Schore, A. N. (2003). *Affect regulation and the repair of the self.* New York: W. W. Norton.

Shane, M., Shane, E., & Gales, M. (1997). *Intimate attachments: Toward a new self psychology.* New York: Guilford Press.

Siegel, D. J. (2013). Brainstorm: The power and purpose of the teenage brain. New York: Penguin Books.

Siegel, D. J. (2007). *The Mindful Brain: Reflection and Attunement in the Cultivation of Well-Being.* New York: W. W. Norton.

Siegel, D. J. (2012). Pocket guide to interpersonal neurobiology: An integrative handbook of the mind. New York: W. W. Norton.

Spitz, R. A. (1959). Countertransference – Comments on its varying role in the analytic situation. *Journal of the American Psychoanalytic Association, 4*, 256–265.
Stern, D. N. (2004). *The present moment in psychotherapy and everyday life.* New York: W. W. Norton.
Strachey, J. (1934). The nature of therapeutic action of psycho-analysis. *The International Journal of Psychoanalysis, 15*, 127–159.
Van Der Kolk, B. A. (2014). *The body keeps the score: Brain, mind, and body in the healing of trauma.* New York: Viking.

Chapter 8

The therapeutic dialogue
Concordant moments

During concordant moments, the initial conditions that the therapeutic dyad faces are in the forefront of the interactions. Both therapists and patients confront the diversity in the neuropsychological makeups, the stability or instability of the relationship, and its openness to change agents. The transference/countertransference provides the measure by which these elements may enhance or detract from the therapeutic process. As part of a system, each member of the dyad brings his own personality profile, history, and vulnerabilities. Consequently, we must view any outcome as a function of the dynamics that are activated in the interaction between therapist and patient rather than simply as a result of the contributions that one or the other makes to the process.

Anna Ornstein (1992, 1995) suggested the concept of "curative fantasy" to describe the hopes and expectations for relief of their distress that patients bring to the clinical setting. This "fantasy" is an expression of the patient's wish to regain a sense of self-cohesion and stability. It contains the seeds of the hoped-for responses for complementarity from the therapist. For their part, therapists direct their efforts in response to those expectations by creating an environment of safety and trust. Spitz (1959) suggested the term "diatrophic attitude" to describe that aspect of the therapist's countertransference. I interpret that to mean that therapists bring to the process an attitude of support and concern that is similar to that parents have for their child. I suggest that the curative fantasy and the diatrophic attitude come together as part of the process of fitting together during concordant moments.

At the beginning of a therapeutic encounter, neither the therapist nor the patient knows what lies ahead. The patient enters into the therapist's world much as a newborn enters into a family. From the therapist's perspective, the anticipation of what is to come sets a tone that the patient detects. From the patient's perspective, the anxiety as to how the therapist responds may either heighten or alleviate the patient's anxieties. If we think of the negotiations that a parent must undertake in getting to know her newborn infant as a model for what occurs during the early hours of the therapeutic encounter, we may then draw a parallel between the two sets of encounters. A family can welcome and/or be apprehensive about the arrival of a newborn into its midst. The mysteries of what lies ahead may intensify either set of feelings. Yet, what is critical is the acceptance and love that parents convey to their newborn.

I often think that as therapists, we carry with us in these first encounters an image – a nonconscious representation of the kind of infant our new patient will be. Will this be an easy to soothe and non-demanding infant? Will she be a special needs infant that will require the mobilization of many resources to attend to her needs? Furthermore, how will the entrance of this new being into our world affect our lives? By consistently maintaining a perspective from within the patient's experience, the therapist demonstrates a willingness to "fit in" with the patient's unique personality, much as a mother must fit in with her infant's unique constellation of temperamental traits. As Wallerstein (1995) maintained:

> The "rapport" [between analyst and patient] . . . elicits the patient's feelings of hope for (and expectation of) the diatrophic response . . . *a meeting of the patient's desire for cure with the analyst's professional commitment to cure*, setting up the anaclitic-diatrophic equation and creating the conditions that would make the new development and new beginning possible.
>
> (p. 293, italics added)

During concordant moments, then, each member of the dyad takes the measure of the other to learn how the other responds. Each becomes aware of anxieties that are generated by topics to which the patient is sensitive. Each tries to find a space in which a level of comfort exists and in which the relationship can unfold. Clinicians have traditionally classified those transactions as pertaining to the therapist's *empathy* for the patient, the creation and maintenance of a *holding environment* (Winnicott, 1987), and the fostering of a *therapeutic alliance* between patient and therapist (Brandchaft & Stolorow, 1990).

Patients will respond differently to those overtures. If patients experience a sense of safety and security in the relationship, then the conditions are set for the possibility of the emergence of feelings that patients associate with their missing functions. Their selfobject and adjunctive deficits emerge as longing for responses that would mitigate their effects and the psychic pain associated with them. Although therapists can create the conditions of safety and provide the understanding that patients require, concordant moments cannot occur until patients can actively engage in the process. The therapeutic alliance is established when both the therapist and the patient, as a functional system, join in the task. Another way to describe this process from a neurobiological perspective is to say that the therapeutic encounter activates the social engagement system that Porges (2004) describes:

> Social engagement and defense behaviors may be adaptive or maladaptive, depending on the level of risk that is present in the environment. From a clinical perspective, the defining features of psychopathology may include either a person's inability to inhibit defense systems in a safe environment or the inability to activate defense systems in a risky environment – or both. Only in a safe environment is it adaptive and appropriate to simultaneously inhibit defense systems and exhibit positive social engagement behavior.
>
> (p. 19)

The initial setting of the therapeutic dialogue

During concordant moments the process that preoccupies both therapists and patients centers around the activation of hope and the diatrophic responses; however, the content of those moments addresses the initial conditions of the system. Among these conditions are the diversity of the patients' neuropsychological deficits, the stability or instability of the patients' sense of self, and their capacity to benefit from change agents – that is, whether as complex adaptive systems they are open or closed to change.

The medium through which many of the transactions are conducted during concordant moments is primarily nonverbal, since during such moments, the primary change agent is the relationship. Nonverbal modes are most often the vehicles through which affects are expressed. All too often, we misinterpret the meaning of a communication because of our desire to articulate verbally what the patient seeks to express. Such misunderstandings can only lead to the derailment of the dialogue. To insist that during these moments patients grasp verbally the essence of the dialogue in which they are engaged is like asking that a person to learn a foreign language before they have mastered their native tongue. As therapeutic interventions, nonverbal communications may serve to formulate a new meaning for an experience or to place an event in a context that is different from that conceived by the patient. These types of interventions provide reinforcement of the presence of the therapist as someone who has shared the experience with the patient (Lyons-Ruth, 1998; Stern, 1998; Tronick, 1998).

The dialogue between therapists and patients initiates a process during which self-organization is determined by the attractors and the preferences that are embedded in each member of the therapeutic dyad. Furthermore, the strains that the relationship places on the intersubjective dyad will buffet its participants. This process will lead the system to lurch from stability to instability and back to stability. As the process unfolds and the communicative exchanges become change agents, the possibility for self-reorganization emerges, although not always necessarily to more hierarchically complex levels. Regressions can occur that may lead to the erosion of current levels of functioning or to fragmentation. This instability may approach what we may call the edge of chaos, a period when outcomes are unpredictable because of the uncertainty introduced by the attractors, the initial conditions, the specific fit between the therapist and patient, and other factors that influence the unfolding process (see Harris, 2011).

The therapeutic relationship that evolves during concordant moments may now be defined as the experiences that result from the dialogue in which the interplay between the transference and countertransference are emergent properties of the interaction between patients and therapists. For patients, within the transference, the dialogue reflects the hope of attaining a stable sense of self-cohesion and self-continuity and the achievement of a measure of self-understanding that permits the tolerance of intense affective experiences. It is possible to say that the relationship becomes a form of "being with" another that diminishes the patient's sense of aloneness and loneliness. For the therapist, attunement and empathy lead to a deepened understanding of the patient. The countertransference mirrors the transference as the intense feeling evoked in both patient and therapist provide therapists with the evidence of the patient's self-deficits and of the devastating effects those have had on the patient's life.

The diversity in patients' neuropsychological deficits

An important consideration in the establishment of concordant moments relates to the information the therapist finds necessary to understand the patient fully. For therapists to understand their patients' experience, they not only must become immersed in the patient's subjectivity but also must place that subjectivity within the context of the factors that give rise to it. Knowing that a patient feels distressed provides only part of the information that is necessary to understand the patient in depth. Basch (1995) noted:

> The more I know about how we are designed to function – what neurophysiology, infant research, affect theory, cognitive psychology, semantics, information theory, evolutionary biology, and other pertinent disciplines can tell me about human development – the better I am prepared to be empathic with a patient's communication at a particular time in his or her treatment.
>
> (p. 372)

Therapists may arrive at a statement of the patients' psychodynamics through different paths. Child and adolescent therapists often receive reams of information, such as neurological, neuropsychological, social work, and teachers' reports, prior to seeing the patient. These reports are often helpful in identifying the diverse non-discreet variables, such as innate givens or social conditions that the therapist will confront. However, there is a danger that such reports may also bias and skew the therapist's view of the patient, setting up expectations that the therapist cannot meet.

In this sense, the relationship is not symmetrical (see Aron, 1996). What the therapist brings to the process is different from that brought by a nonprofessional to a relationship. Continuing with our analogy, much as a mother has greater awareness of her infant's requirements than does the infant, so does the therapist, who is conscious of and reflects on the patient's request for assistance as a demand to which she must respond. Therapists bring to the relationship a body of knowledge, a sensibility, and a diatrophic attitude.

Profound empathy for the patient requires the therapist to be thoroughly acquainted with the details of the patient's neuropsychological profile as obtained through a comprehensive neuropsychological assessment. This knowledge of the patient's neuropsychological strengths and weaknesses will provide a context for understanding the patient's subjective experience and his responses and interactions with the therapist. The uniqueness of the patient's profile will individualize the patient's experiences and responses. It would provide insights into the patient's stability or instability, sense of self-cohesion, and capacity to enter the therapeutic dialogue. Finally, the self-narrative that patients narrate will demonstrate the extent to which their self-understanding includes their realization that their self-deficits contributed to the accommodations they had made to circumstances during their lifetime. Geist (2013) best articulated the issue when he stated:

> During every analytic session, the empathic process exerts both a general healing effect and more specific curative influences. In a general way, mutual empathic processes encourage patient and analyst to search out and understand each other's subjective world, catalyzing what I have described as an evolving connectedness between members of the analytic couple.
>
> (p. 268)

When considering the diversity of the components that contribute to the initial conditions, attempting to identify which of the components – the neuropsychological deficits, the unstable sense of self-cohesion, or the dysfunctional patterns of interpersonal relationships – is primary in its contribution to the patient's unsuccessful accommodation presents therapists with serious challenges. Whereas the contributions of neuropsychological deficits are more easily identified in children and adolescents, by the time patients reach young adulthood, the components are so entangled that any attempt to separate their contribution appears bound to fail.

The dynamic systems perspective leads us to conclude that attempts at identifying the root cause of the patient's problems are in fact fraught with difficulties. It is true that the more severe the neuropsychological deficit, the clearer the contribution made to the patient's emerging personality, as in the case of patients with autism. In such cases, there is little doubt as to the impact the deficit has on the patient's capacity to remain cohesive and to establish stable relationships. However, in instances of less severe deficits, factors other than the neuropsychological deficit may have made a larger contribution to the patient's difficulties.

Ultimately, we must rely on the unfolding transference for clues that would permit us to begin to unravel the Gordian knot of the factors the patient presents. Unraveling this knot involves attending to the affects that served as attractors in the organization of the patient's psychodynamics. As I indicated throughout this work, feelings of shame or beliefs of being a fraud have acted as primary motives in the formation of those attractors. The defenses brought to bear to deal with these intense feelings varied with the initial conditions.

Part of the problem that clinicians face in dealing with the issue of the identification of patients' neuropsychological deficits is that patients may experience the therapist's comments as injunctions that they need to face a "reality" that is painful and that they would rather avoid, the reality being that of the limitations imposed on the patient by the self-deficits. Clinical experience has taught therapists that such approaches are not only counterproductive but also lead patients to feel criticized, as though they should have known better or could have acted differently under the circumstances they faced. From the patients' point of view, their self-deficits were transparent to them. They often had no awareness as to the source of their difficulties. In their bewilderment, they often accept the judgments that others make of them as explanatory of their conduct. Although often overcome with embarrassment when having to perform a task for which they do not have the skills, they muddle through using a variety of strategies and defenses.

Stable or unstable sense of self

Another element to consider during concordant moments is whether the patient's sense of self is stable or unstable. A patient's stability or instability depends on the person's capacity to maintain a dependable state of self-cohesion. Since self-cohesion is always context-dependent, a patient's instability will be an indicator of a failure of complementarity (i.e. the loss of some important selfobject or adjunctive functions). During the early moments of the therapeutic encounter, therapists direct their efforts toward the identification of the self-deficits that are responsible for the instability and to the challenge of finding ways of responding that mitigate the patient's distress.

For patients with neuropsychological deficits, their neuropsychological strengths and deficits accentuate the movement from destabilization to restabilization of their sense of self-cohesion. Depending on the nature and severity of the deficits and of the context's responses to those deficits, the swings between stability and instability may be much greater than in patients without those deficits. They may be stable, having achieved an internal homoeostatic balance. However, they may also become unstable by virtue of the failures of the processes within them. Their stability or instability may also be due to their ability to respond to environmental inputs and to respond with feedback loops to those inputs. Their instability provides opportunities for change, such that further reorganization may take place and hierarchies may emerge. Their instability may also present a danger in that they may lapse into a closed state and become unresponsive to environmental inputs.

For some patients, the capacity for timely self-righting and the restoration of their inner balance is an indicator of the resilience of their self-systems. They learn from the injuries they suffer and gain an understanding that immunizes them from detrimental outcomes. Others seem to teeter between self-cohesion and fragmentation. As clinicians, we are familiar with narcissistic patients who are highly vulnerable to – and who respond to – minor injuries by feeling devastated. They seem "undone" by the insult to their sense of self. In such cases, we may usefully describe their reactions as a state of chaos that has invaded their psychological space. A different example is the effects of severe trauma on a person who then suffers from PTSD. The trauma is so disruptive of the person's psychological organization that instability becomes the prevalent mode of being. Chaos has invaded their lives.

In addition, the capacity for self-reflection – the extent to which patients can understand themselves – may contribute to the stability of their sense of self. The absence of self-understanding or the inability to make sense of one's life may be a powerful generator of instability. Some may be racked with self-doubts, others may be puzzled as to why they are the victims of circumstances, and others still may attribute their failures to reasons that have nothing to do with what actually caused the failure.

Within the therapeutic relationship, the stability or instability of the patient's sense of self is a dimension of the transference/countertransference interaction. The extent to which the therapist meets the patient's expectations, whether in actuality or as projections of the patient's desire for the missing functions, will determine whether a measure of stability will characterize the therapeutic encounter. What this means is that, at least in the clinical setting, the manner in which patients experience the process will determine their capacity to maintain their sense of self-cohesion. Periods of loss of self-cohesion during therapy will be interpreted as resulting from disruptions or disjunction in the process.

Open or closed to change agents

As complex adaptive systems, people may be *open* or *closed* to communications from others. Open systems that are responsive to input from the environment can change over time and can evolve. In such systems, at any given moment, component elements of the system interact or overlap with the processes of other components. These systems are dynamic systems in the sense that they are capable of internal modification to accommodate to external circumstances. As an open system, the self as a complex adaptive system is in continual communication with its component elements and with the environment. These communications affect the self-system as it lurches between stability and instability. From the dynamics that emerge, disorganization or self-organization may result. The disorganization may lead to chaos, in which case dysfunctional states may emerge as the system becomes closed in the face of the danger it faces. The system may then institute defenses to prevent its destabilization. Siegel (1999) aptly describes the brain's functions as a system:

> At the most basic level, the brain can be considered as a living system that is open and dynamic. *It is an integrated collection of component subsystems that interact together in a pattern and changing way to create an irreducible quality of the system as a whole.* The living system must be open to the influences of the environment in order to survive, and the brain is no exception. The system of the brain becomes functionally linked to other systems, especially to other brains. The brain is also dynamic, meaning it is forever in the state of change. An open, dynamic system is one that is in continual emergence with a changing environment and the changing state of its own activity.
>
> (pp. 16–17, italics in original)

If a system cannot absorb the inputs arising either internally or externally, or if its self-organizing capacities become constrained, then a different set of outcomes will follow than if it were an open system. The system may shut down and become resistant to any inputs; it becomes a *closed system*. At times, a closed system may achieve a level of stability that permits it to function adequately, although within limited confines (see Sroufe, 1995). Alternatively, some components may shut down while others continue to operate. Under these conditions, the system may continue to evolve provided no internal or external challenges emerge to strain the system beyond its capacity to operate. Some factors that organize patterns of experience can become sequestered and closed to input, making it impossible to be affected by a change agent.

In closed systems that are impermeable (i.e. where the channels of communication are seriously impaired or closed to inputs from the environment), patients may become isolated from others, particularly when a serious disruption occurs in their internal functioning or when they are under threat from elements in the environment. Such circumstances restrict the system's capacity for change and accommodation. In mental health terms, we may view a paranoid delusion as an example of a closed system that is not modifiable by external inputs. Schore (in Bromberg, 2011) refers to "pathological dissociation, [as] an enduring outcome of early relational trauma, is manifest in a maladaptive highly rigid, closed right brain system" (p. xxiii).

The behaviors of some patients with ADHD may be considered a closed system. Those behaviors are impermeable to modification, except perhaps through medication. Parts of those patients' personalities are unavailable to inputs from others because of past negative interactions with others who have been critical or punitive because of their disruptive behaviors. Furthermore, some may develop what has been labeled as an oppositional/defiant attitude because of their experiences of feeling misunderstood. On the other hand, for a child with dyslexia, the possibility of remediation would be available to mitigate the effects of the child's reading problems because the child may be receptive to the necessary tutorial help. The child's system is still open. However, a boy who feels ashamed of his disorder or who is vulnerable to narcissistic injury may refuse the intervention. His self-system has shut down, and therefore he is, for the time being, impermeable to change.

In past years, patients' inability to respond to change agents was interpreted as "resistance" – that is, they were considered to be in systems terms "closed systems." However, a more helpful characterization is that the system, in its present state, is incapable of changing. A dialogue is only possible if patients present as an "open system," capable of feeling safe enough to take in what the therapist has to offer both cognitively and affectively. Some patients, such as adolescents, whom well-intentioned parents bring to therapy, experience the encounter with the therapist as assaultive or shaming and refuse to participate. At times, they are brought because of a tragic family loss or school failure. In those circumstances, the adolescents' psychic pain is so unbearable that no amount of empathy or support can make it possible for them to expose how they feel. They experience any therapist's efforts at engaging them in a dialogue as a violation of their privacy. For this group of patients, therapists must postpone their therapeutic interventions to a time when they are more predisposed to participate. However, one should not rule out the possibility that with a different therapist or in a different context, such as family or group therapy, the same adolescent may be more willing to participate.

We may now view what psychoanalysis has traditionally called "resistances" as representing the fear of retraumatization. Aron (1996) credits Fairbairn for this conceptualization. Other sources may include unfamiliarity with the process, personal discomfort with the therapist's personality, concerns about costs, or other factors. Any or all of these contribute to the system's stability and consequently represent a threat at the prospect of changing. As Kohut (1984) stated:

> *Defense motivation in analysis will be understood in terms of activities undertaken in the service of psychological survival*, that is, as the patient's attempt to save at least that sector of his nuclear self, however small and precarious reestablish it may be, that he has been able to construct and maintain despite serious insufficiencies in the development-enhancing matrix of the selfobjects of childhood.
>
> (p. 115, italics added)

Most patients begin treatment with some initial hesitancies, which must be recognized and worked through. The fear of retraumatization often motivates these hesitancies. They are indicative that the state of the self-system is closed to the initiation of a dialogue with the therapist (cf. Schore, 2003).

The patient anticipates that the therapist will be no different from others in his past and will inflict the same injuries as had been inflicted by others. The empathic atmosphere may raise the patient's hopes and transference expectations, although these provide little assurance that their fears will not be realized. Time and acquaintance with the therapist can help work through some of these hesitancies, although their articulation through interpretations, which convey a general understanding of their source, may help to move the process on.

However, of equal importance is the therapist's contribution to this aspect of the process. A variety of defenses may be activated in the therapist that could stall or even abort the process. I will deal with these in detail in the chapter on disjunctions.

Once the process permits patients to overcome these initial hesitancies, the process may then unfold. Some selfobject or adjunctive needs may come to the surface as the transference develops, and the countertransference positions and responses begin to emerge. The "curative fantasy" becomes activated. This fantasy, which is often unconscious, embodies within it the unfulfilled longings contained within the deficient self. Another way to think of this fantasy is to understand it as the activation of the patient's hope for self-restoration. The hope is that at last relief from the chronic suffering is in sight, something will change radically, for the better.

Reconfiguring relational patterns

As we have seen, relational interactions that are experienced during a person's formative years are nonconsciously encoded in procedural memory. They become part of a person's patterns of "being with others" (Stern, 1983). Some of these patterns are modifiable through learning from experience. The person is able to adaptively respond to different situations by deploying different modes than those to which he or she was previously exposed. However, some of those patterns are encapsulated within attractors around which nodal experiences became organized. These latter patterns become problematic for patients as they lead to unsuccessful accommodations.

The process through which a reorganization in these patterns occurs during concordant moments deserves our attention. The question we confront is: How is it that without the assistance of verbal interpretation or cognitive processing some patients are able to modify these longstanding patterns? (cf. Lyons-Ruth, 1999). The issue centers on how we understand the process through which a habitual pattern encoded in procedural memory is displaced by a different, less rigid pattern that is more receptive to a context that requires a different response. In short, can habitual patterns change as a result of exposure to the therapeutic milieu created during concordant moments?

As I have repeatedly pointed out, many patients with neuropsychological deficits are oppressed by fears of the exposure of their self-deficits and have experienced great shame or humiliation when those were publicly revealed. When, during concordant moments, patients are able to reveal those deeply distressing feelings, they experience a great deal of relief if the therapist is able to respond with empathy and acceptance. For the first time, they regard what they once felt to be a deep flaw in their personality as no more than a human failing. They feel freed of the inhibitions and constrictions in which they were immured and find it possible to displace the old patterns with new ones that enrich their relationships and their lives.

Such examples illustrate the process through which major changes may occur in patients' lives without the assistance of interpretations of the psychodynamics involved.

Patients' proactive endeavors

Whatever benefits patients may derive from the relationship or interpretations and understanding of their problems, without their feeling empowered to make changes in their lives, these interventions may not bear fruit. Patients with challenges that stem from their neuropsychological deficits must be able to be assertive in advocating for accommodations on their behalf and in engaging in mentoring or educational programs that would help them to compensate for their deficits and acquire skills that would allow them to accommodate successfully to the demands made of them.

In order to acquire new patterns of behavior, patients must also undertake a particular form of learning to modify their responses to the circumstances they confront; the new learning involves facilitating the transfer of knowledge from episodic memory to procedural memory (Gedo, 2005). The attainment of this goal may involve didactic methods that include direct instruction and rehearsal of ways of approaching and solving individual life stressors and problems (Miller, 1992), or it may require actually modeling the function or even providing it to help those patients compensate for their deficit. However, the processes through which these interchanges occur serve to enhance the patient's sense of agency and control over their lives.

Such interventions, when made within the context of the transference and countertransference, at times may depart from traditional modes. Therapists may find it necessary to complement the patient's social and cognitive deficits by providing the patient with missing functions related to the deficits. Specific types of interventions can be designed to address the requirements for complementary function in patients with neuropsychological deficits (see Ogden, 2009; Ogden & Minton, 2000).

When offered, these complementary functions are best provided in the "zone of proximal development" (Vygotsky, 1986, p. 187). This term, used in developmental psychology, refers to a type of scaffolding that others provide to permit the patient to exercise available functions. This term may translate into Tolpin's (2002, 2007) concept of the "forward edge," although it comes from a different theoretical framework. The dilemma that confronts therapists of patients with these deficits is how much to do for them and how much to let them struggle to do for themselves. If too much is done for them, they will be prevented from exerting efforts to do for themselves. They may also regress and develop an inordinate reliance on the therapist. If too little is done, they may become frustrated, fail at a task, give up trying, and lose motivation. Staying within the zone of proximal development means meeting them halfway and challenging them even as they are supported to avoid failure. By using this approach, therapists can avoid having patients become overly dependent or fail to develop potential competencies.

An important caveat to undertaking these departures from traditional modes of intervention must now be stated. The initial reason for instituting these interventions is to inform patients of the nature of their deficits and to deal with the associated psychodynamics. In the absence of adequate motivation to change, the helping efforts would face defeat. Patients require a demonstration of the effectiveness of alternative modes of functioning before being able to take the initiative to bring about change on their own. Once such issues have been dealt with, it is possible to make a referral to an appropriate educational specialist who can provide more extensive strategies to compensate for the learning disabilities. Such specialists are found increasingly in some regions of the country and constitute an excellent resource for such patients.

Compensation

The brain's plasticity and its capacity to take over functions that other areas are incapable of performing are well-known (Arrowsmith-Young, 2012; Doidge, 2007; Taylor, 2008). The phenomenon of compensation for physical disabilities is also well documented. When it comes to compensations for neuropsychological deficits, similar phenomena may be observed, although these are less well-documented in the literature. The concept of compensation implies that a failure of a system's component need not lead to a failure of the total system, as would happen in a mechanical system. Synergy proposes that if a failure occurs in one component, the remaining components will adjust so that the system continues to function and attains the end-goal or completes the task that it was undertaking (see Kelso, 1995).

The compensatory strategies that people with neuropsychological deficits can develop are limited only by their creativity. Kohut (1977) noted:

> [T]he child's selection of certain functions out of the number of those at his disposal (and his developing them into efficacious talents and skills) and the direction of his major pursuits as ultimately laid down permanently in the psyche as the contents of his ambitions and ideals – i.e., the acquisition of compensatory structures – are best explained in the context of his having been able to shift from a frustrating selfobject to a nonfrustrating or less frustrating one.
>
> (p. 83)

Although a patient may develop compensatory structures either spontaneously or through the process, nevertheless some deficits may remain as lifelong impairments; such persons require adjunctive functions for the rest of their lives. Some patients learn to structure their environment to minimize the reliance on areas of weakness. Others, with help, learn to anticipate and avoid encounters with situations that would expose their weaknesses. When a person can use such compensatory strategies, the negative impact of the disorder is attenuated, as are the psychosocial problems. At times, it is possible that without interpretation a patient will discover a talent or skill that begins to provide a way of compensating for the deficits. In those cases, the outcome may be just as successful. Involvement in athletic activities, for example, may become a source of gratification and self-esteem. Eventually, success obtained through compensatory activities may lead to renewed efforts in task performance. The old aversive reactions to work settings may give way to efforts at mastery.

Clearly, not all people compensate for their self-deficits. Some do very well while others do not. It is not clear why it is that some are more efficient at the task of compensation while others seem to be ineffectual at that task. Some, who confront tasks that they find insurmountable and who have marked strengths in other areas, turn to the latter areas to find successes. They then appear to cope much better with areas of deficiencies. At times, they even challenge themselves to undertake what is most difficult for them and to overcome the constraints that limited their capacity to achieve their goals. However, they are seldom able to perform these tasks with the ease and comfort with which a well-endowed person might do.

Compensation then does not mean that the person "outgrows" a deficit. It means that the person could take a perspective regarding the areas of weakness and has dealt with them at some level. This may have been done by depreciating or devaluing what is difficult, therefore neutralizing the negative effects of other people's evaluation of the person's competence. Alternatively, it may come about through a transformation of the meanings of the deficit into a badge that they then proudly display. In either case, the person turns to other areas of competence through which to obtain satisfaction. The consequence of compensation always appears to be a greater sense of coherence, a stronger sense of cohesiveness, and a lesser vulnerability to other people's estimation of them.

Summary

As patients engage in the initial moments of the therapeutic encounter, their hopeful anticipation of relief from their distress organizes the interactions during concordant moments. From the therapists' point of view, these interactions consist in taking a diatrophic attitude toward their patients, whereas patients bring to the process the "curative fantasy" (i.e. the hoped-for relief from their distress). However, the therapeutic path does not follow a predefined course; rather, it is the process that determines the transactions that occur between patient and therapist.

Since the relationship is central as a change agent during concordant moments, the interchanges provide patients with a "corrective emotional experience" that demonstrates to them that not everyone responds to them in the same way that others have in their past. Through this process, therapists provide affirmation, protection, and an enhancement of the patients' sense of well-being that normalizes their differences from other people.

That these changes occur at the nonverbal level is indicative of the fact that implicit forms of communication can be as powerful as explicit ones (i.e. verbal forms) in bringing about changes. Nonverbal communication may serve to create new meanings for experiences or may place events in a context that is different from that originally conceived by the patient. These interventions may reinforce the experience of the therapist as someone who has shared with the patient a meaningful episode that also had a healing effect (Lyons-Ruth, 1998; Stern, 1998). Implicit forms of communication can address the patients' deepest affect states without the necessity of these having to be articulated verbally.

It is important to clarify that because certain experiences cannot be articulated verbally, this does not mean that they originated during the preverbal period (i.e. early during infancy). As stated in an earlier chapter, all preverbal experiences are encoded nonverbally, but not all nonverbal experiences originated during the preverbal period. Empathy failures obviously need not have taken place during the preverbal period for a deficit to occur; in fact, most disorders of the self are the result of experiences that occur after the acquisition of speech. These early experiences are often devoid of verbal content, are encoded in memory iconically, and form the core of future enactments.

Therapists who make the error of interpreting all nonverbally encoded experiences as dating from the preverbal period equate these structures or disavowed material with nonverbal signs. If this were the case, then all nonverbal expressions would reflect regressive trends that are manifestations of archaic periods in development. The problem with this view is that it fails to account for the effects of the nonverbal storage of negative experiences and the enactment of those memories when evoked by contemporary events. It fails to explain the specificity of the shape each transference takes by focusing only on the longing evoked but not on the possible repetitive dimension of what the patient brings to the clinical setting. Any view of enactments must take into account that a different code from a different language than verbal language is being use to give expression to a message that may be incommunicable through verbal means (see Bromberg, 2003). Allowing for this view would lead to a shift in the way we view transferences. It raises the question of whether patients are repeating an experience or are simply saying something about their self-state.

Finally, it is possible that without interpretation a patient will discover a talent or skill that begins to provide a way of compensating for the deficits. In those cases, the outcome may be just as successful. Involvement in athletic activities, for example, may become a source of gratification and self-esteem. Eventually, success obtained through compensatory activities may lead to renewed efforts in the performance of challenging tasks. The old aversive reactions to those situations may give way to efforts at mastery. Furthermore, some find ways of compensating for their self-deficits in creative and unpredictable ways.

As for patients' proactive engagement in making changes in their lives, I draw an analogy to the processes involved in rehabilitation following a physical injury. The healing of the injury that occurs is insufficient to restore the lost functions. What is necessary in addition is the acquisition of the means through which to accommodate successfully to the demands of the context. In the case of patients with adjunctive deficits, what is required of them is that they develop compensatory skills and engage in relationships through which others may complement their deficits.

References

Aron, L. (1996). *A meeting of minds: Mutuality in psychoanalysis.* New York: Routledge.
Arrowsmith-Young, B. (2012). *The woman who changed hr brain: How I left my learning disability behind and other stories of congitive transformation.* New York: Simon & Schuster.
Basch, M. F. (1995). Kohut's contribution. *Psychoanalytic Dialogues, 5*(3), 367–373.
Brandchaft, B., & Stolorow, R. D. (1990). Varieties of therapeutic alliance. *The Annual of Psychoanalysis, 18*, 99–114. Hillsdale, NJ: The Analytic Press.
Bromberg, P. M. (2003). Something wicked this way comes: Trauma, dissociation, an conflict: The space where psychoanalysis, cognitive science, and neuroscience overlap. *Psychoanalytic Psychology, 20*, 558–574.
Bromberg, P. M. (2011). *The shadow of the tsunami and the growth of the relational mind.* New York: Routledge.
Doidge, N. (2007). *The brain that changes itself: Stories of personal triumph from the frontiers of brain science.* New York: Penguin Books.

Gedo, J. E. (2005). *Psychoanalysis as biological science: A comprehensive theory.* Baltimore, MD: Johns Hopkins University Press.

Geist, R. A. (2013). How the empathic process heals: A microprocess perspective. *International Journal of Psychoanalytic Self Psychology, 8,* 265–281.

Harris, A. E. (2011). Gender as a strange attractor: Discussion of the transgender symposium. *Psychoanalytic Dialogues, 21,* 230–238.

Kelso, J. A. S. (1995). *Dynamic patterns: The self organization of brain and behavior.* Cambridge, MA: The MIT Press.

Kohut, H. (1977). *The restoration of the self.* New York: International Universities Press.

Kohut, H. (1984). *How does analysis cure?* Chicago: The University of Chicago Press.

Lyons-Ruth, K. (1998). Implicit relational knowing: Its role in development and psychoanalytic treatment. *Infant Mental Health Journal, 19*(3), 282–289.

Lyons-Ruth, K. (1999). The two-person unconscious: Intersubjective dialogue, enactive relationsal representation, and the emergence of new forms of relational organization. *Psychoanalytic Inquiry, 19*(4), 576–617.

Miller, L. (1992). Cognitive rehabilitation, cognitive therapy, and cognitive style: Toward an integrative model of personality and psychotherapy. *The Journal of Cognitive Rehabilitation, 10*(1), 18–29.

Ogden, P. (2009). Emotion, mindfulness, and movement: Expanding the regulatory boundaries of the window of affect tolerance. In D. Fosha, D. J. Siegel, & M. F. Solomon (Eds.), *The healing power of emotion: Affective neuroscience, development, and clinical practice* (pp. 204–230). New York: W. W. Norton.

Ogden, P., & Minton, K. (2000). Sensorimotor psychotherapy: One method for processing traumatic memory. *Traumatology, 6*(3), 149–173.

Ornstein, A. (1992). The curative fantasy and psychic recovery. *Journal of Psychotherapy Practice and Research, 1*(1), 16–28.

Ornstein, A. (1995). The fate of the curative fantasy in the psychoanalytic treatment process. *Contemporary Psychoanalysis, 31*(1), 113–123.

Porges, S. W. (2004). Neuroception: A subconscious system for detecting threats and safety. *Zero to Three, 5,* 19–24.

Schore, A. N. (2003). *Affect regulation and the repair of the self.* New York: W. W. Norton.

Siegel, D. J. (1999). *The developing mind: Toward a neurobiology of interpersonal experience.* New York: Guilford Press.

Spitz, R. A. (1959). Countertransference: Comments on its varying role in the analytic situation. *Journal of the American Psychoanalytic Association, 4,* 256–265.

Sroufe, L. A. (1995). *Emotional development: The organization of emotional life in the early years.* Cambridge: Cambridge University Press.

Stern, D. N. (1983). The early development of schemas of self, other, and "self with other." In J. D. Lichtenberg & S. Kaplan (Eds.), *Reflections on self psychology* (pp. 49–84). Hillsdale, NJ: The Analytic Press.

Stern, D. N. (1998). The process of therapeutic change involving implicit knowledge: Some implications of developmental observations for adult psychotherapy. *Infant Mental Health Journal, 19*(3), 300–308.

Taylor, J. B. (2008). *My stroke of insight: A brain scientist's personal journey.* New York: Viking.

Tolpin, M. (2002). Doing psychoanalysis of normal development: Forward edge transferences. In A. Goldberg (Ed.), *Progress in self psychology: Postmodern self psychology* (Vol. 18, pp. 167–190). Hillsdale, NJ: The Analytic Press.

Tolpin, M. (2007). The divided self: Shifting an intrapsychic balance the forward edge of a kinship transference: To bleed like everyone else. *Psychoanalytic Inquiry, 27*(1), 50–65.

Tronick, E. Z. (1998). Dyadically expanded states of consciousness and the process of therapeutic change. *Infant Mental Health Journal, 19*(3), 290–299.

Vygotsky, L. (1986). *Thought and Language* (Alex Kozulin, Trans.). Cambridge, MA: The MIT Press.

Wallerstein, R. S. (1995). *The talking cures: The psychoanalyses and the psychotherapies.* New Haven, CT: Yale University Press.

Winnicott, D. W. (1987). *Babies and their mothers.* New York: Addison-Wesley Publishing Co.

Chapter 9

The therapeutic dialogue
Complementary moments

From a dynamic systems perspective, I conceive of the therapeutic dialogue as a collaborative endeavor in which each member of the dyad makes a unique contribution. The central organizing feature of complementary moments that occur during this dialogue is the recognition process, the process of *fitting together* that requires that each member of the dyad modify itself and adjust to the other so as to arrive at the best state of coherence, continuity, and self-organization. During such episodes, through mindsharing, patients nonconsciously attempt to find a match between their selfobject and adjunctive needs and the functions available in the environment that would fill in those needs, whereas therapists are drawn to examine their responses as indicators of what the patients may need. However, members of the dyad filter their perceptions of the others through their own preconceptions about what is transpiring in the process.

Complementary moments are episodes that occur when the transference and countertransference occupy the foreground of the interaction. Patients searching for complementarity reenact, within the transference, the need for complementarity associated with their deficits. In other words, complementary moments represent episodes during which patients' deficits, whether of neuropsychological, self-regulatory, or selfobject functions, become activated, and the patient expects the therapist to respond by providing those functions.

Through their capacity for mindsharing, therapists attune themselves to the patients' deficits and to the expression of those deficits as a search for complementarity. In the countertransference, therapists experience the patients' expectations as demands to which they must respond. These processes occur nonconsciously, since the patients' patterns of expectations were previously encoded in non-declarative memory. The therapeutic process, with all its ambiguities, brings these patterns to the forefront. We may say that the therapeutic process acts as a "priming" agent (Levin, 1997) that brings forth old patterns of expectations.

As we have seen, the active search for complementarity began with patients' experiences that they were unsuccessful in their attempts to accommodate to the demands made of them. Whereas what they lacked may have seemed mysterious to them, the effects of their self-deficits were all too evident. Some patients may have felt cohesive when others silently provided the missing functions, whereas others may have felt devastated when abandoned by those who complemented their sense of self. The greater the activation of the therapists' recognition process and the heightening sense of "fittedness" between them and their patients, the greater the experience of complementarity for the patients.

In what follows, I limit my discussion of this aspect of therapeutic dialogue to the two preferences that are typical for the self as a complex adaptive system: patients' preference for *self-cohesion* over fragmentation and their preference for *self-understanding* through the creation of a coherent self-narrative. As we have seen, the relationship between the experience of self-cohesion and the possession of a coherent narrative is complex. Yet each of these two dimensions of the therapeutic dialogue deserves separate discussion. Whereas there are parallels between the two sets of processes, the two are deeply entwined. The patient's search for complementarity is in the service of the *restoration or maintenance the sense of self-cohesion*, while the *co-construction of a narrative* that integrates the therapist's and the patient's views of what occurred during the patient's life helps to make comprehensible aspects of her life that were incomprehensible.

While during concordant aspects of the relationship moments were primarily instrumental as change agents for patient, during complementary moments a different set of processes is at work. During complementary moments, the therapeutic dialogue shifts from the relational aspect of the interaction to an exploration of the nature of the self-deficits that have organized the patient's psychodynamics, their effect on the trajectory of the patient's life, and to the co-creation of a coherent self-narrative.

The preference for self-cohesion

As we saw earlier, the loss of self-cohesion is a condition in which patients are unable to maintain the experience of inner organization and self-continuity. It is characterized by anxiety, defenses against anxiety, and a variety of symptoms. Anxiety is both an indicator of an unstable sense of self-cohesion and a contributor to it. When a threat to self-cohesion exists, defenses are activated in an attempt at self-rescue. These defenses may manifest as overt symptoms of the patient's distress. Disorders of self-cohesion may result from self-critical attitudes that patients develop in comparing themselves with others, resulting in self-esteem problems. In addition, such experiences are found either when patients cannot avail themselves of the complementary functions caregivers can provide or when those functions are not available to them.

Self-deficits may disrupt the sense of self-cohesion in several ways. Patients' sense of self-cohesion may be disrupted by their responses to their self-deficits. Patients may realize that they have a deficit. They may experience that realization as an injury to their sense of self; they may then feel imperfect or defective. That realization may depress their view of themselves, producing anxieties, depression, discouragement, or feelings of incompetence. The effect on their self-esteem is a destabilized sense of cohesion.

Guided by the patient's preference for self-cohesion, complementary moments offer the dyad an opportunity to create the conditions that would facilitate such an outcome. Earlier, I described this component of the therapeutic dialogue as a "voyage of discovery" in which both patients and therapists engage in the exploration of the impediments to the patient's attainment of a stable sense of self-cohesion. At one level, through the dialogue the patient anticipates regaining a sense of well-being. At another level, the patient fears the re-arousal of past painful events, expecting the therapist to replicate relationships from figures from the past. Critical to this aspect of the process is that understanding without experiencing is mere intellectualization; experiencing without understanding may alleviate the patients' distress, but alone it does not necessarily lead to the integration of the new meanings of the experience.

Traditionally, the processes of *understanding* and *interpreting* (see Kohut, 1984; Ornstein & Ornstein, 1985) were regarded as the instruments through which self-cohesion may be restored. From a dynamic systems perspective, I will suggest that *understanding*, which will deal with the patient's attempt to grasp the nature and function of his self-deficits, is attained through the co-construction of a narrative. I conceptualize what *interpreting* means as the joint exploration by therapists and patients of the nature and effects of the self-deficits on the patient's sense of self.

One way to define the effect that we have as therapists on patients is that we act as catalysts that activate our patients' motives to bring about changes in themselves. What we say or do not only engenders some of the changes that patients make, but patients also make use of what we offer in conjunction with other factors to make changes in how they feel, think, or act. If these processes are successful, the outcome is the enhancement of their sense of cohesion.

Since I examine these processes through the lens of the *transference* and *countertransference*, I begin with a brief review of these concepts as interpreted within this neuropsychodynamic perspective.

Transference and countertransference

For therapists, the entry point to an understanding of their patients' deficits is through transference and countertransference. The patient's transference will manifest both the selfobject deficits and the adjunctive deficits. Based on the insights gained through the countertransference, the patient's psychodynamics are revealed.

From a dynamic systems perspective, *transference* represents the patient's expectation that the new relationship will provide the longed-for functions or will repair the injuries produced by past events. The type of responses that therapists make to these expectations and the types of explanations they give patients determines the outcome. *Countertransference*, on the other hand, represents the therapist's urge to complement the patient's self-deficits by providing the missing functions, whether of selfobject functions or adjunctive functions, that press for satisfaction.

Patients begin to learn about transference as they experience the differences between the therapist's responses as contrasted with those of others in their lives. Transference then refers to the phenomenon through which patients shape their perceptions of current situations and that of their relationships with others so that they conform to past experiences (see Palombo, 2001). The self-similarity that we note in the patient's patterns of interactions now manifests itself in the transference. Transference reflects the fact that past experiences structure patients' personalities into patterns that result from the attractors formed by the self-deficits that led to the dysfunctional accommodations; it is a manifestation of the self-replication of patterns of interaction that were encoded in procedural memory.

As a contrast, we may say that for Kohut, transference is evoked by the longings for experiences that the child did not get – that is, it represents the revival of unsatisfied selfobject needs. If we were to contrast Freud's view with Kohut's, we would say that Freud understood patients as wanting something that they were forbidden from having (the oedipal object) and for which they felt *guilty*, while Kohut saw patients as wanting something they needed to have in order to maintain their self-cohesion (a selfobject function) and for which they felt *ashamed*. While self psychology has emphasized selfobject deficits as central to patients' psychopathology, *I am proposing that equal weight be given to contributions made by deficits in adjunctive functions. These self-deficits will manifest as transference phenomena just as selfobject deficits emerge during the process. The longing will be encrusted with feelings of shame.*

When complementary moments are in the foreground, adjunctive deficits manifest as transferences much as selfobject deficits. These deficits manifest themselves as nonconscious pleas for the provision of cognitive functions, social skills, and other competencies that the patient requires. For patients with a neuropsychological deficit, the search for these competencies parallels the yearnings for mirroring or idealization selfobject functions. Both sets of phenomena, the deficits in selfobject function as well as those related to the neuropsychological deficits, can emerge within the transference. Both represent functions that when provided complement the patient's sense of self. When deprived of a response, patients will experience frustrations that may lead to a breach in the therapeutic process.

From the perspective of the countertransference, it is inevitable that the therapist's experience will parallel and will be a counterpart to what the patient is experiencing in the treatment. The intensity of the transference will lead the therapist to feel either as the patient experienced others to have felt toward the patient or to respond to the patient as the patient may have expected others to respond. The therapist's complementary responses reflect aspects of the context that the patient re-creates.

We may think of the *transference/countertransference configuration* as representing the therapist and patient as components of a system in which each of the members engages the other in a mindsharing process. That is, whereas patients bring to the relationship the experiences formed by their neuropsychological givens, their subjective responses to those givens, and by the context in which their relational patterns arose, similarly, therapists bring their own configuration of experiences. What transpires between the dyad is a function of the factors and of the unfolding processes that follow. The processes of "recognition" and of the fit between therapist and patient are critical to the negotiation of the issues that arise. The therapeutic context then re-creates a setting in which the patient can experience the absence of integration and can experience those areas of unintegrated affects that remain problematic. The patients' experience of mindsharing and fitting together will result in their feeling "recognized" (i.e. their self-deficits are acknowledged and responses to them have been made).

A rich literature on enactments has appeared in recent years presenting differing interpretation of the dynamics involved in that process (Aron, 2003; Aron & Atlas, 2015; Gerhardt & Sweetnam, 2001; Harris & Gold, 2001). In what follows, I present two views, the first is that in the treatment of patients with neuropsychological deficits an enactment represents, in part, the therapist's urge to complement the patient's self-deficits by providing the functions that press for satisfaction, whether these are selfobject functions or adjunctive functions. The second, from a narrative perspective, the therapist becomes "emplotted" into the patient's dynamics. As we saw earlier, emplotment entails being drawn nonconsciously into becoming a character in the other person's narrative. Enactments essentially constitute the participation by the therapist as a character from the patient's past while becoming part of the scenario in the patient's narrative. For both the patient and the therapist, the experience is that of the re-creation of an aspect of the patient's psychic organization.

When patients' expectations take the form of overt behaviors that reflect the patterns that depict the nature of the deficit and in which the therapist participates, we designate those episodes as enactments. Such enactments occur when the patient responds to the "priming" effect that the therapist activates. The patient's expectation is not necessarily that the therapist would respond positively; in fact, it in all likelihood, based on past experience, patients will believe that a replication of past episodes would recur and to which the therapist responds insensitively or even with hostility. The specific form the transference would take represents the patient's perception of the therapist as a figure from her past; the patterns of interaction that emerge reflect the earlier relational patterns. These patterns are encoded in the patient's procedural memory, and patients may have no conscious awareness of when or how they become enacted.

Case illustration[1]

A woman, who had been through a long and bitterly contested divorce, asked to consult a therapist about the problems she was having with her adolescent daughter. The patient was terribly upset that her daughter, who was living with her father, was refusing to have anything to do with her.

As the therapist struggled to understand the dynamics at work between mother and daughter, the following incident occurred that vividly demonstrated the nature of the problem. The therapist was on her way to a critical medical appointment when she received a phone call from the patient. In answering it, she warned the patient that she only had ten minutes and would call her back later should she require more time. The patient, however, was unresponsive to the therapist's urgent requests that she hang up after the ten minutes had elapsed. Multiple attempts to end the conversation were unsuccessful as the patient kept up her tirade at her former husband, accusing him of alienating the daughter from her. After being kept on the phone for 25 minutes, the therapist feeling totally trapped felt she had no option but to hang up on the patient.

In the session that followed that phone call, the patient and therapist reviewed what had occurred. It became evident that this mother's rage at her former husband had so alienated the daughter that she felt desperate that her mother could not hear her. In essence, the daughter felt that she had to "hang up" on her mother as she could not feel heard. When the pattern was revealed to the patient, she burst into tears maintaining that her anger at her husband had blinded her to what she was doing to her daughter.

The mother and therapist had enacted the pattern of the mother-daughter relationship, which allowed the therapeutic process to unfold.

Interpreting

Interpretation becomes a process of discovery to which both therapists and patients make their own unique contribution. It involves dealing with the psychodynamics associated with the patients' self-deficits and the attractor that have crystalized because of those deficits. The psychodynamics relate to the erosion in self-esteem that may have occurred, the beliefs surrounding the meaning associated with the effects of the deficits, the effects of the patients' responses to others and other people's responses to patients that led to relational difficulties, and the impact on the sense of self and self-cohesion.

These interpretations also entail dealing with the defenses that have accrued as a result of patients' efforts to deal with the distressful feelings engendered by their self-deficits. In and of themselves, these interpretations are not "curative" in the sense that the insight does not necessarily lead to a repair of the deficit. The explanations open the possibility for more effective ways of having others complement for the missing functions or for the patient to develop compensatory structures that bypass the effects of the deficits.

Disavowal and dissociation

Once patients have developed a greater sense of confidence, it is possible to approach the psychological tasks of dealing with the injuries the years have inflicted and the associated feelings of shame and humiliation. The experience in therapy is geared to helping them to be valued and appreciated. The interpretations involve dealing with the defensive "wall of shame" that patients built to deal with the painful experiences to which they were exposed. Through the transference, patients experience their longings, expecting that the therapist would satisfy those longings.

Defenses have served as an organizational function for the self as a system – that is, they provided a degree of stability that at times anchored the patient's sense of self, even as the patient struggled to maintain a sense of self-cohesion. Given the outsize role that the defenses of *disavowal* and *dissociation* play in the psychodynamics of patients with neuropsychological deficits, a discussion of their manifestation and the possible intervention that may be useful in addressing them is needed.

Disavowal

As discussed earlier, disavowal is characterized by a conscious awareness of what is disavowed and a simultaneous disregard for the reality of what is disavowed. It serves the purpose of safeguarding the patient's sense of self following a narcissistic injury. The concept of defense, in this context, is indicative of an avoidance of the pain associated with confronting an unacceptable reality. In disavowal, it may appear as though patients with neuropsychological deficits "distort reality." Often, these patients seem to disregard the consequences of their actions even as they realize the "irrationality" of those actions. They filter their experiences through a distinctive set of neuropsychological functions that keeps them from obtaining complete information about the context (Basch, 1975). Because the information is incomplete, it is also often incorrect. Yet, these patients usually carry a conviction that their perceptions are correct and that they are justified in their responses. They are unaware that their failure to meet the demands placed on them is due to their deficits rather than to the obstacles that others place in their path.

We cannot say that these patients distort reality in the same way that patients who suffer from psychotic disorders distort their reality. Within the bounds of their competencies, their perceptions are correct; yet from the perspective of others, their interpretations of events are clearly disparate from those most people make. This disparity leads to maladaptive responses on their part, responses to which others in the patient's context react negatively. Out of step with this context, the patient cannot process what is going on and ends up confused and bewildered. Disavowal as a defense serves to protect the patients from further narcissistic injury and fragmentation.

Dealing with the defense of disavowal requires that the patient get in touch with the disillusionment felt at not receiving the expected responses or not experiencing the feelings associated with having her selfobject needs met. In either case, the feelings that surface during this process begin to undermine the wall of shame. The patient can feel freed to feel greater self-esteem, pride in her accomplishments, and greater self-cohesion.

Although this process addresses the patient's selfobject deficits, the repair to the sense of self that relates to the deficits in adjunctive functions comes from the other change agents that occur simultaneously with the healing of the vertical split caused by the disavowal.

Case example

Dan is a 36-year-old man who was referred by a psychiatrist because the anti-anxiety medication he was taking was not sufficient to control his symptoms. On the phone, Dan stated that in addition he felt the need for some help around a recurring pattern of being fired from jobs because he is habitually late for work and is frequently absent without adequate explanations. Dan was employed as an editor for a specialty journal.

Dan is a single man who has been living on his own since graduating from college. He was verbally highly articulate although he displayed little affect. He has had no long-term stable relationships, although he was in a relationship for the past six months with a woman who broke up with him because she felt they could not get along.

Dan has had a long history of being diagnosed with learning disabilities, which dated back to eighth grade. Testing at ages 24 and 27 revealed a consistent picture of cognitive strengths and weakness across the board. On intelligence testing, results indicated a superior level of verbal processing and average processing of nonverbal and perceptual information. According to the neuropsychologist who had evaluated him, these results suggested that he has a nonverbal learning disability. In addition, Dan was found not to perform well in an environment in which his attention could be drawn away from the task at hand. In particular, he had difficulties in such contexts with tasks that require processing complex information. It took Dan much longer to process general information that required written responses than the average person. The speed with which he was capable of producing responses on a written test was impaired by visual-motor problems. In addition, he had organizational difficulties and had to exert special effort to sequence and organize his thoughts and the tasks at hand.

Dan was 10 minutes late for his first appointment, apologizing that he had lost his way trying to find my office. As he walked in, he made no eye contact, but walked directly to my chair where he began to sit down. He was very apologetic when I redirected him to the patient chair, saying that it is hard for him to get oriented to this new environment.

Dan started out saying that he had a lot of therapy, including breathing exercises, biofeedback, and cognitive therapy. He is currently under the care of a psychiatrist who had prescribed Zoloft, Ritalin, and Xanax. He feels that the therapy has given him a lot of insight but has made no difference in his functioning. He had been instructed in some social techniques to facilitate transactions with people, but none of them works. He would ask for specific principles he could apply to specific situations. He wanted to learn what clues to look for so that he could respond appropriately. He was taught to look at people directly in the eye, but he always found it so uncomfortable that he would avert his eyes. In any case, the principles he sought only confuse him more because he could never apply them to the appropriate situation.

His major problem is that he feels that once more he was fired from his latest job and faces the prospect of being unable to pay his rent. What happened was that he had been consistently arriving late for work. He had difficulty getting himself ready for work. Knowing that he would be late led him to rationalize that he could satisfy his boss with excuses that he made up on his way to work. In addition, on several occasions, he had not gone to work because he had stayed up all night playing a competitive computer game. He would go to bed early in the morning, failing to notify his boss that he would not be coming to work. Again, he rationalized that he could make up the work the next day and no harm would be done. It was evident that while he realized the threat to his job that his behavior created, he minimized its effects and seemed unconcerned about its consequences.

During the two years of twice-a-week therapy that followed, we uncovered several dynamics that helped explain Dan's symptoms as well as his behavior. The unremitting anxiety, which did not respond to the medication, was related to the confusion, indignation, and overwhelming rage at the manager who laid him off. The rage, which he held on to, appeared to be in the service of filling in the void within him. The feelings of devastation and mortification led to feelings shattered by the injury with which he had to deal. Destructive thoughts invaded his mind as he tried to integrate the effects of what he experienced as an assault. He ruminated in a stubborn effort at restoring the sense of balance. At a different level, he realized that the response was unjustified as he had been irresponsible and had given cause for his firing. The helplessness produced by his situation turned into self-hatred. It was no wonder that the medication could not alleviate those symptoms. It was only after considerable work on his rage and mitigating its effects that his anxiety level diminished and became manageable.

A different dynamic was associated with his "irresponsibility." Behind the overt behaviors of arriving late or not showing up for work was a conviction that he was so indispensable for the work that he did that the organization would not survive without him. The grandiosity clouded his judgment as to his contribution to the success of his company. We attributed his poor judgment to the disavowal of the consequences of his actions. Whereas he knew he was jeopardizing his position, he also convinced himself of his immunity to any action by his manager because he saw himself as indispensable to the operation of the department for which he worked.

The defense of disavowal does not respond to the focus on the untoward consequences of the patient's behaviors or to efforts at convincing the patient of the narcissism implied by his grandiosity. The patient's "reality testing" is unimpaired, so that such interventions not only fall on deaf ears but patients experience them as belittling and insensitive. Counterintuitively, permitting the patients to elaborate the belief in their invulnerability allows them to give expression to their selfobject deficits and to reveal their suppressed longing for appreciation and admiration. Once therapists acknowledge this yearning, patients come to a realization of the functions these desires have served and are able to replace the dysfunctional behaviors with more successful accommodations to the demands of the context.

Dissociation

Whereas robust evidence exists that patients with adjunctive deficits have suffered from moderate to severe narcissistic injuries, some of them were victims of abuse that resulted in complex trauma. There is little doubt that some patients were the object of serious bullying by their peers during their school years; some were socially marginalized, while others were berated by teachers and their families because they were thought to make little effort to succeed academically.

Dissociation results when, in the face of a repeated traumas, the fragility of the patient's sense of self and the circumstances in which the event occurs do not permit a response other than conservation/withdrawal. That is, the response represents a deep retreat into oneself and the suppression of the feelings evoked by the events to which the patient was exposed (Bromberg, 2011; Janet, 1907/2012; Ogden, 2009; Schore, 2012). As one of my patients, a 37-year-old woman with a nonverbal learning disorder, described the experience:

> There are moments when I feel nothing, I feel empty, depleted; it is a mindlessness state. I feel overwhelmed with boredom. It isn't like I am in pain, because I feel nothing except exhaustion. Any demand

requires so much effort that I want to curl up and huddle in a corner. I feel paralyzed, I have no confidence that I have what it takes to meet those demands. When I am around people, I feel spacey, immobilized, and disconnected. Then all of a sudden, the feelings of inertness begin to trigger a sense of panic. I am reminded of the recurring nightmare that I had as a child of being buried under an icy avalanche. I find myself living at two levels. I watch myself having those feelings and thinking "What is going on? Why am I being so stupid?" I should just stop feeling sorry for myself and get on with my life.

In the literature, we find two different approaches to dealing with the dissociation associated with trauma, those of Bromberg, which Schore supports, and those of Van Der Kolk. Bromberg (2003) suggests that enactments are the central dynamic that activate the therapeutic process, whereas Van der Kolk (2014) proposes that in addition to talk therapy, other interventions are effective in alleviating patients' symptoms. It may be that Bromberg and Van der Kolk are dealing with different patient populations, for which each of their interventions is appropriate. Bromberg's patients seem to have suffered from the erosive effect of chronic insensitive responses to them, which resemble the effects of complex PTSD, while Vander Kolk's patients were exposed to unusual and dramatic events, such as those of Iraq veterans, which left an indelible imprint on them. If this is the case, then the patients with adjunctive deficits, with whom we are concerned, would fit the population of patients to whom Bromberg's approach is more appropriate.

In either case, the brain changes that occur as a result of trauma are not in dispute. Both Schore and Van Der Kolk describe similar processes as occurring at the neurological level, although each emphasizes a different aspect of those processes as a focus for intervention. Schore chooses the role of the right frontal orbital cortical region and its role in the development of the capacity for self-regulation as central to the healing process. The attachment the patient forms to the therapist is the vehicle through which patients develop the capacity to modulate affect states.

From Van Der Kolk's (2014) perspective:

> Many treatment approaches for traumatic stress focus on desensitizing patients to the past, with the expectation that re-exposure to the

problems will reduce emotional outburst and flashback. I believe this is based on a misunderstanding of what happens in traumatic stress. We must most of all help our patients to live fully and securely in the present. In order to do that we need to help bring their brain structures that deserted them when they were overwhelmed by trauma back desensitization may make you less reactive, but if you cannot feel satisfaction in ordinary everyday living life will pass you by.

(p. 73)

He provides a compelling approach for patients with PTSD: such modalities as EMDR, dance, music, theater, and athletic activities can have beneficial effects in healing the dissociative defenses that the trauma produced. He suggests that the reason these modalities are more effective than talk therapy is that they allow patients to get in touch with the feelings that could not be processed cognitively at the time of the occurrence of the trauma.

The preference for self-understanding

We may conceive of this component of the therapeutic process during complementary moments as a dialogue, a conversation, between two people who have come together to address a task that they will jointly define. The substance of the task is the patient's distress or unsuccessful accommodations. The medium through which they will both address this task is the respective narratives that each brings to the setting. One way to conceptualize this dimension of the therapeutic dialogue is to view the narrative as the central organizer of the process. Patients bring to the clinical setting their self-histories and their unique interpretations of the events of their lives, often unaware of the impact that their neuropsychological deficits have had on them. For their part, therapists construct a narrative that incorporates what they know about the patient based on their experience and knowledge about the conditions that have affected the patient. This narrative includes aspects of the life stories their patients have shared, their understanding of the mental process that they believe contributed to the patient's sense of self.

The task that the dyad faces is that of co-constructing a coherent narrative that includes aspects of both the patient's and the therapist's narrative. This narrative then serves as an orienting text through which interpretations are made. It is subject to revisions and emendations. It reframes for the patient the meaning of past experiences, shedding new light on old stories or revising these stories in a manner that gives them new meanings. This process serves to strengthen the patients' sense of cohesion and permits them to give expression to their life goals and ambitions. Upon completion of this task the patients' sense of cohesion is strengthened and permits them to give expression to life goals and ambitions.

Understanding as a change agent

Patients contribute to the dialogue by presenting their self-narrative, which either is incomplete or contains elements of incoherence. The gaps in the narrative represent aspects of a person's life that are partly unintelligible, meaningless, or are conflictual. Neuropsychological deficits often interfere with the coherence of the self-narrative, leading to personal meanings that are incomprehensible to others or at variance with shared meanings of the culture. We cannot divorce the issues of the coherence or incoherence of the self-narrative from the correspondence between the account given in the self-narrative and the historical events. A fictitious self-narrative (a fantasy) cannot carry the weight required to heal a patient's inability to accommodate to the context or to maintain a sense of self-cohesion. Shared meanings emerge from the sharing of personal memories of events as understood within the context in which these occurred. The coherence of the narrative is related to those shared meanings and by extension to the view of reality as understood within the context.

As therapists, our contribution to the dialogue is to function, in part, as seekers of meaning. In that role, we present as historians who have an understanding of human nature and who are entrusted with the task of constructing a plausible coherent narrative of the patient's life. We are privy to the schisms to which their lives have been exposed. We are in the presence of a stirring struggle to make coherent what was formerly meaningless. By empathically indwelling with the patients in their experiences, we glean clues about their deficits and strengths. But that is only part of our task, because we also bring to the clinical setting the knowledge we have garnered through our empirical observations and apply these to the particular person we are trying to understand. This is especially true for patients with adjunctive deficits. With those patients, we address the self-deficits that served as attractors to organize their experiences and help them seek ways to compensate for or find the means to complement their sense of self.

During such moments, therapists attempt to facilitate the process through which patients acquire an understanding of their neuropsychological strengths and weaknesses in a manner that avoids the danger of aggravating their vulnerable sense of self by heightening their feelings of shame and inadequacy. Since the self-deficits and their effects often were transparent to them, this process requires reviewing previous accounts that the person accepted as explanatory of his feelings, thoughts, and behaviors. Understanding then provides patients with information about the nature of their deficits, whether these are of selfobject functions, self-regulatory difficulties, or adjunction functions.

At times within this dialogue, a tension arises between the patient's perspective and that of the therapist. This tension is particularly evident when a patient comes to therapy with an undiagnosed neuropsychological deficit. With some adults, it may take months to uncover the existence of an undiagnosed learning disorder or neuropsychological deficit, although an experienced therapist may quickly recognize the existence of the deficit from the patient's symptoms and from the transference/countertransference responses. Asking the patient to confront the deficits presents a set of difficulties that require careful negotiation.

For some patients, relief comes with the realization that there were reasons beyond their control that caused the problems they faced. This insight may lead to a reorganization of their view of themselves and their relational patterns. The outcome is an enhancement of the stability of their sense of cohesion. It may also give rise to emergent properties that move the patient to higher levels of organization, which depending on their capacity to integrate the new inputs may lead to a hierarchical or nested set of structures that represent greater maturation – that is, greater differentiation than existed previously and a more distinctive individuation.

Others experience profound distress at the thought that something within them was irreparably broken. They cannot accept the suggestion that they have a brain-based disorder. A clash may ensue between the two different narratives, which requires reconciliation. While neuropsychological testing may provide confirmation of the presence of a disorder, the practicalities may vitiate the value of taking such a step; costs may be prohibitive, neuropsychologists with the expertise to test such patients may not be available, and even if testing were to be completed and results obtained, the opportunities for remediation may not be available.

Ensuring the continuation of the dialogue becomes the urgent priority for the therapist and patient. In my experience, too forceful an insistence on the correctness of the therapist's view is an invitation to the disruption of the treatment. I often suggest that the patient consider the possibility of such a deficit while the work continues. Over time, the preponderance of the evidence wins the day. Data about neuropsychological strength and weakness, about which the patient had no knowledge, leads the patient to reconsider. The outcome is that a different interpretation of past events clarifies many of the issues the patient confronted and provides a more meaningful integration of their experience.

Co-constructing a new narrative

As the dialogue evolves, the patient's current self-understanding is revealed. It is found to contain explanations that incorporate past responses by others, which led to unsuccessful accommodations. For her part, the therapist begins to form an outlook that constitutes a different narrative from the one the patient formulated. The divergence between the two narratives creates a tension that requires resolving.

A major dimension of the process is the co-creation of a new narrative based on shared meanings. This narrative may include what was not present in the old narrative – that is, it brings meanings to events whose meanings were lost or never existed. They may eventually be rendered meaningful, or if that is impossible, as sometimes happens, they may be accepted as part of the constraints imposed on us by our humanity.

With the establishment of a set of shared meanings regarding their respective narratives, the therapist and patient are in a position to co-construct a narrative that weaves together the elements of the patient's past and present experiences in the service of making sense of what occurred historically as well as what is occurring currently in the patient's life. This conscious understanding may be beneficial but of limited value if not accompanied by the affective experience that brings about the change in the patient's patterns of interactions.

Within this reconceptualization of the therapeutic dialogue, interpretations made by a therapist consists in the articulation of the interaction between the dyad or the filling in of a gap in the narrative being co-constructed. In continuity with this view, a self-disclosure may be interpreted as an effort on the part of the therapist to make intelligible some aspect of the narrative that had been obscured by other factors. It consists of a bit of information that is required to add to the coherence of the co-created narrative. Its appropriateness or inappropriateness becomes a function of its success in moving the process along (J. Palombo, 1987). As Aron (1996) emphasized, *"self-revelation is not an option for the analyst, it is an inevitability"* (p. 228, italics in original).

Constructions or reconstructions are new or edited versions of the personal meanings given by patients to their life experiences. They represent the coherent ordering of experiences as viewed through the template of the person's competencies. Since the narrative is a constitutive part of the patient's sense of self, the more coherent, consistent, and comprehensive it is, the greater the experience of cohesion and integration the person will experience.

As Saari (1986b) has stated, the therapeutic process

> involves the organizing of old meanings into newly constructed consciousness. What is curative is not so much the recovery of deeply rooted repressed material but the reordering of structures that underlie personal meaning and the symbolic capacities of the individual so that new meanings can be differentiated, constructed or abstracted.
>
> (p. 27)

To this I would add that an indispensable dimension is the sharing of the unintegrated affects in a context that makes these meaningful with the present re-arousal of those affects. The construction of a meaningful history can only occur if the old meanings are brought forth and the associated affects experienced. The role of the therapist as selfobject who can facilitate the new integration is often indispensable.

However, the therapeutic process is not reducible simply to the construction of a text or a narrative. As therapists, we understand that the functions of motives and their contribution to the organization of themes within the narrative is an integral part of our task. It is not only the content and its coherence with which we are concerned. We are also mindful of the factors that operate to give the narrative its unity, of the way in which the characters are cast, of the setting in which they are placed, and of the props used to fill in the gaps in the plot. This effort is not a cold, dispassionate attempt at making the facts fit into a neat episode in life. It carries the weight of a struggle to attain a sense of cohesion through sense-making. This sense-making comes through understanding, and understanding brings with it a sense of conviction as well as a sense of inner harmony and peace. The result is a feeling of having triumphed over some deep division within their sense of self.

Transference and countertransference: A narrative view

The transactions of the clinical setting are characterized by the unfolding of a transference from the patient to the therapist and by the experiences of a set of countertransferences with which the therapist responds. The transference is the expectation that the new relationship will provide the longed-for functions or will repair the injuries produced by past events when failures to respond to such expectations occurred. In other words, the patient's expectation is that the therapist will complement the patient's self-deficits.

The transference may now be interpreted as representing the themes that have organized the patient's experience of past dialogues; these themes represent the central motifs in the patient's narrative. The therapist may come to represent characters in the patient's past. The therapeutic setting may bring back elements of past settings that were significant to the patient. The countertransference represents the therapist's effort at, and the difficulties in, engaging the patient's dialogue through his system of meanings.

Since facts can only have meaning within the context of the totality of human experience, in treatment, the patient's narrative is examined through the horizons of meanings the therapist and patient bring to the relationship. By horizons of meaning, I mean the worldviews the participants in the dialogue bring to their interactions. During the exploration of the patient's personal meanings, a text is created that is given meaning through the horizons of understanding the therapist brings to the relationship. To the extent that the patient shares and can integrate the horizons of understanding, the text presented is revised and an autobiography is created. This autobiography, which is the product of the dialogue, will make coherent to the patient the past within the context of the present. The sense of continuity and completeness that is established will result in a sense of cohesion that will strengthen the patient's sense of self. The clinical enterprise is conceived in terms of a hermeneutic endeavor (Friedman, 1983, 1985).

From a narrative perspective, the concepts of transference and countertransference take on new meanings in this context. We can consider the transference/countertransference processes as reflecting the efforts of each member of the dyad to emplot the other into his narrative – that is, either the patient or the therapist is drawn to become a character in the plot of the other. What has been described as "enactment" we would consider in this view as the nonconscious or unconscious involvement on the part of one or both members of the dyad into the narrative of the other, which I call emplotment.

The patient nonconsciously relives, in the transference, old patterns with little understanding of the motives for her conduct. Having an understanding for her conduct – that is, having a narrative interpretation that ties disparate events together – provides a road map that serves as a guide to the patient. The therapist's responses serve to reveal the nature of the patterns and to begin to build new patterns for the patient's conduct. As the therapist is informed by the patient of the narrative themes that shape the enactments, the therapist gains an understanding that can provide an explanation to the patient as well as an understanding of the explanation the patient has given to himself for his conduct. As new experiences occur between the therapist and patient, the therapist has an opportunity to reframe the patient's understanding of his patient narrative and even help the patient create an entirely new self-narrative.

Through mindsharing, the therapist is able to empathize with the patient's state and begins to experience the patient's self-deficits, both the selfobject and adjunctive deficits. As the dialogue evolves, the patient's current self-understanding is revealed. It is found to contain explanations that incorporate past responses by others, which led to unsuccessful accommodations. For her part, the therapist begins to form an outlook that constitutes a different narrative from the one the patient formulated. The divergence between the two narratives creates a tension that requires resolving.

When the transference is in the foreground, the therapist may also be able to complement the patient's self-deficits by providing missing adjunctive functions related to the self-deficits. The provision of these adjunctive functions activates the patient's hope that someone is there who understands. At other times, the therapist may wish to demonstrate to the patient that he or she is not like the others in the patient's milieu who got angry, set impossible expectations, or inflicted punishment for nonconformity. The therapist then provides a corrective experience for the patient. The positive transference is instrumental in helping patients maintain a sense of self-cohesion. Through the therapist's empathy for the distress, the therapist creates a context within which the patients feel a sense of connection and complementarity with someone who cares.

The replication of old patterns provides an opportunity through the dialogue to assist the person in the task of integrating self-experiences. If successful, this endeavor will help the patient to attain a more coherent meaning system, which will result in the experience of greater cohesion. As the therapist reveals her narratives, through interpretations, to the patient, if the patient is capable of integrating these explanations, the self-reorganization begins to occur that displaces the old unsuccessful accommodations with newer patterns. Ultimately, as therapists, we serve as interpreters of meanings to our patients. The success or failure of our interpretive efforts is contingent on the consonance of the explanatory metaphor we offer as a substitute for the text the patient presented us with for the patient's self-experience.

Clinical presentation: Pat[2]

Pat wrote this lengthy essay following a neuropsychological evaluation that found her to have the signs of a nonverbal learning disability. In this communication, she attempted to integrate that information with what she knew about herself and what she had experienced in treatment up to that point.

> I have been in psychotherapy with Joseph Palombo for over two years. Recently, I read his article "The Effect of Nonverbal Learning Disabilities on Children's Development: Theoretical & Diagnostic Considerations." In December of 1993, W. R. and J. G. administered a battery of 20 tests to me. Early this year, they returned a neuropsychological evaluation. I believe that the following phrase from the evaluation of me sums up my interest in Dr. Palombo's paper: "... the cluster of visuo-spatial difficulties and affective processing deficits make up an entity known as non-verbal learning disability."
>
> I am a 42-year-old woman. I have never been married and have been physically and financially independent since I was 18. For most of that time, I've

worked for a governmental agency. In the last three years, I have accumulated almost a year of college credit, geared more toward my areas of interests than a degree program. The therapy, the schooling, and a recent emergence in creative writing are slowly pulling me out of wherever I spent the first 40 years of my life. The puzzle that Joe and I have been recently trying to solve, is how much of my prior (and present) difficulties were related to this nonverbal learning disability and how much to other factors.

When I first requested a referral to see a therapist, it was because I was feeling out of control from alcohol abuse. Immediately after I made the call, I stopped drinking. It was at least six weeks later before I met Joe. I now feel that the 15 years that I spent abusing alcohol was more related to clouding over other issues in my life than an "addiction." I am not presently abstinent, though I don't feel conflicted over my alcohol use. The layer underneath the alcohol use, we labeled dysthymia. (In one of the first sessions with Joe, he explained that for insurance reasons, we needed a diagnosis. I was taking Psych 101, got my hands on a *DSM-III-R*, and diagnosed myself as having a schizoid personality disorder. He overruled me on that one.)

Dysthymia (once I learned what it meant) made sense. Although superficially functioning, I was withdrawn, unmotivated in any direction, energy-less, and isolated (except, of course, when I was drinking in my friendly, neighborhood tavern).

It also made sense diachronically. My mother was and is severely clinically depressed. My father probably could be diagnosed as having a schizoid personality disorder, in that he seems to be devoid of human empathy. They divorced when I was 7 and both remarried volatile partners with their own share of diagnosable symptoms. My childhood was spent continually moving, not only physically, but into almost completely different familial situations (kind of a "please pass the kids" syndrome). My brother, at least until I was 14, was the only constant in these ever-changing environments.

During the first year of treatment, Joe probably did little more than try to fill selfobject functions for me. I couldn't say for sure, because I was only occasionally emotionally with him. I don't know that this reaction could be labeled as resistance. I immediately liked and trusted him. I wanted to connect with him. But it has always seemed like there is a transparent barrier, perhaps made of Saran Wrap, which acts to mute connections between anyone and myself. Even now, in my relationship with Joe, the barrier is still there, though thankfully ripped and shredded. Now, he evokes long latent emotions. I respond, with only quiet temper tantrums, in exactly the way he writes on page 11 about children with NVLD: "They respond to affect laden situations with anxiety, withdrawal or sadness. They appear to have problems in the modulation of certain affects. When frustrated, they lose control and have temper tantrums. Their response to most feelings is one of generalized excitement that is unfocused and lacking in content." Joe goes on to explain the effect this has on the adults around the child.

I've probably learned to hide the disorientation I feel when I'm suddenly "attacked" by this sort of disembodied emotion. That's the closest that I could come to describing it, prior to reading Joe's explanation above. It's not a comfortable feeling!

So, first we have a layer of substance abuse. Then we have a layer of dysthymia. Then we have a layer of inadequately filled self-object functions. Now, we have a nonverbal learning disability. Which chicken laid which egg?

It was well over a year ago when I first brought up in therapy a feeling of kinship to something Joe had written about a woman whom he believed suffered from, among other things, a nonverbal learning disability (Palombo, 1993). (I was covertly reading his articles from the time I first learned that he was published. After I confided that, he made life easier for me and local librarians by giving me copies.) It was the first time I considered that my inability to remember faces, places, and things might come from something other than disinterest, stupidity, and/or laziness. It was the first time I considered that there might be a difference between my experience of the world and that of others. It had never come up in therapy before, because I thoroughly believed memory-aid masters who assert that everyone has the ability to develop a photographic memory if they only make an effort. I failed in my effort, so why keep trying? I knew that whenever I found myself in a different environment and with different people, I would only remember the most outstanding characteristics. I had learned to accept that. It wasn't something I would think to bring up in therapy. It was just the way it was. It wasn't something that most therapists would have understood, even if I had brought it up.

So, Joe began to explain some of the normal ramifications of a NVLD. Some fit, some didn't. My handwriting was terrible as a child, but so is most children's. I spent a lot of time working at it. It is now compulsively legible. I never learned arithmetic tables, but I could get around it with a strong understanding of mathematics. (I have never known by rote what 8×7 is, but I could always figure it out.) I hated art and phys ed, because they made me feel incompetent. I am only physically organized with efforts of will which soon deteriorate, so my apartment and my work space are frequently in shambles. I bought my condo six years ago. I have never felt capable of putting up a picture or decorating, because I fear that I would do it "wrong." I find visual entertainment frustrating. I never know "who is who" in movies. I prefer old Westerns where the good guys always wear white hats. I passionately avoid games such as "Trivial Pursuit." I hate puzzles. They underline what I feel are my inadequacies. Likewise, I don't want to engage in sports that require any kind of eye-hand coordination. (I do like to swim.)

These things contributed to my isolation. That brings us to the affective ramifications I've experienced, at least in part, because of this disability.

I remember at an early age forcing myself to learn to make and retain eye contact with people, because someone told me that I should. The neuropsychological evaluation included these observations: "She made clear efforts to engage the examiners appropriately, chatting and sustaining eye contact for long periods of time. Her continuous gaze and lack of nonverbal feedback, such as nodding and smiling during conversation, seemed a bit unnatural and might feel somewhat uncomfortable to others." It is unnatural! Although my gaze appears to be into the other person's eyes, there is that Saran Wrap shield in between. I don't want either of us to see through "the windows of our souls." I probably won't even remember meeting you the next time I see you.

Although nothing significant in the area was noted (or, I believe, tested for) in the evaluation, I also seem to have a poor oral memory of any affect-laden situation. I tape my sessions with Joe. When I listen to them, even immediately afterward, I often wonder where I was. In fact, I've recently begun to tape anything that I truly care about, because I don't trust my memory in this area any more than I trust my visual memory. Perhaps Joe could figure out if there is a tie-in. It probably has to do with strong affect.

I'm presently enrolled in a creative writing course. Most of the work I've done has been slightly fictionalized personal recounting. As I was re-reading some of it, I was struck by the number of times I alluded to going from one "world" to another or of being in a different "world." In many of Joe's papers, he refers to a feeling of fragmenting or incoherent self-narratives, both from a self-psychological perspective when self-object functions are not met and in children with verbal or nonverbal disabilities, which cause them to see the world differently from their caretakers. I believe that I have maintained a reasonably coherent self-narrative because I have been able to fractionalize the world instead of myself.

Each time that I moved – from depressed mother in a rented house to self-involved father in a roach-ridden apartment, to spending summers with my grandmother, to a house in the suburbs with a new obsessive-compulsive stepmother and younger stepbrothers who I was expected to care for, to an apartment with my depressed mother and volatile stepfather – I experienced "another" world.

Each school I was transplanted to (nine through high school) apparently had different rules. I had nothing to take with me; each time life changed. It seemed that none of the previously learned behavior was applicable to the new situation. I was always starting from scratch.

Starting from scratch meant almost complete initial withdrawal. I had to figure out this new world. I had to categorize the new cast of characters. After a time, I usually made one close friend who was also marked as "an outsider." These friends may have acted as buffers by explaining the parts of the world I didn't understand. Their "outsideness" generally related to overt shyness, being "the fat kid," or coming from "the wrong side of the tracks." Since I never understood any of these concepts, I'm sure that I filled equal needs by just accepting them. Then it was time to move on. We would vow perpetual friendship. For a time, we'd write. But again, I was in a new world that had no connection with the older world. My energy was sapped in learning the new rules. I could not maintain a friendship.

Similar withdrawal accompanied new family situations. Actually, by the time I was 10, I learned to build a barrier between myself and all new and old family members. In this arena, there was no one to explain the new rules. My brother was just as confused as I was and four years older. He had the escape of high school and after-school work. I learned to love to read in my bedroom with my door locked.

How does this apply to Joe's paper? I don't believe that in early childhood I had any sense of viewing the world "idiosyncratically," as he refers to it. I believe that both my brother and my father share my nonverbal disability. Confusion as to which waitress was ours in a restaurant, which beach we had last been to, and which bush bore black raspberries was shared by all of us. Our responses, though perhaps confusing to those around us, seemed perfectly normal (from page 9 of Joe's paper, it seems likely that he would not agree that this would be the expected outcome when people live together with shared NVLDs.) It was only at 10 years old, when my world changed to a completely "different world" that difficulties arose.

When my father remarried, he turned me over to my stepmother and for all practical purposes withdrew from my life. My brother began high school. Suddenly, everything seemed "idiosyncratic." Looking back on the time, I always thought that it was my stepmother's emotional difficulties that started my own. In light of Joe's paper, it may have been that I was suddenly thrust into a world which was viewed completely differently by those closest to me. Now, there was a lack of cohesion.

But however it came about, I had 10 years of a reasonably coherent self-narrative built up. My aunt, Dodie, taught psychological testing at Western Michigan University in Kalamazoo. She used me as a "testing guinea pig for her class" when I was 10. I loved it – wonderful attention! Not only did I score a high IQ, but I was also assessed to be abnormally well-adjusted, considering the trauma of living through a divorce, an infrequent phenomenon at the time. When my father remarried, I did withdraw. I became hyper-vigilant. But I never disintegrated. It was the world that was different. Not me. All I had to do was keep learning new rules. Sure, it wore me out. Sure, I escaped into mild, chronic depression. Sure, the 15-year sojourn in my local tavern gave me a feeling of belonging that I had never had. But, it seems that in many areas, I was able to compensate without paying too high a price.

I have used two areas of compensation that Joe mentions (page 18) for as long as I can remember: I almost always "verbally mediate" nonverbal tasks and "rehearse verbally what is to occur in anticipation of an encounter with a new function." Now, with the knowledge of the disability, I am further able to compensate by unashamedly questioning others in order to aid in the rehearsal. I'm more able to admit that I have no recall of previous meetings with people. (The conclusion that Joe has come to, that NVLD people don't have a good sense of what is a socially acceptable confidence, is a great aid in this area. I just blurt out that I have this peculiar problem and they tell me who they are. Of course, they then may want to run!) Often I used to try to cleverly finesse my way through uncomfortable situations, or more frequently, just avoid them. This isn't uncommon for people, even without my visual memory deficits. The difference was that often I had met these people many times before, not just once. They knew me and things about me. It turned out that I had often had intimate prior conversations with them, but I had no recall. All my memory told me, was that given certain situations, it was probable that I should recognize them. In the last six months, now that I have an understanding of what is going on, I've learned to take notes, write down names with brief descriptions of a memorable peculiarity, and rehearse the lists prior to entering a situation when I'm likely to see the same people again. I've learned not to expect to recognize another person as a gestalt until after many meetings. I didn't even recognize a picture of myself taken at a recent work-related meeting.

Joe also writes of caretakers complementing these sorts of disabilities or being unable to, because the child's behavior seems so foreign. When I first read Joe's paper, I wondered whether my impression of my mother's emotional absence could have something to do with my misreading her intentions and, because of the disability, reacting unusually toward her. Maybe so; however, other sources do attest to her clinical depression. Likewise, I wondered about my father. If anything, until I was 10, he related more empathically with me than he probably ever has with anyone. After that, I think that I just emotionally outgrew him. Obviously, from this upbringing, there was no chance of someone else performing a complementary function, with the possible exception of the short-term friends that I mentioned, or any chance of a developing symbiosis.

Would it have helped me if I had been diagnosed with a nonverbal learning disability at an early age, even with everything else remaining the same in my upbringing? I have no doubt that it would have, provided I was at an age where I could at least partially understand it. No caretaker could have, but at 10, I think that I would have. This would be where some of the negative affective results could have been avoided. Children born with other sorts of handicaps learn to understand them and are probably less likely to blame themselves for things beyond their control. In the range of possible handicaps, a nonverbal learning disability would certainly not rate highly in its disabling features. Looking back on ways I adjusted to the world, the only truly harmful outcomes came from the elusiveness of the problem. As I said at the beginning, the world translates the effect as being caused from laziness, inattention, or stupidity. It is similar to the way children with verbal disabilities were looked at prior to the discoveries of such things as dyslexia. With the knowledge that there is a cause outside of my control, I could have learned at a much earlier age to modulate the control that I do have to fit the context.

Instead, I reacted by trying to hide my laziness, inattention, and stupidity. I withdrew to the extent possible. And, although I'm not sure that Joe follows me on this one, I think that I divided the world rather than myself, thus maintaining a certain coherence. I conceptualize my moves from Chicago to Arlington Heights to Riverside to Evanston (all in the Chicagoland area) as being similar to an untraveled American who only understands English going from Japan to Australia to Greece. In order to survive, I believed that each situation had to be treated as a "different" world. If, from early on, I had a better understanding of the dynamics of the disability that made this true, maybe I could have applied learning from the past to the present and the future and not forever have felt like "a stranger in a strange land."

Summary

During complementary moments, the issues in the foreground of the interaction between patients and therapists center on the recognition process. This process involves the re-creation of the match between the patient's self-deficits and the complementary functions that would restore to the patient the sense of well-being that was lost. I focused on two aspects of the relationship that could be instrumental in the achievement of that goal: the preference for self-cohesion and the co-creation of a coherent narrative.

Seen through the lens of the transference/countertransference during moments when the preference for self-cohesion is dominant, patients in the transference replicate their inner world, their past relationships, as well as the attractors formed by their self-deficits. We encounter the central dynamics that organize patients' psychological functions, which are the nonconscious awareness of their self-deficits and their reparative efforts to fill in those deficits. Mending the person's sense of self-cohesion requires restoring the system's capacity to accommodate successfully to the circumstances in which patients find themselves (see Jaenicke, 2013).

In the countertransference, therapists experience the urge to complement the patients' missing functions; they also experience the pressure to conform to patients' expectations that they responded as others had in the patients' past. These dual facets of the transference/countertransference become central themes of the dialogue.

In this view, what was traditionally characterized as "interpretation" of aspects of this process, I now reframe as a joint endeavor in which both therapists and patients undertake the task of uncovering the various mental processes that patients had used to maintain a stable sense of self in spite of their self-deficits. Central to this aspect of the dialogue is the focus on the wall of shame built by patients behind which to hide so as to not reveal their self-deficits. The defenses of dissociation and disavowal are exemplars of these efforts.

The second component of the dialogue during complementary moments is the preference for a coherent narrative. When such moments are in the foreground of the interaction, we may conceive of the dialogue as a conversation in which patients present their narratives to explain their interpretations of their experiences and those associated with the events in their lives. For their part, therapists have constructed their own narratives (psychodynamic formulation) to explain what they believe happened to the patients. The conversation then centers on finding a shared set of meanings that could result in the co-construction of a narrative that incorporates elements of both the patient's and the therapist's narratives.

As the patient's narrative unfolds, the themes will reveal the place of each of these factors in the patient's history, self-deficits, and relational patterns. However, the connections between events and the patient's self-understanding will reveal the personal meanings the patient has drawn from his experiences and the patterns of interaction that emerged. Often left out of this self-understanding will be the place of the neuropsychological deficits in the patient's life. Therapists address this gap in self-understanding during complementary moments.

Part of the conversation now includes the delicate tasks of introducing to the patient the nature of their neuropsychological deficits and to re-examine in light of these deficits the role these played in the patient's life. Such understanding is central to the emergence of a narrative, as without it a large segment of the contribution to the patient's wall of shame will be missing. During moments when *understanding* is in the forefront of interactions, therapists provide patients with information about their self-deficits. This information will raise their awareness of the nature of the self-deficits and demonstrate to them the effects these have had on their lives. As patients relive the pain associated with the narcissistic injuries they suffered and the anxieties that engulfed their lives, therapists will assist them to deal with the wall of shame they had built to deal with those experiences.

Within the therapeutic dialogue, what is replicated is the meaning that patients attached to their experiences. A tension arises between the patient's perspective and that of the therapist. The tension is related to the personal experiences and expectations the patient brings that the therapist must understand. This tension reveals itself in the ways shared experiences between patient and therapist are understood and the ways in which the patient feels misunderstood. The patient sees aspects of the present through the past. The therapist at first does not share the same perspective. The reinterpretations given by the therapist serve as points of departure for the patient to engage in the dialogue (Beebe & Lachmann, 1998; Beebe, Rustin, Sorter, & Knoblauch, 2005).

From the perspective of this preference for a coherent self-narrative, new meanings are found in the concept of transference and countertransference. Since each narrative has a plot (central theme that acts as an attractor) and a protagonist, each member of the dyad may find herself emplotted into the other's narrative. This form of "enactment" becomes central to understanding the patients' self-deficits as well as to the structure of past relationships. In the countertransference, therapists may bring their own histories, their theoretical biases, or their own nonconscious conformity to the patient's expectations by becoming one of the characters in the patient's narratives.

The task of co-constructing a new narrative then becomes more than simply arriving at a shared narrative to which both agree (see Spence, 1982). It is essential that elements of the narrative conform with historical facts as well as facts established by neuropsychological data. What is curative is not so much the recovery of deeply rooted repressed material but the reordering of the personal meaning around which attractors were formed so that new meanings can replace the old beliefs. It is the reordering of structures that underlies personal meaning and the symbolic capacities of the individual so that new meanings can be differentiated, constructed, or abstracted (Saari, 1986a).

The evidence for the greater integration of the patient's experiences is found in the greater coherence of the patient's self-narrative. Themes that formerly reflected the construal personal meanings now encompass a set of shared meanings that grew out of the patient's maturation and experiences in therapy. It is difficult to point to specific events or interventions that produce this greater sense of coherence; it usually results from the cumulative effects of the therapeutic dialogue.

Notes

1 I am indebted to Kacie Liput for this vivid illustration of an enactment.
2 From Palombo, J. (2000). A disorder of the self in an adult with a nonverbal learning disability. In Goldberg (Ed.), *Progress in self psychology* (Vol. 16, pp. 311–335). Hillsdale, NJ: The Analytic Press.

References

Aron, L. (1996). *A meeting of minds: Mutuality in psychoanalysis.* New York: Routledge.
Aron, L. (2003). The paradoxical place of enactment in psychoanalysis: Introduction. *Psychoanalytic Dialogues, 13,* 623–631.
Aron, L., & Atlas, G. (2015). Generative enactment: Memories from the future. *Psychoanalytic Dialogues, 25,* 309–324.
Basch, M. F. (1975). *External reality and disavowal.* Unpublished Manuscript.
Beebe, B., & Lachmann, F. M. (1998). Co-constructing inner and relational processes: Self- and mutual regulation in infant research and adult treatment. *Psychoanalytic Psychology, 15*(4), 480–516.
Beebe, B., Rustin, J., Sorter, D., & Knoblauch, S. (2005). An expanded view of forms of intersubjectivity in infancy and their application to psychoanalysis. In B. Beebe, S. Knoblauch, J. Rustin, & D. Sorter (Eds.), *Forms of intersubjectivity in infant research and adult treatment* (pp. 55–88). New York: Other Press.
Bromberg, P. M. (2003). Something wicked this way comes: Trauma, dissociation, an conflict: The space where psychoanalysis, cognitive science, and neuroscience overlap. *Psychoanalytic Psychology, 20,* 558–574.
Bromberg, P. M. (2011). *The shadow of the tsunami and the growth of the relational mind.* New York: Routledge.
Friedman, L. (1983). Seeing something new in something old. In A. Goldberg (Ed.), *The Future of Psychoanalysis* (pp. 137–164). New York: International Universities Press.
Friedman, L. (1985). Toward a comprehensive theory of treatment. *Psychoanalytic Inquiry, 5,* 589–600.
Gerhardt, J., & Sweetnam, A. (2001). The intersubjective turn in psychoanalysis: A comparison of contemporary theories: part 2: Christopher Bollas. *Psychoanalytic Dialogues, 11,* 43–92.
Harris, A., & Gold, B. H. (2001). The fog rolled in: Induced dissociative states in clinical process. *Psychoanalytic Dialogues, 11,* 357–384.
Jaenicke, C. (2013). When the bell tolls: A systems view of cure. *International Journal of Psychoanalytic Self Psychology, 8,* 245–264.
Janet, P. (1907/2012). *The major symptoms of hysteria: Fifteen lectures given in the medical school of Harvard university.* Retrieved from www.forgottenbooks.org.
Kohut, H. (1984). *How does analysis cure?* Chicago: The University of Chicago Press.
Levin, F. M. (1997). Integrating some mind and brain views of transference: The phenomena. *Journal of the American Psychoanalytic Association, 45*(4), 1121–1151.
Ogden, P. (2009). Emotion, mindfulness, and movement: Expanding the regulatory boundaries of the window of affect tolerance. In D. Fosha, D. J. Siegel, & M. F. Solomon (Eds.), *The healing power of emotion: Affective neuroscience, development, and clinical practice* (pp. 204–230). New York: W. W. Norton.

Ornstein, P. H., & Ornstein, A. (1985). Clinical understanding and explaining: The empathic vantage point. In A. Goldberg (Ed.), *Progress in self psychology* (Vol. 1, pp. 43–61). Hillsdale, NJ: The Analytic Press.

Palombo, J. (1993). Neurocognitive deficits, developmental distortions, and incoherent narratives. Psychoanalytic Inquiry, 13(1), 85–102.

Palombo, J. (1987). Spontaneous self disclosure in psychotherapy. *Clinical Social Work Journal*, 15(2), 107–120.

Palombo, J. (2001). The therapeutic process with children with learning disorders. *Psychoanalytic Social Work*, 8(3/4), 143–168.

Saari, C. (1986a). The created relationship: Transference, countertransference and the therapeutic culture. *Clinical Social Work Journal*, 14(1), 39–51.

Saari, C. (1986b). The use of metaphor in therapeutic communication with young adolescents. *Child & Adolescent Social Work Journal*, 3(1), 15–25.

Schore, A. N. (2012). *The science of the art of psychotherapy*. New York: W. W. Norton.

Spence, D. P. (1982). *Narrative truth and historical truth*. New York: W. W. Norton.

Van Der Kolk, B. A. (2014). *The body keeps the score: Brain, mind, and body in the healing of trauma*. New York: Viking.

Chapter 10

The therapeutic dialogue

Disjunctive moments

The feature that organizes disjunctive moments is the *rupture and repair process* (cf. Beebe & Lachmann, 2002; Schore, 2003). The *rupture* represents a failure in the system's functionality. The members of the therapeutic dyad appear to go their separate ways. Disruptions in mindsharing are evident and the fittedness between patient and therapist fails to provide the complementarity necessary for the therapeutic process to progress. Attractors may emerge within the system that lead to stalemates or that impede the mindsharing process (cf. Sandmeyer, 2016).

The *repair* process involves the reestablishment of the therapeutic alliance that characterized concordant moments. Through this process, therapist and patient acknowledge the breakdown and set about remediating the situation. This remediation entails the participation of both members of the dyad in the restoration of the dialogue. To assign responsibility to either member alone for the rupture or the repair is to undercut the view that the participants are part of a system and that each is not the sole contributor to the process. Such occurrences are an inevitable part of the process; however, they provide an opportunity for therapeutic work. This ebb and flow in the process is a major component of the curative dimension.

When disjunctive moments occur, they present both dangers and opportunities for both members of the dyad. On one hand, they present a danger to patients that may frighten them into fleeing from the treatment, while therapists may be drawn into enactments of the dynamics or to defend against the intense feelings generated. On the other hand, these moments offer an opportunity to undo the patient's withdrawal and isolation, bringing renewed hope for a deeper connection with another person, while the therapist's acknowledgment of her contribution to the rupture becomes a transformative moment for the patient, who then feels recognized and empowered. A repair of the breach may ensue.

Ruptures

As stated earlier, ruptures are episodes during which *a derailment of the therapeutic dialogue has* occurred (see Beebe & Lachmann, 2002). Such ruptures in the therapeutic process will invariably occur. The issue is not whether it is therapeutic or un-therapeutic that they occur, but rather that once having occurred, how they are managed determines the course of the treatment. Many factors may cause such derailments, some internal to the process and some triggered by external circumstances. Among the external factors is the therapist's unfamiliarity with neuropsychological deficits that may lead the therapist to misinterpret the motives for a patient's thoughts or actions. Therapists may interpret thoughts or actions that were driven by impaired functional brain systems that were not under the patient's control, such as their inability to read or their impulsive behaviors, as motivated by unconscious intentions. The patient experiences these interpretations as a repetition of the trauma of being misunderstood or at best as puzzling and missing the mark. The derailed dialogue represents a repetition of patterns of responses by others in the patient's past. A rupture ensues.

In this chapter, I limit myself to a discussion of two contributors to these ruptures: those that are related to the *fear of retraumatization* and those that result from *failures in the recognition process* that lead to the loss of self-cohesion in the patient. Both of these processes represent miscarriages of mindsharing. When such disjunctions occur, *the treatment is in crisis*; one or more components of the system have ceased to function, and the dialogue between the participants is derailed. It is then essential that the therapist and patient heal the rupture and reestablish the concordance between them.

Fears of retraumatization

Many patients with neuropsychological deficits have histories of having been exposed to humiliating experiences early in their lives. Some were bullied and marginalized by their peers. These patients fear the revival of these experiences. They tend to anticipate that a retraumatization will occur in the therapeutic relationship. This anticipation arises out of their expectation that old patterns will recur in new situations. In the transference, they may experience the therapist as the embodiment of those who had injured them in the past. Something about the therapist, whether embedded in his personality or in a particular response to the patient, primes the patient to respond as though the therapist were a "character" in her narrative, or as one of my patients put it, "They want to put him [the therapist] into their movie!" In the complementary interplay between patient and therapist, a nucleus of reality embedded in the activities or the personality of the therapist may become the focus of the interaction for the patient. The patient may attach meanings that set off negative expectations or revive past traumatic experiences.

The conditions for the activation of those fears is a "seed" of reality in the transference/countertransference configuration that permits the patient to structure her perceptions in accordance with past experiences or with current sources of anxiety. This may occur as a result of some small, perhaps inadvertent response on the part of the therapist who misses the mark and that the patient experiences as intentional or even as maliciously inflicted. Patients have a compelling need to bind their anxiety by anchoring their concerns into some concrete manifestation to which they may attribute their fears. The stage is set for an enactment of a segment of the patient's past. Therapists may contribute to the enactment by nonconsciously responding as others had done in the past. At times, such breaches may represent titrated replications of the past, which can assist in the reconstruction of the patient's original experience.

If the therapist is unable to respond to the patient's fears, the patient will experience that incapacity as an intentional assault. In a sense, the therapist's motives are irrelevant; only the effect on the patient is relevant. Such disjunctions become crises in the treatment that requires repair to make further work possible. For example, there are moments when the frustration and rage that have accumulated in the patient from years of feeling isolated and misunderstood may surface in the relationship with the therapist. The therapist in turn responds with impatience, anger, puzzlement, or distancing. The patient's rage at others must be distinguished from the frustration and rage the patient may feel toward the therapist. While both are understandable, the therapist must be able to look at and acknowledge any contribution he or she has made to provoke the patient's response. That piece of reality must first be addressed before the transference dimensions can be dealt with.

Such ruptures must not be seen only as indicators of the therapist's or the patient's psychopathology. If the obligatory nature of the therapist's response is seen as representing the limits of the capacity for a relationship with that patient, then it is possible to conceive of the interactions as the dramatic unfolding and convergence of the flaws in the personalities of both patient and therapist. From such a perspective, the inevitability of the clash is present from the day of the first encounter. However, since such collisions can neither be predicted nor avoided, it is not helpful to say that with greater self-awareness or more treatment, the therapist might have avoided the incident (Searles, 1975).

Failures in recognition

As we have seen, the recognition process involves the "fitting together" between the patient's longing for a complementary response and the therapist's response to that patient's desire. Depending on the nature of the therapist's response, the patient may feel emotionally restored, in which case the patient can regain or maintain a sense of self-cohesion. Or the patient may experience the response as at best not addressing his needs or at worse replicating a traumatic past. If the latter occurs, then a breach in the empathic bond will occur. The question we confront is: How are we to understand the dynamics of the breach that occurs because of a failure in recognition?

An example may best illustrate the dilemmas that the dyad faces when such a failure threatens the therapeutic dialogue. Gary was a 42-year-old successful investor, who had made a fortune through his impulsive speculative strategies. However, his personal life was in total disarray. He was twice married and divorced, his relationships with his young children were disordered because he could never predictably arrange visitations with them, and he was constantly being taken to court for his failure to make the alimony payments due to his former wives in a timely manner. It is not surprising, then, that in the twice-a-week treatment these same patterns were manifested. He could not arrive on time for his sessions, sometimes he "forgot" appointments, and his bills were never paid on time.

At first, the therapist found himself irritated by the patient's disruptive behavior. He interpreted the dynamics as resulting from the chaotic circumstances of the patient's childhood. When these interpretations were ineffective in bringing about any changes, he felt that the patient's resistance to change made him unable to benefit from the treatment. In the meantime, the patient's life grew more chaotic as he despaired of finding relief from his symptoms. The treatment was at an impasse. A serious rupture was in the offing.

At this juncture, the therapist sought a consultation. Fortunately, the consultant was familiar with these situations and suggested that the patient suffered from a serious executive function disorder, which subsequent neuropsychological testing confirmed. The therapist's unfamiliarity with the condition led him to attribute the motives for the patient's actions exclusively to relational difficulties. While these difficulties were part of the patient's problems, without the added understanding of the other factors, the therapy replicated the repeated misunderstandings to which the patient had been exposed.

Repairs

Once a rupture has occurred, there are many hazards to negotiate and obstacles for both the therapist and the patient to overcome before they can reestablish a therapeutic alliance. Repairs of breaches that result from the fear of retraumatization are less complicated that those related to failures in recognition.

Addressing the fear of retraumatization requires that the flow of empathy between the patient and therapist be reestablished, which necessitates a return to concordant moments. We see, then, that as the therapist responds differently from the way others have, a new set of experiences is generated for the patient. This new set of experiences lays the groundwork for what is to be curative in the process. Through the therapeutic process, patients experience patterns that are different from those to which they resorted in the past and gain an understanding of the old patterns through the therapist's interpretations. Patients are then in a position to compensate for their deficits. The new patterns include the meanings of past experiences and the new meanings gained through the relationship with the therapist. The understanding that patients acquire through this set of shared experiences with the therapist serves to break through their former isolation. Patterns that were central in the configuration of the patient personality are reshaped. New patterns come into play, and the patient's expectations are modified. These new patterns give the patient greater hope for success than was possible in the past.

From a dynamic systems perspective, repairs to the failures in recognition involve addressing the patient's need for a complementary function.

From the patient's perspective, the breach had occurred because the therapist was unable or unwilling to provide the needed function. From the therapist's perspective, the struggle centered around what constituted providing the function. If the therapist limited his responses to an interpretation of what the patient needed, the patient may have experienced such interventions as insufficient to allay her anxiety. Some patients require that the therapist provide the function, whether a selfobject or an adjunctive function. During such critical moments, a failure to respond on the part of the therapist will lead to a rupture. The complexity that the therapist faces is that, at times, such ruptures are a necessary part of the therapeutic process.

The issue centers on the patient's capacity to maintain a sense of self-cohesion without the function that is critical to the capacity to accommodate successfully to their context. Some patients find that an understanding of the function they seek as sufficient, whereas others seem to urgently need the function. For the latter group of patients, they are impaired in their ability to function without the assurance of someone that is available to provide the function.

In the previous illustration of Gary, the circumstances necessitated a response that included providing the function until other interventions were possible. The therapist arranged for his secretary to remind the patient of his appointment each morning on the day of the appointment. The patient created a bank account from which the therapist could draw for the timely payment of his bills. The therapist recommended that the patient hire an "executive secretary" who could take charge of many of the details in the patient's life that were often unattended. With the assistance of the "auxiliary functions," the patient's life was stabilized sufficiently so that the work of dealing with the relational issues that had resulted from the patient's neuropsychological deficits could be undertaken.

Finally, for each therapist, a number of narcissistic issues are raised in the course of attempting to repair the breaches that have occurred. First, there is the painful confession of unresolved issues that are stirred by the welter of memories and feelings brought forth by the patient. Second, there is the concession that the therapist's competence as a clinician is not as perfect as he or she would like to think it is. The therapist may feel that she has failed to live up to her ideal of what a therapist should be (see Morrison, 2008). Third, there is the resentment toward the patient for being the agent that brings these irritants to the foreground. The therapist's therapeutic ambitions are defeated and he or she is revealed as vulnerable and human. If the therapist can overcome these narcissistic injuries, he or she is able to move on in the process.

The task of healing the rupture and of remaining as the benign selfobject and restoring the capacity to listen to the patient becomes focal to the treatment at that point. The therapist may acknowledge the contribution to the rupture. Yet, that alone does not heal the rupture, nor does it have a prolonged therapeutic effect. What must follow is the recognition that a repetition has occurred and that this pattern must be all too familiar to the patient. The repetition of the past in the present becomes the shared experience that both therapist and patient can now use to repair the patient's deficit. Patients must be able to move on, beyond their rage at the therapist, to a higher ground on which the relationship can be restored.

For Kohut (1971, 1977), the rupture is prompted by a failure in the therapist's empathy for the patient. The therapist placed heavy reliance on the repair as a change agent in that it results in the "transmuting internalization" of the selfobject function that the patient requires to maintain a sense of self-cohesion. Atwood and Stolorow (1984) disparagingly called this process the "translocation" of psychic function, which they attributed to Kohut's one-person view of the process. This criticism does not diminish the effectiveness of the process that Kohut is describing as a change agent, even though his metapsychological explanation harks back to his roots in drive theory.

The desire for the restoration of the relationship is not always present in some patients; in spite of the therapist's best efforts, some will continue to brood and act out their rage with no thought of ever merging again with the therapist. Perhaps for these patients the rage must be seen and understood as an organizing experience, which prevents further disintegration. For them to give up their hatred would mean fragmentation. One may conceptualize such rage as a necessary dynamic for remaining cohesive. The therapist's forbearance is therefore called on to live with such a patient for as long as it seems necessary in the hope that an eventual attenuation of the rage can occur and a substitution of a benign therapeutic selfobject instead of rage will eventually occur.

Reorganization, individuation, and an enhanced sense of agency

The repair of the rupture leads patients to feel empowered by the process and of having their sense of agency affirmed. The establishment of a shared understanding of the events that led to the rupture and their roots in earlier experiences begins to breach the patient's sense of isolation and opens the possibility for new patterns of relating.

The hoped for outcome is that a reorganization of the patient's dynamics occurs and concordant and complementary moments are reestablished. The evidence for the greater integration of the patient's experiences is found in the greater sense of cohesiveness that patient experiences. Themes that formerly reflected the construal of personal meanings now encompass a set of shared meanings that grew out of the patient's maturation and experiences in therapy. Specific events or interventions that produce this greater sense of coherence are difficult to specify; a greater sense of cohesiveness usually results from the cumulative effects of the implementation of the broad therapeutic endeavor. The patient's rehabilitation and restoration to better function can be credited to the combination of greater understanding, improved social functioning, enhanced self-esteem, and the therapist's educative, corrective, and interpretive efforts.

Reflections on the limitations of the therapeutic encounter

One way to characterize the therapeutic relationship is in the terms that Stern (1983) used as a process involving "being with" a patient. The concept of "being with" is an experience near clinical expression that denotes a complex process. Being with someone is being available as a person with whom meaningful affective experiences can be shared. It raises the hope in the patient that the therapist will acknowledge and respond to the patient's unsatisfied longings. For the therapist to allow herself to be so experienced requires the discipline of letting her own longings into the background. This disciplined self-denial constitutes the essence of professional integrity.

This process highlights a paradox inherent in the therapeutic encounter: an ambiguous setting created to provide the conditions for a maximum amount of closeness within the context of safety and predictability, and at the same time, a distance created by the limits inherent in the emotional and social constraints imposed by the therapeutic "frame" – that is, by the limitations set by professional conduct.

With the evocation of the diatrophic attitude, which denotes warmth, caring, and compassion, and the curative fantasy, which also denotes hope for relief from anguish, a setting in which protectiveness and generativity is created. There are, however, sharply defined boundaries within this setting. While the therapist may try to imaginatively re-create what the patient experiences and attend to the feelings and thoughts evoked by these recreations, the therapist cannot immerse himself to the point of losing a dispassionate attitude that permits him to monitor the process. Each therapist is limited in the depth to which closeness may be reached. These limits will set the outer perimeter of what the therapist and patient will be able to explore.

The patient understands that while the therapist may on occasion disclose some personal information, an area of privacy exists which is not violated. Neither therapist nor patient may intrude into those areas as a demonstration of the respect each has for the other. The privacy of the therapist's life is maintained not only because of the possibility of clouding the transference but also because the context prescribes that the focus is on the patient. To be overly self-revelatory leads to a distraction away from that focus. It is also not always true that revealing personal facts to the patient dilutes the transference. Transferences often emerge in spite of what the patient knows about the therapist. The issue is that such revelations may confound the therapist in attempts to distinguish what is transference from non-transference, although, as I have noted elsewhere, there may be moments when a self-disclosure by the therapist may produce unexpected beneficial results (J. Palombo, 1987).

The standards of social propriety consistent with the cultural context in which the therapeutic atmosphere is created in the clinical setting always dictate the therapist's conduct. These standards assume an unqualified acceptance of, and respect for, the patient. The demeanor is not just part of the empathic stance that is proper for the conduct of the therapy; rather, it is implied by the code of conduct that society and the professional code of ethics prescribe. To deviate from such standards in its more serious forms can represent a betrayal of the patient's trust. At times, minor deviations from social propriety, such as not responding to questions with no explanation or not acknowledging a significant event in the patient's life, inserts into the setting an element of artificiality that cannot help but bring discomfort and/or embarrassment to the patient. Patients may perceive the deviations as reflective of the therapist's detachment or as a power play. Since the assurance of safety and respect that the therapist owes the patient are conditions for the possibility of conducting therapeutic work, therapists ought to explain to the patient the reasons for these deviations. Failure to adhere to these standards may introduce an iatrogenic element that will add to the patient's suffering.

In addition, an understanding must exist, whether explicit or implicit, that while much is disclosed between the patient and therapist, the patient may withhold some things. The expectation that the patient should disclose intensely private matters does not mean that the patient does not have the latitude to defer revealing information that may be greatly embarrassing. The injunction that the patient must reveal all of her thoughts and feeling was based on Freud's conviction that the demand created a conflict for the patient. The problem with the basic rule, as it was called, is that the insistence to follow it leads to compliance with the therapist's wishes, and compliance of this sort can take the form of an unresolvable resistance. It seems to me that what is critical in the process is not that the patient must comply with the basic rule but rather that the patient feel responsible about what is not disclosed. The issue centers on the meaning of the non-disclosure rather than the actual compliance with the demand.

Summary

A seemingly inevitable occurrence that is part of the therapeutic dialogue is that a rupture will occur. Therapists and patients then confront a failure that each may interpret as an intentional breach that is caused by the other. The relationship between the dyad appears irreparably broken and the process is now in crisis. There is an urgent need to repair this breach.

The causes of such ruptures are too numerous to catalog. In this chapter, I focus on two in particular: the fear of retraumatization and failures in the recognition process. The fear of retraumatization may be activated by the revival in the patient of some old reminiscences or by an action or attitude on the part of the therapist that the patient interprets as hurtful or sensitive. The failure in the recognition process highlights a mismatch between the patient's needs and the therapist's ability to respond to those needs. The movement of the therapeutic process comes to a standstill until a resolution can be found. Otherwise, an impasse may ensue, or even worse, the patient may decide to end the treatment.

The repair of such ruptures requires a close examination of their triggers. Such ruptures are usually profoundly meaningful in that they embody elements of the transference/countertransference dynamics that are at play between patient and therapist. The issue, then, is not so much to assign responsibility as to who caused the rupture, but rather to arrive at an understanding of the meaning of the rupture. Whether it is a replication of a pattern of relating to others that becomes enacted in the process, or whether it is a failed attempt at furthering the recognition process, a resolution requires that each member of the dyad acknowledge his contribution to what occurred. If that resolution is successful, it will bring with it insights into the dynamics that were involved and should permit patients to accommodate successfully to the context.

References

Atwood, G. E., & Stolorow, R. D. (1984). *Structures of subjectivity: Explorations in psychoanalytic phenomenology*. Hillsdale, NJ: The Analytic Press.

Beebe, B., & Lachmann, F. M. (2002). *Infant research and adult treatment: Co-constructing interactions*. Mahwah, NJ: The Analytic Press.

Kohut, H. (1971). *The analysis of the self*. New York: International Universities Press.

Kohut, H. (1977). *The restoration of the self*. New York: International Universities Press.

Morrison, A. P. (2008). The analyst's shame. *Contemporary Psychoanalysis*, *44*, 65–82.

Palombo, J. (1987). Spontaneous self disclosure in psychotherapy. *Clinical Social Work Journal*, *15*(2), 107–120.

Sandmeyer, J. (2016). The interplay between empathy and authenticity in moments of clinical disjunction. *International Journal of Psychoanalytic Self Psychology*, *11*(1), 60–74.

Schore, A. N. (2003). *Affect regulation and the repair of the self*. New York: W. W. Norton.

Searles, H. F. (1975). The patient as therapist to his analyst. In P. Giovacchini (Ed.), *Tactics in psychoanalytic therapy: Countertransference* (Vol. 2, pp. 95–151). New York: Jason Aronson.

Stern, D. N. (1983). The early development of schemas of self, other, and "self with other." In J. D. Lichtenberg & S. Kaplan (Eds.), *Reflections on self psychology* (pp. 49–84). Hillsdale, NJ: The Analytic Press.

Chapter 11
Conclusion

Clinicians who deal with patients with neuropsychological deficits face a major problem. That is, no psychodynamic theory exists to undergird a clinical theory that integrates neuropsychological, introspective, and interpersonal factors. In an effort to remedy this problem, I proposed in this contribution a neuropsychodynamic perspective, based on evolutionary principles, that offers an updated view of development, a redefinition of psychopathology, and a set of interventions that can help to improve the lives of these patients.

Nonlinear dynamic systems theories attempt to articulate the principles that govern the operations of the processes involved in the changes that occur within and among human beings. When applied to human conduct, those principles provide a powerful tool with which we can cross traditional disciplinary lines and integrate knowledge acquired by different disciplines into a broad understanding of human beings as biological, psychological, and social beings (Palombo, 2013). In this work, I offered a neuropsychodynamic systems perspective of self-deficits that, by using nonlinear dynamic systems theory and a complexity view of phenomena, attempts to integrate what we know about brain-based dysfunctions with concepts from psychoanalytic self psychology.

To do justice to our understanding of human nature, I proposed a three *levels-of-analysis* perspective that includes the neuropsychological, the introspective, and the interpersonal domain of knowledge. The levels-of-analysis perspective provides a phenomenological description of patients' experiences, with a particular focus on the affect states generated by the presence of self-deficits. The levels-of-analysis perspective is a heuristic that permits the use of a nonlinear dynamic systems view for the foundation of a clinical theory that addresses the issues of patients with neuropsychological deficits. A premise of the systems perspective is the proposition that all phenomena are part of a system and can have no existence outside of a system. Observations of phenomena therefore may only occur from within a system. I called this view the *neuropsychodynamic perspective*. This approach permits the integration of knowledge from multiple disciplines and perhaps dissipates some of the apparent conflict among the various schools that currently exist.

Based on these premises, I offered the construct of the self as a *complex adaptive system*, which made possible an updated view of development as a process rather than as a linear sequential set of phases or stages. It also provided for a view of psychopathology that envisions self-deficits that have their origins either in early emotional deprivation (i.e. selfobject deficits) or in innate impairments in particular areas of the brain (i.e. neuropsychological deficits). The outcome of such self-deficits often is an unsuccessful accommodation to the context that patients inhabit. Not all problems associated with the human condition result from brain dysfunctions, but brain function does affect the specific expression of all human feelings, thoughts, and behaviors.

A common response of patients with self-deficits is the nonconscious search for others to complement their deficient sense of self. What Stern (1983) calls "self-other complementing" refers to the patient's needs for complementarity. It consists in the provision of selfobject and adjunctive functions to assist in the restoration of a sense of self-cohesion. I proposed the construct of *mindsharing* to conceptualize the process through which self/other complementarity occurs as well as an empathic connection is maintained. Through mindsharing, patients feel understood, which reduces the sense of isolation into which they had withdrawn, and have their sense of self-cohesion stabilized or restored.

The clinical principles that emerge from these considerations expand the traditional view of the transference and countertransference and modify the recommended interventions. The expansion of the transference consists in the inclusion of the adjunctive deficits in its manifestations. Two types of interventions, understanding and complementing, added to other interventions that the therapist might use, produce a transformation of the person's affect state. During concordant moments, the person moves from conditions of uncertainty, anxiety, or depression to feeling reassured, comforted, and at peace. The outcome of these moments is a nonconscious reorganization of the patients' relational patterns such that new patterns that are less problematic replace old patterns that led to unsuccessful accommodations.

During complementary moments, the modifications of the treatment consists of the necessity of adding to the traditional view explanations of the nature of the brain dysfunction and the consequences these have had on the person's life and the empowerment of the patient to become a proactive participant in her recovery. Patients thirst for stability and continuity within the context of making changes to their ways of relating. Their capacity for self-reflection may enhance their understanding and serve as a catalyst to change. If the process produces changes in the patient's psychic organization, then the outcome that is hoped for is greater openness, greater stability, greater self-understanding, and greater capacity for flexible relatedness. These processes lead to the emergence of a self as a complex adaptive system that is more hierarchically structured, more complex, and more capable of successfully accommodating to the demands placed on them. The therapist and patient co-construct a new self-narrative that takes into account the neuropsychological, the introspective, and the interpersonal factors that influenced the patients' lives.

Finally, the pattern of rupture and repair that is endemic to all therapeutic relationships becomes a vehicle through which greater understanding of dysfunctional patterns occurs and the possibility of healing old wounds becomes available.

While I have applied the neuropsychodynamic systems perspective narrowly to the specific population of patients with neuropsychological deficits, I believe that this perspective has broader applicability to other populations. The issue centers on the applicability of the principle that all brain functions affect how people view the world and how they structure their experiences. In a previous publication, I drew an analogy between brain structures and a prism (J. Palombo, 2001). Much as a prism breaks up the light that passes through it, so do the various brain systems act as filters of our experiences. The various neuropsychological strengths and weakness with which we are endowed provide a distinctive shape to our experiences and consequently contribute to their uniqueness.

The need for a grand vision

The psychoanalytic landscape today is populated with theories that subscribe to different philosophical presuppositions that integrate dynamic systems approaches (for summaries, see Aron, 1996; Fosshage, 2003). Among these are the advocates of intersubjectivity theory, as articulated by Stolorow and his colleagues (Orange, 1995, 2013; Stolorow & Atwood, 1983), who are firmly committed to a variant of continental phenomenology (Stolorow, 1997). Lichtenberg and his colleagues recently revised their theoretical outlook, founded on self psychology and motivational theory, to include nonlinear dynamic systems (Lichtenberg, Lachmann, & Fosshage, 2011). Schore's integration of attachment theory seems firmly founded on scientific realism that also uses a systems perspective (Schore, 1997a, 1997b).

The verification problem

The broad question all theories face is: How do we propose hypotheses to verify or falsify conjectures that use different concepts from different paradigms? Until we arrive at a unified psychoanalytic theory that encompasses the biological, the psychological, and the social dimensions of human functioning, it is difficult to conceive of the possibility of formulating specific hypotheses to verify components of particular theories. The research strategy that is best suited to current conditions is that of qualitative exploratory studies. Such studies may expand our knowledge base while eliminating unsustainable conjectures. Ultimately, the value of the neuropsychodynamic perspective will be in whether it can generate testable hypotheses and whether the interventions it proposes can produce the anticipated outcomes.

A further challenge we face is that of reconciling a perspective that wishes to avoid an "essentialist view" of patients' conditions with the necessity of finding commonalities among groups of patients. Without being able to categorize conditions, we are left with each patient's individual dynamics as unique and unlike that of any others. Yet, it is only by identifying entities that highlight the common characteristics of a group of patients and by labeling those characteristics that we can open the possibility of conducting research into the underlying causes of the condition. The progress that has been made in the treatment of PTSD, for example, has come from the detailed description not only of the symptoms from which patients suffer, but also from an understanding of the brain changes that occur in patients who have suffered a trauma. This progress has been invaluable to clinicians treating those conditions. It has led to experimentation with a variety of interventions and to a better understanding of the effectiveness or ineffectiveness of some those interventions. In particular, it has led to a broad appreciation of the defense of dissociation, which is considered critical to the management of these cases.

Like Pirandello's characters in his play, *Six Characters in Search of an Author* (1998), we have psychoanalytic theories that are in search of a unifying paradigm that would bring together a theory of brain function, of psychological and of social development, and that have clinical relevance to psychoanalysis. We appear to be on the cusp of a paradigm shift. Such a paradigm would not only encompass these domains, but would also provide specific research agendas through which we can turn our conjectures into hypotheses that are verifiable or falsifiable. For too long, psychoanalysis remained isolated from other disciplines. This isolation resulted in the impoverishment of the explanatory power of the paradigm and was detrimental to patients who required the knowledge possessed by other disciplines for a full understanding of their problems.

Fortunately, doors to the integration of other bodies of knowledge that will enrich psychoanalytic theory are now opening. In spite of the methodological constraints inherent in such a task, nonlinear dynamic theory offers new insights into our understanding of psychological phenomena. Since all advances in the sciences entail the exploration of new territories, with all the attendant risks, perhaps we should not feel great apprehension at directing our investigations in domains where angels fear to tread. Ultimately, we will be rewarded by the survival of our discoveries and the value that accrues from their clinical application.

I conclude with the following quote by Dennett (1995):

> There is a familiar trio of reactions by scientists to a purportedly radical hypothesis: (a) "You must be out of your mind!" (b) "What else is new? Everybody knows that!" and later – if the hypothesis is still standing – (c) "Hmm. You might be onto something!" Sometimes these phases take years to unfold, one after another, but I have seen all three merge in near synchrony in the course of half an hour's heated discussion following a conference paper.
>
> (p. 283)

It is my hope that the contribution made by this work will find its way to the third response.

References

Aron, L. (1996). *A meeting of minds: Mutuality in psychoanalysis*. New York: Routledge.

Dennett, D. C. (1995). *Darwin's dangerous idea: Evolution and the meanings of life*. New York: Simon & Schuster.

Fosshage, J. L. (2003). Contextualizing self psychology and relational psychoanalysis: Bidirectional influence and proposed syntheses. *Contemporary Psychoanalysis*, *39*(3), 411–447.

Lichtenberg, J., Lachmann, F. M., & Fosshage, J. L. (2011). *Psychoanalysis and motivational systems: A new look*. New York: Routledge.

Orange, D. M. (1995). *Emotional understanding: Studies in psychoanalytic epistemology*. New York: Guilford Press.

Orange, D. M. (2013). A pre-Cartesian self. *International Journal of Psychoanalytic Self Psychology*, *8*, 488–494.

Palombo, J. (2001). *Learning disorders and disorders of the self in children and adolescents*. New York: W. W. Norton.

Palombo, J. (2013). The self as a complex adaptive system, part I: Complexity, metapsychology, and developmental theories. *Psychoanalytic Social Work*, *20*(1), 1–25.

Pirandello, L. (1998). *Six characters in search of an author* (E. Bentley, Trans.). New York: Signet Classic.

Schore, A. N. (1997a). A century after Freud's *Project*: Is a rapprochement between psychoanalysis and neurobiology at hand? *Journal of the American Psychoanalytic Association*, *45*(3), 807–840.

Schore, A. N. (1997b). Interdisciplinary developmental research as a source of clinical models. In M. Moskowitz, C. Monk, C. Kaye, & S. J. Ellman (Eds.), *The neurobiological and developmental basis for psychotherapeutic intervention* (pp. 1–72). Northdale, NJ: Jason Aronson.

Stern, D. N. (1983). The early development of schemas of self, other, and "self with other." In J. D. Lichtenberg & S. Kaplan (Eds.), *Reflections on self psychology* (pp. 49–84). Hillsdale, NJ: The Analytic Press.

Stolorow, R. D. (1997). Dynamic, dyadic, intersubjective systems: An evolving paradigm for psychoanalysis. *Psychoanalytic Psychology*, *14*(3), 337–346.

Stolorow, R. D., & Atwood, G. E. (1983). Psychoanalytic phenomenology: Progress toward a theory of personality. In A. Goldberg (Ed.), *The future of psychoanalysis* (pp. 97–110). New York: International Universities Press.

Index

accommodations, unsuccessful, and self-deficits 61–3, 66–7
ADHD (attention deficit/hyperactivity disorder) 127, 200; *see also* Ryan case study
adjunctive deficits/self-deficits 3, 55
adjunctive functions: mindsharing and 143, 144, 152, 153–4; overview 3, 59; selfobject functions and 157–8
adventitious organizers 57
affect regulation 159
affects and self-cohesion 90–2
agency, sense of 43–5, 89–90, 178, 249
attachment and regulatory functions 123–6
attachment theory 29, 32–3; *see also* interconnectedness
attention deficit/hyperactivity disorder (ADHD) 127, 200; *see also* Ryan case study
attractors 56–7, 83
autobiographical memory 121

"being with" patient 194, 249
beliefs, self-narratives compared to 102
Bowlby, J. 32–3
brain, as self-organizing system 41–2
brain functions: development, attachment, and 34–6; mind as emergent property of 144–5; as system 199

capacity for dialogue: case study 133–8; medium for dialogue 130–1; overview 117, 130; types of communication 131–3
case study: as approach to theory-building 1; of capacity for dialogue 133–8; of complementary moments 217, 231–7; of disavowal 219–22; of dissociation 97–8;

of mindsharing and nonverbal dialogue 159–64; of relational patterns 127–30; of self-understanding 106–10; *see also* Ryan case study
causality, nonlinear 10–11
change agent: communication as 159; patient as open or closed to 199–202; proactive activity as 178–80; sense of agency as 44; in therapeutic process 173–4; therapeutic relationship as 175–6, 183; understanding as 225–7
closed systems 200–1
co-created narratives 177–8, 227–9
cognitive domain of function 56, 59
coherence: cohesion compared to 88–9; of self-narratives 103–6; *see also* self-cohesion
communication: as change agent 159; types of 131–3, 139, 193–4; *see also* capacity for dialogue; mindsharing and nonverbal dialogue; therapeutic dialogue
communication domain 30
compensation 205–6
complementarity, search for 3, 176–80, 211–12
complementary functions 18–19, 42–3, 148–9, 151–2; *see also* adjunctive functions; selfobject functions
complementary moments: case study 217, 231–7; overview 17, 183–4, 211–12, 237–9, 255; preference for self-cohesion and 213–14; transference, countertransference, and 214–17
complex adaptive system: from developmental perspective 39–41; therapeutic dyad as 15, 172–3, 180; *see also* self as complex adaptive system

complexity view of human development 38–9
conceptual problem for clinicians 3–4
concordant moments: change agents and 199–202; compensation for self-deficits and 205–6; diversity of neuropsychological deficits and 195–7; initial conditions of system and 193–202; overview 16–17, 182–3, 191–3, 206–8; proactive activities and 203–5; reconfiguration of relational patterns 202–3; sense of self and 197–9
context: endowment, experience, and 65; endowment and 60–1; person as embedded in 42, 47; self-cohesion and 90; of social interactions 131
"continuous construction" 62
conventionalization of narratives 105–6
core shame 91–2
countertransference 211–12, 214–17, 229–31, 254–5
Cozolino, L. 36
"curative fantasy" 16, 182, 191

data: for formulation of patient psychodynamics 77–9; patient experience as 5–6; sources of 7
declarative memory subsystem 120
deficits see neuropsychological deficits; self-deficits; selfobject deficits
developmental dialogue 29, 180–1
developmental theories: Bowlby 32–3; Cozolino 36; differentiation 43–5; individuation 45–6; nonlinear dynamic theory and 37–9; Palombo 36–7; revised view of development 39–41; Sander 37–8; Schore 34–6; from simple to complex levels of organization 41–3; Stern 33–4; trends contributing to revised views 31–2
developmental viewpoint 25
dialogue 29, 30; see also capacity for dialogue; nonverbal dialogue and mindsharing; therapeutic dialogue
"diatrophic attitude" 16, 182, 191
differentiation 43–5
disavowal 93–5, 112, 218–22
disjunctive moments: limitations of therapeutic encounter 249–51; overview 17, 184, 242, 251–2; reorganization, individuation, and sense of agency 249; repairs 246–8; ruptures 243–6

"disruption and repair sequence" 184
dissociation 95–6, 97–8, 218, 222–4
diversity: in endowment 58–9, 79–80; of neuropsychological deficits 27–8, 195–7
domains of experience/knowledge see interpersonal (social) domain of knowledge; introspective (psychological) domain of knowledge; neuropsychological (biological) domain of knowledge
"dual aspect" theory of mind/body problem 145
dynamic systems view: diversity and endowment 58–9; environment and endowment 60–1; overview 253; of self-deficits 55–8, 253; self-deficits and unsuccessful accommodations 61–3; see also nonlinear dynamic systems theory
dynamic viewpoint 25
dyslexia and self-esteem 105

emotional (affective) domain of function 56, 59
empathy: capacity for 144, 148, 149–50; of therapist 192, 196
emplotment 106, 216–17
enactments 216–17
encoding of relational patterns 122
endowment: diversity in 58–9, 79–80; environment and 60–1; experience, context, and 65
environment and endowment 60–1
episodic memory 120–1
evolutionary viewpoint 7–10
executive function disorder 85n2; see also Ryan case study
experience: self-narratives as organizers of 100–3; therapeutic process as engaging patient in 175–6
experience of being self see sense of self

fantasies, self-narratives compared to 102
fear of retraumatization 200–2, 243–5, 246
fitting together process 8–9, 211
"forward edge" 204
fragmentation 28, 62–3
functionality of therapeutic dyad 172–3

idealizing selfobject functions 156
implicit memory 122

implicit relational knowing 118–19, 123, 138, 182
individuation 45–6, 249
initial conditions: neuropsychological deficits and 64, 66; of therapeutic dialogue 193–202; therapeutic dyad and 172
interactive regulatory functions 146
interconnectedness 29, 119, 158–9, 170; *see also* relational patterns
Internal Working Models 118, 132
interpersonal domain of function 56
interpersonal (social) domain of knowledge (L-III): capacity for dialogue 117, 130–8; complementary functions and 42–3; interplay with other levels 13–14, 19; modes of interaction among components 27, 29–30; modes of interaction with others 117–18; overview 12–13, 117, 138–9; person as embedded in context 42; *see also* relational patterns
interpreting: disavowal and 218–22; dissociation and 218, 222–4; process of 176–7, 213–14, 217–24
intersubjectivity theory 256
introspective (psychological) domain of knowledge (L-II): interplay with other levels 13–14, 19; overview 12–13, 87; preferences 27, 28–9, 87–9; self-cohesion 89–99; self-understanding 99–106; sense of self 42

learning disorders 5–7, 124–6; *see also* nonverbal learning disability
levels-of-analysis perspective 12–14, 27–31, 253–4; *see also* interpersonal (social) domain of knowledge; introspective (psychological) domain of knowledge; neuropsychological (biological) domain of knowledge
loss of self-cohesion 92–3

medium for dialogue 130–1
memory and relational patterns 119–23
mental processes of patients, understanding 2, 18, 82–4
mind: as emergent property of brain function 144–5; shared 145–8
mindsharing and nonverbal dialogue: case study 159–64; complementary functions 151–2; deficits in interconnectedness 158–9; empathy 149–50; neuropsychological deficits 152–5; overview 14–15, 18–19, 143–4, 164–5, 254; search for complementarity and 211; selfobject deficits 155–8; senses of term 148
mirroring selfobject functions 156
mirror-neurons 150
modes of interaction 81–2, 117–18
moments in therapy 16–17, 180–2; *see also* complementary moments; concordant moments; disjunctive moments
mutative factors in therapeutic process: co-created narratives 177–8; overview 173–5; proactive activities as change agents 178–80; relationship as change agent 175–6; restoration of self-cohesion 176–7; search for complementarity 176–80
"mutuality" 117

narcissistic issues for therapist in repair process 247–8
narratives *see* self-narratives
negation 40
neuropsychodynamic perspective: development and 40; interplay among three levels 13–14; nonverbal dialogue and mindsharing 14–15; overview 7, 254–5; self as complex adaptive system 7–10, 11–12; self-deficits 12–13; *see also* self as complex adaptive system
neuropsychological deficits: attachment and 124–6; as contributors to symptoms 18; development of 9–10, 64–6; diversity of 27–8, 195–7; dynamic systems view of 55–8; impact of 5–7; mindsharing and 152–5; narrative incoherence and 103–6; outcome of 11; overview 3–5; *see also* self-deficits
neuropsychological (biological) domain of knowledge (L-I): brain as self-organizing system 41–2; diversity of components 27; interplay with other levels 13–14, 19; overview 12–13, 54–5; *see also* self-deficits
neuropsychological problems, effects on functioning and psychodynamics 2–3
neuropsychological testing 7
NLD (nonverbal learning disability) 85n3, 133–8, 231–7

non-declarative memory subsystem 120, 121
nonlinear dynamic systems theory: developmental theories and 37–9; overview 4–5, 10–11, 257–8; self-deficits and 56–8
nonverbal communication 131–3, 139, 193–4
nonverbal dialogue and mindsharing 14–15, 18–19, 143–4; *see also* mindsharing and nonverbal dialogue
nonverbal learning disability (NLD) 85n3, 133–8, 231–7

object relatedness 117, 118
one-person psychology 30–1
open systems 199–200, 201
organization, from simple to complex levels of 41–3

Palombo, J. 36–7
patients: "being with" 194, 249; engaging in therapeutic process 175–6; mental processes of, understanding 2, 18, 82–4; as open or closed to change agent 199–202; *see also* psychodynamic profiles of patients
person, as embedded in context 42
preferences *see* self-cohesion; self-understanding
preverbal communication 132, 139
priming agent, therapeutic process as 212
proactive activities 178–80, 203–5
procedural memory 121, 122
processes of conditions 4–5
psychodynamic profiles of patients: formulation of 77–9, 177–8; mindsharing 162; relational patterns 128–30; self-understanding 109–10
psychological functions 143, 145, 151, 157; *see also* adjunctive functions; selfobject functions
psychopathology, defined 54

recognition process: adaptation and 38; complementary moments and 211; evolutionary viewpoint on 147; failures in 243, 245–7; overview 8–9; therapeutic dyad and 173
regulatory functions and attachment 123–6
relational patterns: attachment and regulatory functions 123–6; case study 127–30; encoding and retrieval of 119–23; overview 29, 118–19; reconfiguration of 202–3

relational theory 4
reorganization of patient dynamics 249
repair process 246–8; *see also* rupture and repair process
"resistance," as fear of retraumatization 200–2
retraumatization, fear of 200–2, 243–5, 246
retrieval of relational patterns 123
rupture and repair process 17, 184, 242, 243–8, 255
Ryan case study: background and history 68–70; diversity in endowment 79–80; initial diagnosis and recommendation 70–1; initial phase of treatment 71–3; modes of interaction 81–2; overview 67–8; preferences and biases 81; processes guiding functioning 82–4; psychodynamics 77–85; treatment outcome 84; treatment process 73–7

Sander, L. W. 37–8
scaffolding 148
Schore, A. N. 34–6
script theory 100–1
search for complementarity *see* complementarity, search for
secondary elaborations 102
self: being a self 26–7, 144; restoring and healing 15–17; sense of 87, 144, 197–9
self as complex adaptive system: evolutionary viewpoint 7–10; initial conditions of 66; levels of analysis 27–31; overview 11–12, 26–7, 46–8, 254; preferences guiding 110–11; *see also* developmental theories
self-cohesion: affects, self-experience, and 90–2; disavowal 93–5; dissociation 95–9; loss of 92–3; mindsharing and 154; preference for 28, 87–9, 110–11, 213–14; restoration of 176–7; Ryan case study 81
self-deficits (neuropsychological): adjunctive 3, 55; compensation for 205–6; dynamic systems view of 55–8, 253; levels-of-analysis perspective on 12–14; overview 18, 66–7; remediation of 178–9; unsuccessful accommodations and 61–3; *see also* introspective (psychological) domain of knowledge; neuropsychological (biological) domain of knowledge
self-experience and self-cohesion 90–2

self-narratives: co-created 177–8, 227–9; neuropsychological deficits and incoherence of 103–6; as organizers of experience 100–3; over lifespan 111–12; transference, countertransference, and 229–31
selfobject deficits 55–6, 155–8
selfobject functions: complementary functions and 152; defined 55; mindsharing and 143, 144, 146; mirroring 156; twinship (alter ego) 156–7
self psychology 4
self-understanding: case study 106–10; as change agent 225–7; co-construction of new narrative 227–9; during development 41; preference for 28–9, 81, 87–8, 99, 111, 224–31; self-narratives and 100–3; transference and countertransference 229–31
semantic memory 120
sense of self 87, 144, 197–9
series of moments, therapeutic process as 16–17
shame: self-cohesion and 91–2; transference and 215; wall of 1–2
shared minds 145–8; *see also* mindsharing and nonverbal dialogue
smiling response 40
social domain of function 56, 59
social engagement system 193
social synapse 36
Solms, Mark 2
sources of data 7
specificity 59
Stern, D. N. 33–4
stranger anxiety 40
subjectivity of infants 33–4

termination of treatment 185
theoretical perspective: need for unified psychoanalytic theory 256–8; nonlinear dynamic systems view 4–5, 10–11, 37–9, 55–63, 257–8; overview 4, 169–70; *see also* developmental theories
theory-building, case study approach to 1
therapeutic dialogue: as moments 180–4; overview 29, 170–2, 174–5, 185–8; termination as conclusion to 185; *see also* complementary moments; concordant moments; disjunctive moments
therapeutic dyads 15, 172–3
therapeutic process: limitations of 249–51; mutative factors in 173–80; as priming agent 212; sense of agency in 44; *see also* therapeutic dialogue
transference 211, 214–17, 229–31, 254–5
twinship (alter ego) selfobject functions 156–7
two-person psychology 30–1

understanding: as change agent 225–7; mental processes of patients 2, 18, 82–4; process of 213–14; *see also* self-understanding
unified psychoanalytic theory, need for 256–7

verbal communication 131–2

wall of shame 1–2
world view 103

zone of proximal development 204